Training, Civil Services and Personnel Administration

Golden Jubilee Volume Series–2
Changing Contours of Administration Since Independence

Training, Civil Services and Personnel Administration

EDITORS
SUNEEL DHARIWAL
K.K. PARNAMI

SERIES EDITOR
RAKESH HOOJA

The HCM Rajasthan State Institute of Public Administration
Jaipur

RAWAT PUBLICATIONS
Jaipur • New Delhi • Bangalore • Mumbai • Hyderabad • Guwahati

ISBN 81-316-0111-0

Published by
Prem Rawat for **Rawat Publications**
Satyam Apts, Sector 3, Jawahar Nagar, Jaipur 302 004 (India)
Phone: 0141 265 1748 / 7006 Fax: 0141 265 1748
E-mail: info@rawatbooks.com
Website: www.rawatbooks.com

New Delhi Office
4858/24, Ansari Road, Daryaganj, New Delhi 110 002
Phone: 011 2326 3290

Also at Bangalore, Mumbai, Hyderabad and Guwahati

Typeset by Rawat Computers, Jaipur
Printed at Chaman Enterprises, New Delhi

Contents

Series Editor's Introduction

RAKESH HOOJA

It is most likely that all possible types of developmental, governmental, regulatory and administrative initiatives have been tried out in some part or the other of India over the last 60 years since the country gained independence. With governments of different ideological hues having remained in power at difference points of time in different states of the Indian Union and at the Centre, and with different ideas about development, governance, planning, state welfarism, market-orientation, administration, nation-building etc. having been fashionable or accepted in different time frames, as well as a willingness to try out and emulate what was being attempted in countries of the West, or of the Soviet bloc, or in other developing areas, all forms of administrative and governmental action and all types of development schemes, as well as types of organizational arrangements, have been tried out somewhere or the other in India and have been commented upon by experts, scholars, researchers, practitioners, journalists and the ordinary laymen. In fact, Public Administration is a well-established discipline in India and has been regularly analyzing changes in the field, as also in administrative thinking, and in policy making, over the years. These debates, discussions, descriptions, analyses, comments, opinions, findings and administrative prescriptions have been duly covered in the various articles published in the two journals of the HCM Rajasthan State Institute of Public Administration (HCM RIPA), which contain useful and valuable reference material.

It is in this context that we have undertaken this project of preparing thematic volumes, which would indicate some of the important *Changing Contours of Indian Administration Since Independence*. We wanted to look at how concepts, approaches, organizational structures, procedures, policies, programmes, projects, working styles, and modes of observation, analysis and evaluation, have all emerged and undergone change over time.

Accordingly, to celebrate 50 years of HCM RIPA, we felt it appropriate to select the best and most appropriate articles from the issues of the over 33 years that our journal *Prashashnika* is being published as well as the 11 years that our second journal *Development Policy and Administrative Review* used to be simultaneously printed. Deliberately wanting the articles selected for inclusion in this series to retain the flavour of the period in which they were written and to reflect the thinking and practice of that time, we have chosen not to modify the selected articles, except in some cases to slightly change the titles of the articles. The words, descriptions and analyses are of the authors as they had originally written the pieces. However, the articles selected have their intrinsic value, and by putting them together into separate thematic volumes, we have, hopefully, enabled readers to visualize how certain administrative concepts, or governmental and developmental programmes (or experiments) and policies, have been initially conceptualized and implemented, and have subsequently evolved over time. We have also attempted to provide a judicious blend of the theoretical and the practical in each book as also in the series as a whole.

Having gone through the back issues of *Prashasnika* and of *Development Policy and Administrative Review*, we have selected the following as the themes for each of the separate volumes:

1. Development Administration and Rural Development
2. Training, Civil Services and Personnel Administration
3. Panchayati Raj, Participation and Decentralization
4. Administration of Health and Education Sectors
5. Welfare and Tribal Development Administration
6. Administration of Public Sector Enterprises and Industrial Development: Changing Trends Since Independence
7. Administrative Theories: Approaches, Concepts and Thinkers in Public Administration
8. Prashasnik Parivartan (in Hindi)
9. Plan and Project Formulation and Implementation: Theoretical and Applied Aspects
10. Urban Development and Administration
11. Governance and Reforms
12. District Level Administration and the Role of the Collector
13. Administration of Desert, Drought Prone and Dry Farming Areas
14. Administration of Water Management and Command Area Development
15. Administration for the Empowerment and Welfare of Women
16. Organizational Behaviour, Managerial Change and Human Resource Development
17. Land Use Revenue Administration and Land Reforms

Other titles may be added as we go along.

I have received able support from the my colleagues on the Series Editorial Board, namely, Mr. Suneel Dhariwal, Mr. Sandeep Varma and Mr. K.K. Parnami in finalizing the themes for the individual volumes and identifying the possible thematic volume editors. Mr. Parnami got a cumulative index prepared of all matter published in our two journals without which this exercise could not have been started. We are also gratified that the two publishers Subodh Bhushan Gupta of Aalekh Publishers and Pranit Rawat of Rawat Publications respectively agreed to jointly co-publish the books with HCM RIPA, and to distribute them. The editors of each volume also are to be thanked for their efforts at meticulously culling out and selecting the best and most relevant articles for our consideration for inclusion in the respective volumes, and for their writing appropriate volume introductions.

It is hoped that this series of volumes shall prove to be a useful source of reference contributing to better understanding of the themes covered and acting as a stimulus for further reflection to all those interested in Indian administration, and that readers shall enjoy and appreciate reading the books as much as we in the Series Editorial Board, and the volume editors, did while preparing the books for publication.

Introduction

SUNEEL DHARIWAL AND K.K. PARNAMI

'Training', 'Civil Services' and 'Personnel Administration' are three interlinked terms. While 'Personnel Administration' is a holistic term, 'Civil Services' and 'Training' are parts of it. This anthology contains essays on these themes in three separate parts.

Training

'Training in the public service' is defined in the *UN Handbook of Training* as "instruction in an art, a profession, or an occupation, consisting of teaching, drill or discipline by which powers of mind or body are developed...With particular reference to civil service, training is the reciprocal process of teaching and learning a body of knowledge and the related methods of work". Today, training of civil servants has acquired a significant place for itself in the public personnel administrative system. Not only does it help develop the competence of a trained officer, but it also inculcates in him a set of values, which may be desirable in a particular socio-administrative milieu.

Civil service training in India has, since long, been recognized as an important means of improving the human potential and increasing the administrative efficiency of those who run the government machinery. Today, India is considered among the countries having a most advanced system of civil service training. There has been a phenomenal growth of training institutions, faculty, training programmes, training materials, training techniques, and above all, a training consciousness.

Part I of the present volume includes eight papers by the eminent experts in the field on different dimensions of training, particularly in the Indian context. While the first paper by T.N. Chaturvedi delineates the role of training in administration, B. Mehta, in his paper, outlines the role training plays in the executive development. Then comes the paper by C. Richard Parkins on the importance of human relations training in civil services. The oft-repeated exhortation that one of the main objectives of civil service training is to inculcate 'right attitudes' among the civil servants suggests the appropriateness and relevance of human relations training. Human relations training is offered as one possible vehicle for accelerating understanding about behaviour as a component of government service. The intention of this discussion is therefore to suggest relationship between government service and individual behaviour and ways in which human relations training can participate constructively in associating or reconciling the two.

Mohan Mukerji, in his paper, discusses some aspects of inter-institutional coordination in training such as faculty, multidisciplinary approach and specialization. Likewise, in a small piece, R.G. Sood describes some issues in in-service training such as training of trainers, post-training utilization of training, subordinate staff's attitudes and effectiveness, newer techniques and selective approach. These two papers are followed by another paper on evolution and growth of training by K.K. Parnami. The emergence of training idea in the civil service is not accidental. Actually, it is the result of innumerable efforts made both at international and national levels, which the author has very succinctly described in his write-up.

Recognizing the need and significance of networking training institutes in the state, the Government of Rajasthan, over the years, has taken several measures, which B.K. Khunteta, in his paper, has recounted in detail. He also described the initiatives taken by HCM RIPA, as an apex institution, in this direction.

The last paper in this section is on decentralized training in support of urban development by A.N. Krishnamurthy and Harry A. Mengers. This essay mainly focuses on making a movement towards the change in the urban development sector in which training is visualized as a catalyst in the process.

Civil Services

Part II of the volume, delineating the salient features of the civil service system in India, has five papers. Civil services in India are the backbone of its administrative machinery. They have played a vital role in the task of nation-building, right from the time we achieved independence, to the present day. The values of integrity, partiality and merit have remained the guiding principles of our civil services.

Along with the maturing of the nation, the role of civil service has also been changing. However, throughout this process of change that the country has been experiencing, the civil services have continued to be an important instrument for initiating and managing change. Much of this change has been in areas and activities that had a strong presence of the government and its resources. Where development was driven by the government, the civil servant has been a key instrument, along with the political leadership, in initiating and managing change and delivering services.

Today, the Indian civil service system, which is one of the oldest in the world, is composed of the central and provincial civil services. The central civil service system comprise of three all-India, viz., IAS, IPS and IFS, and many other civil services. The provincial civil services follow a similar pattern.

This part begins with a paper (which is in fact a talk delivered by the author) by Dharma Vira, an eminent civil servant of his times, entitled "The Services of Modern Times". In his write-up, the author has narrated the journey connected with the changeover from the bureaucratic system to the democratic system.

"The Anatomy of Civil Administration" is the title of next essay written by G.B.K. Hooja. Then, in his long essay, R.K. Mishra attempts a critical overview of the national civil service system in India. The Indian civil service system has a long history and had its origin in the Mauryan times. It has seen many developments during the Mughal and British eras and is today one of the best civil service systems in the world. Despite acquiring the traits of serving party in power, the tendency today has been to tread the path very carefully and avoid any confrontation with the political bosses.

Then comes the V. Jagannadham's paper in which the author has examined the relationships of civil servants with citizens, pressure groups and the people's representatives.

The last paper in this section is by Rakesh Hooja on career and cadre planning for the IAS officers. The author is of the view that the career and cadre planning for IAS should be such that the best countrymen from all walks of life are available in the service and that they are given appropriate formal as well as informal training and used in such a manner that all state governments as also the Centre have the best possible manpower available to them to undertake the jobs that our administrative system is called upon to perform.

Personnel Administration

Indian polity is passing through critical times. Not only is the socio-economic and political structure of the country undergoing a phenomenal change, but also the expectations of people in terms of the availability of superior goods are getting echoed in different forums repeatedly. Added to this is the dilemma of rendering effective and efficient administrative support to people by sprawling bureaucracy which has been labelled as 'status-quoist' and obstructive to the factors which could be harbingers of change. The recent amendments to the Constitution of India have intended to restore power to the common people. This has resulted in creating forces against the present excess of power, seeking a change in the real relations between the executives and people. The country has reached a stage where it has been widely felt that what is important is not giving Constitution to the country but running it. It is in the backdrop that the role of personnel administration in India assumes a critical dimension.

Section III of the present volume, on the personnel administration, includes a total of five articles, four of them deal with different dimensions of bureaucracy. Bureaucracy determines the major administrative styles and influences a large section of the society. In our country, although it has taken long strides in the direction of developmental work, the basic character continues to remain towards the maintenance of law and order. In the present scenario, this goes against the spirit of democratic values and need to be changed. It is in this context that Udai Pareek, in his paper, has discussed this topic and also suggested a framework for introducing a change in bureaucracy.

In the next article, P.K. Chaubey has attempted a short critique of Indian bureaucracy. One may find many people holding pejorative views about bureaucracy but not a single to say words of praise. Why, this is so? In this paper, the author has tried to answer this question. According to him, not only the bureaucrats themselves but largely the administration is responsible for all this malaise.

"Bureaucratic Sensitivity and Human Rights" is the title of next paper contributed by Amit Lodha. Quoting a few instances of bureaucratic apathy towards the plight of masses, such as Bhopal gas disaster, the author is of the view that there is an urgent need for a paradigm shift in the thinking of bureaucracy and it simply has to be more proactive, sensitive and progressive in nature.

After becoming free independent states, most of the nations in the South Asian region made efforts in reforming and restructuring their administrative system, particularly in their rural areas. The paper by Richard M. Tom is a modest attempt to present an overview of efforts made by South Asian countries like China, Nepal, Bhutan, Pakistan, Bangladesh, Sri Lanka and India in constituting a separate rural local-self government/rural development administration at the grassroots level. It also reviews the various administrative structures presently functioning and assesses the administrative problems prevailing in the countries.

The last article in this volume is contributed by Rajendra Bhanawat on "Delays in Disposal". It is often said that delay breeds corruption. Today, it has become an accepted way of life in almost all spheres of public utility services. However, it cannot be more relevant to the public delivery system whether of the government or any other agency. In this paper, the author looks into some of the dimensions of the problem. He has also suggested some measures for reducing the delays in disposal.

I

Training

1

Role of Training in Administration

T.N. CHATURVEDI

> "There is only one thing that will train the human mind and that is the voluntary use of the mind by man himself. You may aid him, you may guide him, you may inspire him; but the only thing worth having is that which he gets by his own exertions and what he gets is in direct proportion to what he puts into it."
>
> — A. Lowrence Lowell

Meaning and Objectives of Training

'Training in the public service' is defined in the U.N. Handbook of Training as "instruction in an art, a profession, or an occupation, consisting of teaching, drill or discipline by which powers of mind or body are developed....with particular reference to the civil service, training is the reciprocal process of teaching and learning a body of knowledge and the related methods of work."[1] Broadly, training helps to promote, maintain or enhance the employee's effectiveness in his present assignment and prepares him for future work or promotional opportunities, i.e., assumption of higher responsibilities through the cultivation and development of habits of thought and action, skills (conceptual, social and procedural), knowledge, attitudes and behavioural patterns. All this goes to promote organizational effectiveness as functional efficiency and morale of employees will be reflected in the totality of effectiveness, output and overall performance of the organization. Training has thus a personal as well as an organizational angle to it.

Assheton Committee on Aims of Training

The five-fold aims of training, as laid down by the Assheton Committee[2], are:

(1) Training should endeavour to produce a civil servant whose precision and clarity in the transaction of business can be taken for granted.

(2) The civil servant must be attuned to the tasks he will be called upon to perform in a changing world. The civil servant must continuously and boldly adjust its outlook and its methods to the new needs of new times.

(3) The civil servant should not be allowed to fall into danger of becoming mechanized by machine. The recruit from the start should be made aware of the relation of his work to the service rendered by his department to the community. The capacity to see what he is doing in a wider setting will make the work not only more valuable to his department, but more stimulating to himself also. In addition, therefore, to purely vocational training directed to the proper performance of his day-to-day work, he should receive instruction on a broader basis as well as encouragement to persevere with his own educational development.

(4) Even as regards vocational training, it is not sufficient to train solely for the job which lies immediately at hand. Training must be directed not only to enabling an individual to perform his current work more efficiently, but also to fitting him for other duties, and, where appropriate, developing his capacity for higher work and greater responsibilities.

(5) The training plans, to be successful, must pay substantial regard to staff morale to off-set the dull monotony of routine work. It is of utmost importance that every probationer should realize that he is entering the life of service, and that he should be a servant of the people and not their master. The civil servants should be given proper training in the methods of dealing with the members of the public. "Nothing could be more disastrous than that the civil service and the public should think of themselves as in two separate camps. The inculcation of the right attitude towards the public and towards business should therefore be one of the principal aims of civil service training. The civil servant must never forget that he is the servant, and not the master, of the community, and that official competence need not involve the loss of the human touch."[3]

The ARC Report on Personnel administration has also devoted a chapter to training indicating objectives, suggesting need for national policy on civil service training, preparation of training plans, mechanics of training etc.

Training and Emerging Problems in Administration

The role of training in administration is increasingly gaining recognition in the developed as well as the developing countries. It is being realized that new developments in administration necessitate a well-planned attention to the problem of training. The need for the projection of an adequate image of public service in a fast changing society becomes an essential function of training in administration. Purposes of administration are undergoing reorientation. Not that the old functions are necessarily becoming irrelevant, actually, their nature is changing. New dimensions to traditional tasks are arising thus underscoring the need for new knowledge, new skills and new attitudes. As Professor E.S. Wengert has stated: "What we mean by administration we can abstract from the social, economic and political context of endeavours at social change and control. We can study it in the setting of ideas, opinions, and purposes of people. It is performed within the framework of a particular technology." Again, the variety, complexity and volume of administrative tasks or operations are on the increase. Moreover, administration has slowly evolved into a well-defined scientific discipline reinforced by scientific technological developments as well as by fresh insights in social and behavioural sciences. As has been said, the behavioural sciences have made a contribution to the illumination of particular elements of the world of the administrator. Besides, physical sciences have identified and provided some of the tools of action and analysis which the administrator may use to simplify, rationalize and control his decisions. Training in public administration as such will mainly depend on the nature, volume and variety of socio-economic plans, programmes and activities as are being undertaken in the country. Training programmes will have to be diversified and variegated. Training requirements will have to be identified in terms of functional content and responsibilities and apposite pattern worked out. Manpower planning, quantitatively and qualitatively, is intimately associated as a prerequisite for working out useful training programmes.

Training: A Comprehensive and Integrated Concept

Training in public administration is a comprehensive concept. Training can be effective only if there is a clear-cut realization of the objectives and needs of public administration. It is conditioned by the needs and requirements of various categories of public service. Again, it implies a stage-wise approach. Training has to be designed for various stages in the career of a public servant. Training can thus be viewed as follows in this perspective: (a) training for fresh recruits or entrants to public service; (b) refresher or mid-career training; and (c) training for senior executives and administrators. Training in administration is a comprehensive concept also in the sense that it seeks to promote efficiency, morale and improvements in the generalist, managerial, functional and technical streams of public service. Training for administrative effectiveness, whether viewed horizontally or vertically, is an integrated concept. Training effort has to have a broad coverage. Training cannot be confined to only higher echelons or middle levels in administration. It is as much necessary for junior levels. Authority in administration is functional and functional efficiency at all levels need sharpening. The totality of administrative effectiveness will be determined by the basic quality of all categories of public servants and at all levels. The scope and nature of training for different kinds or levels of public service will be related to their nature of work and authority. But, there are bound to be certain common parameters, the understanding of which may be useful for all. This is all the more so in a developing society with its developmental imperatives and in the context of a democratic system of government where the public servants have to be cognizant of the need for public relations and participation as well as the concept of democratic accountability. Training in administration has obviously to be in conformity with the rules of the contemporary administration and structure of contemporary administration. This provides a dynamic element to the raining process. As has been said, "The education of administrators is no new problem. In the *Republic*, Plato constructed an educational state designed to prepare administrators. Confucious sought to educate men for government. Moralists and speculative philosophers through the ages have devoted themselves to the tasks of teaching princes and kings and others in places of authority to rule over the affairs of the public. Some elements of the problem of educating administrators are undoubtedly as old as Plato, but other ingredients are contemporary."[4]

Training and Personnel System

Training is also related to the totality of personnel system in the country.[5] It is an essential part of the system. But it is also beyond it. Training goes to reinforce a sound and scientific personnel system. Training is thus geared to the aims and objectives of the personnel policy. Training is a tool of flexible and democratic personnel policy which provides scope for the meritorious to rise to the top irrespective of origins or service affiliations. Training even without being backed by any formal compulsive element can serve as an instrument for screening and selecting the deserving and the competent with promise and potential. Training, however, scientifically conceived and implemented, cannot yield desired results unless other essentials of a sound personnel policy exist. Training in order to be effective has to be sustained by adequate career planning, placement and promotion policy. There will only be cynicism and frustration in the field of training if these essentials are not properly realized. The role of training in administration will get vitiated and the entire training effort get denigrated in the eyes of the public servant, the government or its component unit and the public who pays and to serve whom the instrumentality of public service has been designed. Planning of training programmes is functionally obligatory and this would broadly take into account the organization, goals, contents, techniques and information or data as the basis for such planning.[6] The curriculum-building is one of its basic ingredients and it is also not a once-for-all exercise. The role of training in administration is thus not a self-generating and self-reinforcing isolate but contingent on many other cognate factors. The quality and character of training will be an overriding consideration as regards its convincibility and credibility. It is in view of the interrelated role of training in administration in the contextual background of other factors that the training must not be advocated as the cure of all maladies in administration. If needless disenchantment has to be avoided, the training function has to be seen in a more realistic perspective.

Need for Political and Administrative Support

This brings us to the question of administrative and political support to the training function in the government if the role of training in administration is to be operationally effective. It cannot be honestly denied that even in higher levels in administration, there is a good deal of reservation about the need for or efficacy of training. At times there is grudging acceptance because it tends to become a status symbol of a modern organization or 'forward-looking' administrative leadership. The skeleton remains and the spirit withers away. Planning for training becomes unimaginative and ineffectual. The higher echelons of administrative leadership have also to appreciate that training is not effective in a vacuum and they have requisite inputs to provide. This process cannot be separated from the role of political leadership too. Political leadership has to be convinced and it must develop faith that the role of training in administration is of basic significance. It has an important part to play in policies relating to career planning, placement and promotions. Political leadership may have to develop a modicum of self-restraint despite democratic constraints and compulsions if the possibilities of training in administration for larger and lasting public good are not to be fettered by narrow walls of partisan of parochial interests. It ought to be realized that good administration cannot be ensured only by criticism and denigration of public servants but by a set of concrete steps—both of positive and negative character. Training is one of such effective measures. In the public service itself, training—not necessarily in a formal sense—has to be looked at as a continuing function if it has to counteract intellectual obsolescence and has to retain the resilience, flexibility and receptivity to respond to the multitudinous issues and problems as arise in "the web of government" which has profound human implications and far-reaching impact on man and society.[7]

Certain Operating Problems Meriting High Level Political and Administrative Support

Now, what are the areas which need particular attention of the higher political and administrative leadership. In the first instance, it is the question of formulation and crystallization of training objectives. In the second step it is a question of the location of training function in government. It simply means the position of effectiveness of those concerned with training in government—the relationship of trust and confidence they enjoy in the total governmental set-up. Again, it is a question of selecting both the trainers and trainees. It so happens that quite often the trainers are not chosen on the basis of interest, aptitude of professional competence. The turnover is also fairly rapid. The demand of recognition, as exists in the defence forces, is usually absent. Similarly, the trainees are not selected because they have either the potential for development or because they fit in the emerging picture of organizational needs. Sometimes, the 'laggards' and the 'sparables' find themselves as trainees, especially in the in-service programmes. The need is to link training to an appraisal of each promising public servant's points of strengths and weaknesses. What role can training play in administration when such a group of trainees meets a similar group of trainers? The desideratum of a successful training programme is the selection of properly equipped trainers and trainees with potential for growth. Besides, it is the interest and sincerity of purpose on the part of higher political and administrative leadership which can ensure that the public servants trained are so posted that the training is not infructious. The fact of the matter is that these matters get neglected even if there is ample lip homage to the role of training in administration.

Training: Stimulus for Self-Development

In the next place, it is a question of providing adequate financial and organizational resources to be made available in order that meaningful training programmes are planned and conducted. Training is intended to create a climate of awareness, to show the possibilities of improvement in administration and to equip as to how those possibilities can be actualized. Follow-up, as an essential ingredient of training programme, may necessitate the scope for continuing staff-development. Training is expected to provide self-stimulus for further development. [8]

Linkage with Educational System and Character of Training Imparted by Government

Training in administration is invariably linked with educational system in the country which provides general, professional and technical education. The quality and character of the education will have a profound impact on the nature and scope of training that the government proposes to impart. It has been mentioned that the government is best suited to provide training:

(a) in specialization dealing intensively with specific applications of theory and practice to government programmes;

(b) on departmental or governmental policies, programmes and procedures;

(c) in techniques related to work performance; and

(d) on government administrative techniques and procedures.[9]

We can profitably add to the aforesaid broad categorization—Human Relations in Administration and Staff Relations. This is so because the administration has to inspire confidence and evoke cooperation from the people—be it in the planning process or performance of more conventional tasks in administration. Staff relations in an age of greater unionization and political articulation may make or mar the total administrative effort.

Forms and Types of Training

Training can conveniently be divided into two principal types:

(1) On-the-job training; and

(2) Formal training. It can be further divided into :

  (a) post-entry initial training, and

  (b) in-service training.

These categories are not exclusive. They can be and are often happily blended. Formal training is often, though not necessarily always, called institutional training—be it a special institution set up by the government or be it organized in a university or any other such forum. It is also possible to combine the two. All these depend upon the organizational needs and their identification. On-the-job training is most common. The U.N. Handbook of Training in Public Service defines it as "the instruction received by civil servants in a more or less informal manner from colleagues of greater experience or higher rank." Obviously, it imparted in the work situation or the place of work. It has been said that it is more "a method of training rather than a type". The effectiveness of this type of training largely depends on the quality and interest of the senior officer or supervisor. Methods like specific delegation of responsibilities, group discussions and planned rotation or postings are used to impart greater effectiveness to on-the-job training. No amount of background training and skill training can supplant the need for on-the-job training. Every senior civil servant should have an ingredient of training ability as a part of his functional competence and as integral to the progression of the career in public service.[10]

Formal training implies a planned and well-structured training programme and course. Training for new entrants is formalized. It can be in the nature of orientation training or induction training. It all depends on the level of recruitment and the type of work the new recruited are expected to perform. Both are often combined and followed by functional or professional training. Foundation Course for Class I Officers at the National Academy of Administration partakes the nature of orientation training. Orientation training can be an ingredient of middle or senior level in-service training programme too.

Objectives of Post-entry Initial Training

Basically, the aims and objectives of the post-entry initial training can be summarized as follows:

(a) Developing an understanding and appreciation of government's role in society.

(b) Developing a working knowledge of the tools and skills necessary to a career in government.

(c) Developing a familiarity with the substantive field of public administration, including such aspects as personnel management, budgeting, organization and work methods.

(d) Developing an awareness of the economic, administrative and social problems of the country and the efforts made to solve them. [11]

The duration, contents of the course, reading material to be used, the training methods and techniques are some of the problems of planning, designing and organizing such training programmes.

Nature and Objectives of Training

In-service training programme can be for middle management in public service as well as for senior administrators. In-service programmes also relate to functional and technical areas in administration. The main objective of in-service training programme is to accelerate the maturity process of the officer, to reorient him in ideas and outlook and to prepare him well with new techniques and skills. Objectives of the middle management and development to top administrators may partly be in common. In other ways, there has to be some variation too. All this will naturally reflect in the nature of training course, its duration, reading material and teaching techniques. But this much has to be all along kept in view that there has to be much greater flexibility in working out these programmes. Participative methods become more fruitful as this group of trainees constitute by itself 'resource personnel' can contribute to mutual development by interaction and interchange of views and experience. The basic essential for the success of such a programme is a climate receptive to change and development. In the case of in-service programme for senior administrators, apart from managerial or conceptual skills, factors which enhance capacity for decision-making, increase ability and willingness to accept responsibility, broaden managerial skills and perspectives, infuse confidence to delegate authority and develop subordinates, need particular attention. In-service training has to be more individualized in orientation. There has to be the recognition that in view of the compulsions of long-range thinking and perspective planning or programming in all the spheres of life today, the administration has to be much more intellectualized today than before. If the civil servants presume to advise on policy formulation, it is obligatory for them to keep abreast of the trends and temper of the time as well as the latest thinking on vital issues facing the society. The conventional frontiers between administration and management are breaking down. There is increasing need for managerial perspectives to be woven in the conceptual as well as operational framework of training in administration.[12]

Multidimensional Nature of, and Approach to, Training

Administration is concerned with regulation, management and administration of human affairs. The approach to training is therefore to encompass the entire gamut of human behaviour and reactions. Training has therefore to be conceptual, technique-oriented as well as programme-based. The level of trainees will determine the emphasis which any of these approaches will have. In certain cases, especially for entrants to senior services, a happy amalgam will have to be worked out. Moreover, as human affairs are complex and variegated, the approach has to be necessarily interdisciplinary. It is the insights of many developing disciplines and social sciences which provide meaningful insights into human motivations and human behaviour. Similarly, many techniques and aids are provided by developments in sciences and technology. An integrative angle to the study and understanding of administrative problems has to be consciously and continuously developed. Even, as a matter of pure methodology, an administrative problem acquires multidimensional illumination, realism and understanding when it is x-rayed from historical, legal, structural, sociological, behavioural and analytical viewpoints. In the evaluation of the study of administration, they are not mere stages but concurrent circles. Training in administration is a creative framework.

Training Methods and Techniques

The role of training in administration depends to a great extent on the training methods and techniques. Some of these techniques have developed in the teaching of social sciences or law. New experiments have been made in training programmes both in the fields of defence, and industry and business. There is a fair amount of mythology that has grown around the jargon of techniques only with a view to look really modern. Fair amount of experimentation in training techniques is called for. All the techniques are not applicable to all levels and variety of trainees or all branches of knowledge. Happy blending of one and more of these techniques is possible and desirable. Moreover, in our circumstances requiring diversified and multiple training needs, no single method will suffice. The conscious attempt all along has to be as to which of these techniques creates better involvement of participants, evokes greater response and leaves long-lasting impact. Initially, the core problem of learning of training process is as to how to catch and maintain attention or receptivity of participants. Techniques are group-centred or individual-oriented. They can be classified: (1) according to the degree of participant response; (2) according to the participant's exposure to administrative reality; and (3) according to participant motivation. Many of the techniques are not separate ones but just variants. It is not proposed to enumerate all the techniques or discuss them in any detail. I feel that the time honoured lecture method cannot be completely dispensed with. But it is possible to combine it with tutorials, discussion groups effectively and even to make it more lively by presentation of incidents or illustrations. Audio-visual aids can be combined with lecture method and other techniques. Seminars, conferences, syndicates and case studies based on indigenous experience can be very useful. It will depend on the trainer and those entrusted with training function to identify the techniques effective for a particular group since the choice is largely determined by the nature of the group of participants and as to the nature of objectives of particular training course or programme.

Training Aids

Sometimes training aids are apt to be equated with training techniques. Training aids are mainly designed for trainers, though in certain cases they can be used by individual trainee on his own. Similarly, training materials and training aids are also to be broadly distinguished. However, the interrelated nature of training techniques, training aids and training material has to be realized. Training aids, which appeal to the eye, are called visual (e.g., slides or posters). There are those which appeal to the ear (audio), e.g., tape recorders. Again, there are those which appeal to both ear and eye (audio-visual), e.g., television, cinema, projectors etc. The videoscope and overhead projectors as well as tape recorders (e.g., in role playing or for taped talks or interviews) are useful in utilizing all types of training materials and can be combined with various training techniques. Suitability and adoption of these techniques depend again on the insight of the trainer.

Training and Instructional Material

Efficacy of training and administration depends also on the instruction or teaching material which is scarce. In order to be effective, it has to be suffused with environmental realism and based on indigenous experience. The preparation of training material to meet the needs of various groups and at different levels (of responsibilities) in public service merits attention all along. Select reading lists with a concise annotated bibliography are useful. The need to build adequate library services with magazines, periodicals, laws, reports etc. is immense. Library has to become an active centre and not a mere passive collection of documents or books. Memoirs or reminiscences of former administrators or public men with administrative experience contain a mine of useful information. They help to pierce the veil of formal governmental processes. Similarly, if processed properly, the reports of legislative committees can provide basic training material of all types.[13]

Evaluation of Training Effectiveness

Evaluation of training programme is essential if training has to play an effective role in administration. Continuing qualitative assessment and reassessment of the training programmes is invariably necessary if they have to be intellectually 'live' and adequate as well as operationally meaningful and attractive. The effectiveness of a training course is not necessarily linked with the popularity of a course due to many extraneous factors. Evaluation has to be in-built in any system or programme of training in public service. It is always useful if the system of evaluation has been visualized and designed along with the planning and organizing of a training programme. It has also to be kept in view that no fool-proof evaluation device has been worked out. But, the very fact of the consciousness and need for evaluation helps to bring about improvement. It is a step towards quest for excellence. Evaluation has broadly two aims or is of two kinds. In the first place, it seeks to assess the training programme in order to work out better contents, design and improve methods of teaching. This can be done by a review session on the part of the trainers after the close of the programme. It can be done through a well-structured questionnaire along with room for general comments by participants and with facility for remaining anonymous if they so desire. In the second place, evaluation seeks to evaluate the impact of training on the performance of the public servants. This is rather difficult, but can be achieved to a certain degree through interviews with trainee and his supervisor, examinations in certain cases, visits by trainers to field and continuing contacts with the trainees and departmental superiors. The trainees can be called back after a year or two for exchange of views and to assess the impact of training. Apart from these, the evaluation can also aim at the appraisal of the competence and effectiveness of the trainer or instructor in relation to a training programme. Donald L. Kirkpatrick, in his article on "Evaluation of Training"[14] mentions four categories of evaluation of training programmes: reaction, learning, behaviour and results. Certainly, all these parameters merit attention while organizing training programmes. "If attendance on a course is to have any lasting effect it is necessary for the participants to acquire or regain the habit of learning so that they can keep themselves abreast of new developments besides acquiring a new tempo of self-learning."[15]

Management and Organization of Training Function: Role of Training Coordinator/Manager/Director

We have made a reference earlier to the need for political and administrative support of training function. In this connection mention was also made of the adequate location of training function. The management of training function or responsibility for training is very important. Training function is closely related to the overall responsibility for personnel management. It is essential that every organization/department in the government should have somebody specifically charged with this responsibility. If this function is to receive adequate attention, he should not be overburdened with other work. It is his responsibility to identify training needs, work out training programmes, find out as to where the training needs can be fulfilled and so on. He will be concerned at times with the selection and development of institutional staff. In consultation with the head of the department, he must work out the objectives of training programmes as may be needed. He will have to develop a training plan to achieve these objectives. He will have to make budgetary arrangements and administer the training plan. He would also be concerned with appraisal of the implementation of the programme from the angle of cost and overall organizational effectiveness. Convincing the top man regarding the utility of training, not always tangible, is his job. It is for him to ensure that the follow-up of training programme is carried out. He has to be alive to the organizational and instructional or substantive aspects of training apart from training effectiveness. It should be his responsibility to make optimum use of all training resources as may be available in a planned manner for the betterment of his organization. It may be essential to have a Directorate of Training for planning and coordination if a particular organization has many components units. There may be need for formal or informal training programmes even for Training Coordinators or Training Directors so that they are fully aware of the problems and obligations of training.

Training of Trainers: Nature and Role

We have earlier referred to the vital importance of the right type of trainers. But they also need to be trained and developed if they have to conduct manifold training courses and programmes in consonance with training requirements in administration. Training of trainers will aim to familiarize them in the background of the contemporary administrative scenario with modern methods of training and help to improve their competence in imparting instruction and designing courses. In certain cases these may be needed for updating of select specialisms. The role of trainers is underlined by the aphorism that "training is what trainers do". Thus, a proper mix of administrative experience and scholastic base is needed in any group of trainers concerned with training in administration. Apart from personality and educational factors, work experience as well as professional stature or standing have to be looked for in one who has to assume the role of a trainer. He must have aptitude and the quality of "competence of empathy"—interest in others—if he has to build proper rapport with trainees. But whatever his profession he will make no real impact if the trainees think he is not sincere. Trainers must also have a variety of ways and scope for self-development. Developing a professional awareness and opportunities for interaction and exchange of views and experience within the training profession will contribute greatly to an effective role of training in administration. [16]

Relevance of Training and Relationship with Programme Function

Mention has been made earlier about the quality of training as mediocrity undermines faith in its very purposes. But, in order to make training relevant, it is essential to relate it to programme functions. This can only be achieved if there is continuing liaison and contract between the training institution or those conducting a training programme and the officials responsible for working in particular organizations. It is only through this interaction that in the context of a realistic assessment of training lags or gaps, meaningful programmes can be evolved and even requisite resource personnel located. This will make it easier for translating training into action since an atmosphere for organizational change and receptivity will be created. Not only will training imparted achieve credibility and administrative support, it may act as an instrument of innovation and administrative reform in the organization. As a writer has said, "Training and development should not be thought of as a mere programme or an impressive collection of techniques and courses but as a philosophy. Development takes place only when every individual in an organization feels that he is expected, encouraged and helped to grow." It is this spirit, climate and attitude which are important; the mechanics of training are not so important, though they are necessary to bring about conditions which result in systematic development."[17]

Training for Development Administration

In a developing society, it is often said that the traditional administration has to transmute itself into development administration. Such a dichotomy is, however, conceptually and operationally sterile. No development is possible unless there is stability of law and order in society. It is also recognized that immense resources or revenues have to be mobilized if the development has to be self-generating process. Moreover, even development administration has to be regulatory in nature due to compulsion of social justice. The position really is for administration at any point of time to be aware of emerging problems and to prepare itself to cope with them. But, the cliches continue to operate that training in administration should prepare for 'development administration'.[18] Any way, development administration has to take into consideration and is concerned with five 'Ps', viz., (a) Policies, (b) Plans, (c) Programmes, (d) Projects, and (e) People. The last ingredient signifies democratic accountability, need for motivating employees, evoking public cooperation and the need for synthesizing technical, economic and administrative aspects in public interest. It goes without saying that in the larger perspective of a changing society and a democratic set-up, no public servant can either have a sense of achievement or even narrowly justify himself unless he is conscious of these aspects in his day-to-day working. The role of training in administration is thus to provide knowledge and social and professional skills as well as generate necessary attitudes and behavioural patterns in the public service as a whole in order to make it functionally adequate and socially sensitive. Training, if conceived wisely and implemented scientifically, would go a long way in establishing professional norms and promoting public service ethics. Public service, which is functionally adequate and has well-recognized professional and ethical standards, may be swayed by occasional gusts of ill-informed or misinformed criticism but not swept away to the brink of demoralization.

Organizational and Operating Problems of Training

The rationale of the role of training in administration is gaining acceptance. This underlines the need for planning training programmes imaginatively and realistically. The quality and competence of trainers will have much contribution to make to the effectiveness of training. The report of the Administrative Reforms Commission on Personnel Administration has classified the segments in public service as junior, middle and senior management levels. The ARC Study Team on Recruitment, Selection, UPSC/State PSCs and Training has mentioned three categories: (a) policy and managerial, (b) middle management and supervisory, and (c) the infrastructure. Training programmes have to cater to all these levels. This underlines the need for scientific organizational analysis for identification of training group and needs and formulation of plans and specific programmes accordingly. The contents and techniques of training will be conditioned by the objectives and levels of training. Responsibility for training within the organization must be that of the superior official. Institutions and organizational arrangements outside may act as catalytic or service agents. The complete character of approach to training in public service has to take into account research and consultancy. If training has to be realistic, meaningful and willingly acceptable to the operating agencies in administration, institution-building for training in administration has to reckon with this compulsive factor.[19]

Training Strategy

The operating problems of training in terms of working out goals of training, involvement of departments, responsibility for training, arrangements for training, identification of training needs for gaps, organization of faculty, training contents and design of curriculum, selection of techniques, preparation of material, feedback of evaluation, linkage with personal management—all point out to the need for a long-term strategy of planning. The actual implementation, phasing and determination of priorities will be required. The need may be to locate certain strategic areas as a starting point so as to create maximum of impact and which may have snowball effect. Training in administration has multidimensional problems and they merit continuing and comprehensive approach. In view of the developing dimensions and emerging problems in administration, the entire approach to training in public administration has to be in an exploratory and programmatic spirit. Any sound training strategy has to be backed by commitments to the role of training in administration as a matter of policy, if we aim at a creative and achievement-oriented administration responsive to the needs of the people and capable of meeting the challenges of a changing society.

Notes

1. Hand Book of Training in the Public Service (U.N., 1966).
2. Report of the Committee on the Training of Civil Servants, Cmd. 6525, 1944, pp. 10-11.
3. Ibid.
4. Education of the Administrator by Wengert in *The Study of Public Administration* (University of Oregon, 1961).
5. B. Lal, *Personnel Administration* (Training Division, Cabinet Secretariat, 1970).
6. A.P. Saxena, *The Training Function: Identification and Implementation* (Training Division, 1969).
7. T.N. Chaturvedi, *Public Service and Modern Challenges: Need for Continuing Administration* (Training Division, 1970).
8. T.N. Chaturvedi, *Some Common Problems of Training Institutions* (The Training Institution and the Trainer, N.A.A., Mussoorie).
9. M.A. Niaz, *Training Programmes for Various Categories of Civil Servants* (IIAS, Brussels).
10. T.N. Chaturvedi, Training for Trainers: Concept and Organisational Problems (mimeographed), Papers and Proceedings of

the Conference of the Training Institutions, N.A.A., Mussoorie, June 1969.

11. M.A. Niaz, op. cit.
12. L.P. Singh, Valedictory Address, "Conference on Training", IIPA, February 1969. Also refer to R.P. Saxena, *Management Training for Trainers* (Training Division, 1969).
13. Education in Public Administration (A Symposium on Teaching Methods and Materials) ed. by Donald C. Stone (IIAS, Brussels, 1963) & Some Common Problems of Training Institutions (mimeographed) by T.N. Chaturvedi.
14. R.L. Craig and L.R. Bittel (eds.), *Training and Development Handbook* (McGraw-Hill, 1967).
15. Training Managers, Action Society Trust, 1962.
16. Training for Trainers: Concept and Organisational Problems, by T.N. Chaturvedi (mimeographed) and Training of the Trainers, by A.R. Tyagi (mimeographed).
17. M.A. Niaz, op. cit.
18. Education for Development Administration (A Symposium)—IIAS, Brussels, 1966.
19. T.N. Chaturvedi, Institution Building for Training in Administration, *Management in Government*, Vol. 11, No. 1, April-June 1970.

2

Training and Executive Development

B. MEHTA

For running an organization, the management has five major functions. They are: (1) selection, (2) training, (3) control, (4) delegation, and (5) remuneration.

I have purposely put selection and training at the top. Every company must have right type of material processed to get the final product. Wise selection and proper training are, therefore, very necessary. It is only when right type of persons are selected, training, remuneration and incentives will have a meaning.

It will not be wrong to say that in India in our endeavour to procure the machine and tools, to build factories and dams, and to find the money to finance it all, we have become a little too materialistic and have forgotten the human factor. The findings of the survey conducted by the All India Management Association are revealing:

- 27.6 per cent of the managers surveyed do not possess a university degree.
- 54 per cent of supervisory staff are non-graduates.

- 62 per cent of supervisors have less than ten years' experience. This would imply that they have another twenty-five years of service, without an opportunity of training.
- 20 per cent of the managers have undergone training.

Investment in human resource development or what the great economist Marshall calls 'personal capital' is so important in the economic growth of a nation that it should not be left to chance. There is, however, new recognition of the importance of the development of the management personnel. For human resource development right selection has the top place and very great care has to be taken in selecting persons for different jobs, whether they are directly recruited or lent by the state government. In the interest of the organization the practice of sending officers on deputation needs to be discouraged. The public sector organizations should develop their own services.

Selection of direct recruits does not mean a mere interview. It will be useful to have a 'job analysis' to put in writing the questions required from the man for doing a job. I mean 'man specification'. It is only then that the selection board will know what type of person is needed. The idea is that executives should not be chosen on the basis of their apparent possession of behaviour, characteristics or traits, but on the basis of their possession of the requisite skills for the specific level of responsibility involved.

Many people are of the opinion that leadership ability is inherent in certain chosen individuals. There is no denying the fact that certain people, naturally or innately, possess greater aptitude or ability in certain skills. But it is also a fact that those having strong aptitudes and abilities can improve their skills through practice and training, even those lacking in natural ability can improve their performance through practice and training.

Different people learn in different ways, but the skills are developed through practice, relating to one's own personal experience and background and institutional training. If this is properly done, training in these basic managerial skills should develop executive abilities more surely and more rapidly than the unorganized experience. What, then, are the important ways in which a training can be conducted for the executives in the organization itself?

An executive is one who (1) directs the activities or other persons, and (2) undertakes the responsibility for achieving objectives set or may be set for the organization. This definition requires the executive to have technical, human and conceptual skills. These skills are interrelated but have to be developed independently.

Technical Skill

Technical skill involves specialized knowledge, analytical ability within that speciality and facility in the use of the tools and techniques of this specific discipline. Development of technical skill has received the necessary attention and is being, to a large extent, attended to. Sound grounding in the technical institutions and actual practice and experience should suffice. The entrant should, however, be put under a qualified and experienced senior in the initial stages of the service. This, I think, will be an effective training.

Human Skill

Human skill, which is the most important and difficult skill of management, is primarily concerned with working with people. This will be demonstrated in the way executive perceives his superiors, equals and subordinates and behaves subsequently. At every level human skill is very essential for securing integrated team effort. Only that executive will be effective in whom this skill has become an integrated part. Human relations are based on the four fundamental concepts, which constitute the philosophical framework of the subject. They are:

(i) *Motivation*: The means by which the executive creates and maintains the desire of his people to achieve the planned goals.

(ii) *Individual differences*: The existence of these differences precludes the possibility of repeating an experiment under standard conditions.

(iii) *Mutual interest*: The cooperative association of the workers and the company would enable both the parties to secure their respective goals.

(iv) *Human dignity*: The recognition of the fact that each person is a separate personality, free to pursue happiness within the bonds of responsibility.

At this stage, I would like to mention that human relations should not be taken as the practice of amiability. For satisfactory human relations, firmness, when necessary, is essential. Interest in human relations should not be equated with tender mindedness, sentimentality and an unrealistic desire to make everybody happy. In our particular context, it will be necessary to evolve our own working methods.

If the basic concepts of human relations are properly put into practice, it will help in building up the morale of the employees. Without confusing morale with mere group enthusiasms and excitements, we can define it in terms of the individual's integration with the group, his acceptance of group goals and his active participation in the achievement of these goals. It generates loyalty to the organization and causes the organization to function with efficiency notwithstanding occasional difficulties. The studies of Daucel Katz and his associates have shown that morale and productivity have a circular casual relationship, i.e., better morale leads to better productivity and vice versa.

The human skill can be acquired by some individuals without a formalized training. Others can be individually aided by their superiors.

Conceptual Skill

Conceptual skill, like human skill, has not been very widely understood. This skill involves the capacity to visualize, plan, and act in the best interest of the organization. This is the trusteeship responsibility of a top level executive.

The American experience has shown that some of the best results have been achieved through the 'coaching' of the subordinates by superiors. It should be the responsibility of the executive to help his juniors to develop this skill. The senior executive could help the growth of his subordinate by (1) assigning a particular responsibility and by encouraging and helping him to take his own decision; (2) moving promising youngman through different functions of the business at the same level; (3) putting on special assignments which involve inter-departmental problems; and (4) putting junior executive as advisers to top management on policy matters.

Thus, effective management depends on three basic skills, namely, technical, human and conceptual. The relative importance of these three skills varies with the levels of responsibility. At lower levels, the major need is for technical and human skills. At higher levels it is the human and conceptual skills that will be required. At the top, conceptual skill is the most important for efficient running of the organization.

It may also be useful to organize 'Study Circles' in the organization, where the executives of the same specialization could meet and discuss new developments as well as their problems. For such discussions papers should be prepared in advance.

In the former princely states there was a practice to allow youngmen to work as apprentice in a government department and then select the best out of them for appointment in the service. Some such thing should also be introduced in our public sectors. A certain number of apprentice trainees should be selected on the basis of merit and attached to the departments of the trainee's interest—selection of the department should be left to the trainees. The apprentice trainees may be given broad training which should concentrate upon their learning the fundamentals of the subject. Men who perform satisfactorily during this training should be assigned to responsible posts in that speciality or department. Those who show unusual potential and have also demonstrated that they will benefit from additional training should be selected for further training. To start with, this can be tried with those employees of the government who want to work in public sector organizations.

The objectives of management apprenticeship programme may be:

(i) to supply an adequate number of qualified and trained persons to fill the posts of executives; and

(ii) to ensure that complete opportunity is afforded to apprise and develop the full administrative and technical potential of the trainees.

Having dealt with as to what can be done to develop executives in an organization, I will now deal with institutionalized training. Is it necessary? If so, why?

Training outside the organization is a new development in modern business industry and administration. It is being realized in business as in other fields that what the executives had learnt a decade or two before was no longer enough with new concepts and techniques developing at a very fast rate. There is new professionalization of management and there are skills that cannot be learnt on the job. Therefore, there is need for training in institutions specializing in management education.

Outside programmes have many advantages while taking a man away from his regular job. The management institutions and universities specializing in management education offer a variety of subjects which one organization cannot provide. Training outside the organization also makes available the experience of men from other organization. It also means vacation from daily routine.

At Harvard, two separate courses aimed at different levels of management are organized. We could, with advantage, follow the Harvard practice and organize two courses, the higher or advanced management and middle management programmes for the state public sector organizations. Both the programmes should employ case study method, using material taken from business. However, the management course should be concerned with technical and human skills and the other with conceptual skills. These programmes should be of fairly long duration. For mature and experienced ones seminars could be organized in small and intimate groups, without formal rituals. They may meet anywhere between one week to two weeks with the following objectives:

1. Improvement in one's own personality.
2. Development of general skills.
3. Improved conceptual skills.
4. Increased human relations skills.

I would like to emphasize that the approach to executive development outlined above will be effective only if it is part of the business of managing the organization. It does not depend solely on formal or informal programmes. They can only be strengthened by these suggested activities. Development of this sort can be perfected effectively by one executive or by the organization as a whole. Development of executives should become a part of the day-to-day activity. It is only then that it will become meaningful and important. I will close with the following lines from Robert Townsends' book *Up the Organisation*, the world's best seller:

> "Remember, you really want them (executives) to take some important decisions and some mistakes (see mistakes). That's how they grow."

3

Human Relations Training and Civil Servants

C. RICHARD PARKINS

The oft-repeated exhortation that one of the critical objectives of civil service training should be to inculcate 'right attitudes' suggests an appropriate role for human relation training in the civil service, for human relations training has as its basic concern the issue of attitudes. The question of attitudes as raised by human relations experts is raised not for its own sake but rather as a corollary of performance within the organization. A major premise of human relation training, sometimes referred to as applied behavioural science, is that behaviour is a critical determinant of one's effectiveness within an organization; and that the objective or mission of an organization implies certain behavioural responses. Therefore, human relations training provides a possible link between the requirements of the organization and the behaviour of its members. This paper is an attempt to discuss broadly the possible utility of human relations training in enhancing the behavioural capacity of public servants to respond more effectively to the tasks of public service.

To appreciate the relevance of human relations training to the education of civil servants, one must first examine fundamental questions about the relationship of civil servants to their work. The business of government or public service places certain responsibilities, both implicit and explicit, upon civil servants; and one cannot necessarily assume that all those entering the service are temperamentally or psychologically equipped to exercise these responsibilities or that they will automatically develop the appropriate behavioural attributes while on the job. To the contrary, the rewards and punishments of the system may nullify the very attitudes which are thought of as ideal for effective performance. Human relations training is offered as one possible vehicle for accelerating understanding about behaviour as a component of government service. A detailed discussion of the mechanics of human relations training is outside the scope of this paper; and other articles in this collection contain specific information on this subject. The intention of this discussion is to suggest relationship between government service and individual behaviour and ways in which human relations training can participate constructively in associating or reconciling the two.

Individual Values

Most critical is the individual himself. He does not come to his assignment in the public service without his ideological baggage. Feelings, sentiments, values, beliefs and convictions are a part of the psychological equipment, which is basic to our social existence. Yet, the public service itself operates with certain normative assumptions. Democracy, secularism and socialism are not devoid of normative considerations. These concepts suggest an administrative system committed to equality, toleration and nationalism. Yet, the residue of the past, i.e., casteism, provincialism, religious exclusiveness, and the social and political authoritarianism of a feudal and colonial heritage, are not eradicated solely by directives and exhortation. Yet, most would agree that adherence to these anachronisms retard democracy and development. There are instances of incompatibility between personal values and the articulated

development work calls for certain attitudes from those charged with the task of programme implementation, then he must also ponder the question of how these attitudes are to be identified, cultivated, and nourished. Again, the presence or absence of these attitudes may not be immediately observable; and thus an approach to training which is both diagnostic and remedial needs to be considered.

Relations with Public

One hears frequent lamentations about the inability of public servants to deal sympathetically and promptly with the public. Although no one disputes the fact that civil servants must serve the public, the very act of service can be troublesome for many of us. Implicit in the concept of service is the notion of a grater regard for other than for oneself. The public to be served is another dimension of the public life of the government officer which has behavioural implications. The public is hardly a monolithic entity. There are, in fact, many publics; and the variety of client group which complete for the attention of the government requires civil servants to be sensitive to the wide range of interest which comprise this collectivity. The civil servant must have the capacity to discern among various public and to recognize the different approaches which must be taken to respond adequately to their concerns. Obviously, an indigent rural farmer who may still be cynical about participative democracy or who has had his expectations raised unduly is different from an urban merchant who has had practice in working with complicated systems or who can possibly bring more resources to bear upon the administrative and political system. But, both are legitimate constituencies to be served by the government. This raises the question of adaptable styles in relating to this disparate entity. The problem is intensified by the expanding role of government which directly or indirectly touches upon more aspects of the lives of more people. Thus, the opportunities for interaction between administrator and public have multiplied. This self-evident point does not require elaboration. What does require emphasis is the difficulty which the official encounters when he must confront various publics all anger to press for the recognition of what seem to them to be legitimate claims. Many officers may have the intuitive capacity to handle such situations, but no doubt an overwhelming number could profit from some guidance in evolving an appropriate role in relating to the public. The resolution of this problem may be the acid test of democracy. It may also be the problem which ouches most profoundly the beliers and attitudes of the individual civil servant as an executor of public policy. Conflicts and tensions are probably most acute in this sphere of his public life.

Civil Servant and Changing Roles

The context of government service is one of change in other respects. In the first instance, not all postings are similar. Work in a remote and poverty ridden district contrasts sharply with an assignment in a more advanced urban centre. For example, isolated rural areas require administration which can promote change, inject confidence in citizens, and project an image of government which is accessible. These same concerns may exist in urban settings but here one can expect that other catalytic agents and service agencies may be available to the citizenry. Also, in more urban areas, social, political and economic tensions possibly resulting in open conflict may necessitate a greater interest in law and order upon the part of the civil officer. Obviously, the settings are not mutually exclusive in their administrative needs, but the dynamics of urban and rural life are certainly different enough to require a different perspective upon the part of the administrator.

In the same vein, work in the field is distinguishable from work in the secretariat. Work in the field brings the officer into more frequent and direct contact with citizens. Secretariat work may put the officer closer to policy formulation. A staff position is different from a line position. A regulatory posting may be different from a developmental job which demands a promotional effort. Yet, in all instances, we assume that officers are virtually interchangeable. If this premise continues to prevail in the placement of officers, are there any attempts which can be made to facilitate the adjustment of officers to the various types of roles which they are expected to perform? Part of the problem is solved through experience and the prior knowledge which the officer has that his participation in government demands this versatility of him. But, since movement among various situations is an endemic and significant feature of the Indian civil service, certainly measures which can enhance the ability of officers to adapt to a multiple role set should be welcomed.

One of the most important demanding resolutions by the civil servant is his relationship to political leaders. The civil servant invariably finds himself juxtaposed between the public and the political leaders. In addition to his own norms and values, he must accommodate to those other forces which legitimately circumscribe his behaviour. He cannot always take refuge in the sanctity of rules and procedures. Since the administrative environment is largely defined by both public and politician, the administrator will find conflict situations to be a part of his daily routine. Such a setting calls into play the full behavioural resources of the public servant. He must satisfy his own standards of conduct; he must react to a shifting and demanding public; and he must recognize the legitimacy of the political official as the very essence of participatory democracy. The training of civil servants must assist officers in contending with what is potentially a tension producing environment.

Civil Servant as Manager

Of immediate concern o the civil servant is his role as a manager of persons. He must motivate individuals to perform effectively. He must encourage their ingenuity while at the same time controlling their actions with respect to the prescribed norms and requirements of the department of programme in which they are operating. The familiar principles of management such as delegation, control, and employee motivation are all essentially behavioural concepts. Delegation implies conferring trust upon a subordinate. It also implies accepting responsibility for his mistakes. Motivation is the most complicated of these principles since such conventional rewards as salary increases or promotions are not often within the administrative purview of the supervisor. The alternative may be to emphasize job satisfaction or a sense of accomplishment upon the part of the employee; although this is not easily accomplished when security or physical needs may be a dominant part of the employee's concerns. Ultimately, if one accepts a major premise of the management by objectives approach, managers must make efforts, to the extent feasible, it mesh personal goals with organizational goals. This can be a formidable task, one requiring maximum interpersonal skills. The problem of molding a governmental organization and motivating its members is exacerbated by the shifting of individuals within departments, thus making it more troublesome to be in tune with the interpersonal dynamics (tensions and conflicts) of the organization. Yet, this inherent responsibility of government managers must be tackled.

This simple and incomplete enumeration of the behavioural issues relating to public service is presented only to suggest that many of the skills and attributes of the civil servant are maters of temperament, personality, or behaviour. If this is accepted, it is incumbent upon those interested in the training and education of civil servants to recognize these issues as being important to training content and method. One approach is to assume that behavioural properties are basically immutable, but modern behavioural science does not permit us this dismal conclusion. Others might argue that attitudes will change only through the unfolding of experience as a normal part of life. But this belief condemns us to a slow, encertain, and unreliable process in developing an adequate body of qualified officers. No one disputes that affecting behaviour or attitudes is an enormously difficult task. But professionals in the human relations or applied behavioural science field, influenced by their research and training efforts contend that behavioural change can be stimulated and accelerated through intensive learning experiences. The balance of this paper will attempt to suggest possible role for human relations training in the total training-cum-educational effort of public servants.

Self-knowledge

Human relations training begins with the premise that the individual is the main ingredient of an organization. Human relations training also assumes that much of the behaviour which the individual exhibits within his respective organization is a function of his total personality. This premise disputes the idea that an individual who is presumably technically qualified for job will ipso facto adjust to it and perform satisfactorily. Particular situations within an organization call forth certain behavioural reactions. The extent to which these are exhibited may be determined by circumstances which transcend the job and which are dependent upon the emotional or temperamental qualities of the individual. Thus, human relations training attempts to use individual behaviour as its content.

A related assumption is that many of the motivating forces which govern one's behaviour, particularly in group or organizational situations, are submerged. Much of who we are and what we do is precipitated by influences which are possibly not known to ourselves. Therefore, awareness of self becomes a first step in the learning process which human relations training attempts to stimulate. Enhanced self-awareness includes that part of the self as viewed by others. This is important within the context of organizational participation, for effectiveness within an organization is inextricably linked to the view which other hold of our behaviour. Behind all of this is the assumption that many organizational difficulties, both internal as well as those relating to the outside community, can be attributed to faulty communication. Faulty communication is not always deliberate. The covert communication which takes place can be every bit as injurious to a harmonious organization or to the clients of an organization as the international or overt communication which transpires, yet the impact of the former is rarely understood or appreciated.

The root of poor interpersonal relations is frequently caused by our inability to see ourselves as others see us. We consciously or unconsciously misread other persons; and likewise are misread. A constant process of misreading can produce internal organizational maladies. The same phenomenon can hamper our relations with external groups to whom the organization must render some service or from whom it must take counsel. It is important to know how we are viewed by others, not necessarily with the intention of changing ourselves; although this will hopefully occur in some cases, but also to understand more fully the responses that we receive from others. Knowledge about oneself which includes the part of self as seen by others is the initial step in working effectively within a group and among groups. This principle obviously have relevance for the civil servant who is both a group member as well as representative of public policy to the citizenry and, more specifically, to some client group.

Relating to Different Persons and Groups

The composition of a human relation session usually provides a cross-section of personality types. This produces a situation in microcosm that may correspond to the types of individuals invariably confronted in the job situation. The variety of behavioural experience offered by a human relations laboratory allows individuals to experience intensive interaction with an extensive range of personality types. But it is not only a particular relationship to particular relationship to a particular person that it crucial. It is also the opportunity to receive feedback about one's self and to learn about others from the different sources which comprise the group. Related to this is the demand placed upon participants to experience contact with persons who in the external environment might be avoided or feared but who in the lab demand recognition.

Human relations training makes it difficult to evade interaction with difficult unpleasant, or threatening personality types. The interaction is facilitated by the trust and thus the honesty which a skilfully conducted session will presumably encourage. Also, in such training every effort is made to induce a sense of equality among group members, at least as far as the immediate group is concerned. Thus, the sanctions and status considerations which inhibit candid interaction in the outside world cannot operate with the same effect in the training session. A training session which can produce such a climate obviously encourages individuals to relate to individuals who may be similar to persons whom he encounters in the outside world but with whom he has never learned to cope. Interaction with such types and the subsequent analysis of that interaction is virtually obligatory within a human relations session; and thus unique learning experience are provided. This aspect of human relations training has implications for the government servant who may be submissive to authority while at the same time resenting the authority or his submissive state. Such experience may also increase his understanding of individuals and groups which would ordinarily be seen as adversaries but who nonetheless occupy an important place in his work.

One of the objectives of any training experience should be to approximate reality. Because human relations training is experience based (upon the real experiences of real people), the strength of reality is greater. Granted, the intensive and possibly contrived quality of human relations training is somewhat unreal when compared to the restraint and is somewhat unreal when compared to the restraint and superficiality of the outside world; yet it is nevertheless perceptibly closer to that world than he more normal class room experiences which characterize most training courses. One might assert that a human relations lab is 'heightened reality', that is a strong does of reality.

Experimentation

From the content and dynamics (interactions) of a human relations experience, an individual gains more knowledge about himself and others. If properly organized and conducted, the individual should learn how to employ that knowledge to his advantage and to he advantage of his organization. This introduces the question of application.

In the outside world, individuals may be hesitant to experiment with different behavioural styles or approaches. The sanctions against doing so may seem to be too severe or the opportunities too limited. The change to try different approaches in communicating and getting along with others is a salient feature of human relations training. A major contention of the human relations exponent is that a person's manner of interacting with others is put to the pragmatic test in human relations training, for here behavioural experimentation is encouraged and its workability assessed. The fact that human relations training sessions are referred to as laboratories suggests the experimental and testing aspect of the training. Such experimentation might also be viewed as a kind of risk taking, since one ventures to express himself differently with no assurance that the results will be satisfactory. But in the laboratory, the cost is reduced by the acceptance of other members of the group that it is permissible to take a chance and that they have an obligation to support the individual in his efforts.

Two objectives are served by the process of experimentation: (1) individuals learn to recognize the effect of their style upon various categories of individuals and to accommodate to the variety of persons to whom they are exposed; and (2) individuals gain insight into the thinking of persons quite different from themselves and hopefully develop an appreciation of the motives governing the behaviour of others. One of the greatest handicaps to cooperative effort within an organization or effective organizational effort with potential recipients of its services, and the government is no expectation, is partial or misunderstanding of the premise upon which the other party acts. Human relations training may have something to contribute in minimising this difficulty.

It should be pointed out that the lab would not be particularly instructive if generalization could not occur, for the validity of the training experience rests with its transferability to the world to which the trainee returns. Under a skillful trainer, the individual and his colleagues not only examine specific instances of interaction but also learn to recognize elements of the process which go beyond the specific incident and have relevance to situations common to the individual's personal and professional life. This feature of the training is most important with respect to experimentation, for the isolated experience of a group situation would mean nothing unless the individual could be helped to project himself into other more common settings where he is required to make responses.

Help through Shared Experiences

Candour and freedom have been mentioned as characteristics of human relations training. This stimulates a sharing of experiences. One consequence of this sharing is the realization that ones concerns and problems are not peculiar to ones self but often correspond to similar problems experienced by others. In the context of the laboratory, the collective expertise of the group is employed to help persons find solutions to some of these problems, particularly those of an interpersonal nature. It is often helpful to realize that our difficulties are not unique to us. It is even more helpful to receive guidance and encouragement from others who can vicariously identify with our problems because of similar experience which they have had experiences which can be openly shared in the supportive environment of a human relations session.

Innovation and Change

Thus far the discussion has emphasized human relations training as a means of helping persons to get along with others. There is, however, another service which this training can provide. Certain kinds of human relation experiences can strengthen the individual who insists upon his individuality and whose non-conformity may be a positive influence within an organization. All systems need change agents, otherwise, sterility and inertia result. The government can ill-afford either. Therefore, organizations should learn how to take advantage of innovative members who can produce needed change for the organization; and potential change agents of innovators should be helped to evolve an effective strategy for implementing change.

There are obviously different ways where by change can be attempted; and they are not all equally effective or particularly suited to a certain organizational setting. There are times when confrontation will work and times when it is dysfunctional. Other situations may demand greater diplomacy and discretion. Many persons who can be instruments of creativity and innovation within an organization either fail because they needlessly offer or, more frequently, because they lack the self-confidence or personal esteem to take the risk which change often involves. The strategy of change is a legitimate focus of human relations training. Certain labs are designed specifically for this purpose. This is stressed function of human relations training is stressed so that we will recognize that the sole purpose of human relation training is not only to help persons adjust to the organizational climate but also to change it. Since change is a dynamic and complex process, persons can be benefitted through a human relations lab in analyzing its dynamics vis-à-vis their own participation in the change process.

Conclusions

The previous commentary does not exhaustively cover the possible benefits of human relation training. These few paragraphs merely attempt to point out a possible relationship between the requirements and pressures of the life of a civil servant and a possible place for human relations training in coping with these. But, if human relations training is to have a useful role in the training and education of civil servants, there are certain requirements which it should meet. Obviously, a training method must be employed in terms of the organizational objectives being pursued and must be exercised with considerable professional competence. The method per se has no validity independent of the circumstances in which it is used.

Human relations training should be conducted by professionally competent individuals. Amateurism is inappropriate when the raw material of training are the values and attitudes of individuals. Moreover, the task of synthesis and generalization which gives utility to human relations training can best be achieved by persons experienced in psychology, learning, or some related discipline. A rare few may be intuitively equipped to do this task, but must require training. Fortunately, India has made good progress in developing a body of training expertise in this area.

The informal, unstructured and experimental character of human relations training affords participants the opportunity to witness under close and guided scrutiny the behaviour of others. The observation is not a detached or impersonal process; it is a vital one since it is derived from experiences of interaction. One might argue that interaction and subsequent observation occur routinely in the life of all individuals; and thus human relations training provides nothing new. The crucial difference is that the observation process is intentional in human relations training, and it occurs under the supervision of one who has skill in guiding observation. More importantly, the feedback principle is a paramount feature of human relations training. Direct and honest feedback is expected in human relations training, and the equality among the participants as well as the atmosphere of trust and sharing which the trainer generates means that no one escapes it. Feedback allows one to know the reactions of others. He may not accept the validity of their views, but their perception are nevertheless a reality insofar as interpersonal relations are concerned. Rarely in the outside world is candid feedback, we may remain ignorant about an important dimension of our personality. It is this dimension which is important to our working with others.

The composition of a human relations training group can vary depending upon objectives. The initial efforts of the H.C. Mathur State Institute in this field were focused upon foundational trainees with the purpose of helping them to understand their role as government servants. In other organizations, the objective of such training has been to bring together at either the same time or at different times various tiers or echelons of the organization. Presumably, this will enhance inter-hierarchical communication and understanding. A case can also be made for bringing together persons who operate in different functional or organizational spheres but who perform tasks which are interrelated. The objective in such instances is to facilitate inter-departmental or inter-organizational cooperation. Regardless of the mix of the group, it should not be random (at least if the participant are sent by the government) but rather it should be based upon some rationale which reflects the relationship of members to a particular organizational framework. Only by observing this principle can the objective of organizational effectiveness be achieved. It is not only because of the functional interdependence of the participants that this criterion should be observed. It has also been demonstrated that persons who undergo such training can more readily utilize the training in the "back-home" situation if they have the support and assistance of fellow co-workers who have shared the experience and appreciate its dimensions.

Another way of efficiently using human relations training in government is to make it "task-oriented". In short, human relations training, if it is to be useful to government departments, should be directed toward specific governmental problems where behavioural considerations play a part. Human relations training is not a verbal free-for-all where every conceivable feeling is offered up for analysis in some kind of a laissez-faire fashion. The elements of informality and lack of structure do not necessarily mean a lack of substance or purpose. Of course, the extent to which substance and purpose are accounted for in the training depends very much on the quality of the trainer, the planning involved, the diagnosis of organizational maladies upon which the training is predicated, and ultimately the composition of the training group. The impact of the training cannot be measured independent of these variables.

No grandiose claims can or should be made for human relations training as a cure for organizational difficulties. Such training only relates to one segment of organizational disturbances. Moreover, such training must be linked to other aspects of the organization.

Many proponents of human relations training have become progressively more committed to the notion that this training must be fused with a comprehensive organizational development programme; that it, is should not be pursued in isolation but rather should be connected to an overall strategy or organizational growth and improvement. Also, human relations training will have limited effect if offered sporadically. In the best of circumstances, it is an initial step which with a conducive organizational climate and adequate support and follow-through may have beneficial consequences for the organization. Like every other training strategy or method, it functions only as a service to the administration or management of an organization.

The advocacy tone of this note is motivated by the observation that human relations training possibly has potential for dealing with many of the motivational, interpersonal and role conflict problems which often plague governmental operations. In addition, the human relations approach remains relatively untested within the confines of civil service training. Possibly both excessive enthusiasm and excessive fear about the effects of such training would be tempered by more actual experience with human relations training. Unless empirical information is derived through application of the approach, claims and counter-claims remain groundless. Thus, carefully conceived efforts should be made to test the applicability of human relations training against the host of problems confronting trainers of government personnel problems which appear to be fairly intractable when dealt with by more conventional training methods.

4

Training: Some Aspects of Inter-Institutional Coordination

MOHAN MUKERJI

There is a general feeling that our ancestors believed in "plain living and high thinking". However, looking at the architecture, sculpture, painting and some of the literature of ancient times one could conclude that, like their descendants today, our forefathers maintained substantial differences between paper (rather palm-leaf), plans and practice. Anyway, except for a few persons above 70, the general policy today is "high living and plain thinking" to make such living possible. National planning is with the objective of increasing per capita GNP. The poorest of the poor is now not accepting the explanation that lie is paying the penalty for some sin in a previous birth or that his sufferings in this world will be compensated by happiness in paradise.

With the objective of achieving a higher and higher standard of living for an ever increasing percentage of the population, we obviously have to produce more and more persons specializing in a rapidly widening variety of subjects. Our educational system has, no doubt, been undergoing changes to meet the requirement of the growing variety of specialists. Still, we do not turn out from our educational institutions, persons who are fit to take up jobs of a really specialized nature. I have heard irrigation engineers complain that an Agriculture Engineer prepared plans for a water course which bad to climb over a little hillock. I pacified them by telling them about a collector who had little experience in Revenue administration, when he was on tour, villagers complained, *"Hamara* settlement *nahi hua."* He told them, *"Batao kya Jhagra hai mei* settle *kar deunga."* Sometimes ago, the ambassador of a developed country visited the Regional Engineering College. He was asked by a student whether separate courses for civil, electrical and mechanical existed in his country. He explained that there were over thirty different courses. While in the Central Ministry of Education, I once faced the problem of determining equation of a foreign degree in Heavy Earth-Moving Machine Engineering. Our medical college perhaps provide more detailed specialization than other professional institutions.

What I want to emphasize is that, today, our educational system does produce a wide variety of specialists, but they still do not meet our need for a much greater range of specialization. Because of our tremendous population and unemployment problem, a highly specialized person can never be sure of getting a job. Therefore, young people like to have options open to accept a variety of jobs. Educational institutions cannot adopt a policy of providing highly specialized courses and cause more educated employment in a country where education is largely at public expense.

This leads to the need to accept the position that for some time to come, real specialization will be after a person has been appointed to a job. This is true for higher as well as lower jobs—for example, a Roadways Engineer, a Patwari, an Assistant Registrar, Cooperatives, a booking clerk and so on. This is the position in private sector also. I recollect a discussion on the alleged inability of degree-holding specialist, to immediately attend to their specialized duties as soon as they are recruited. A well-known industrialist said that the needs of various industries varied so much that it would be impossible to design courses to meet everybody's requirement; he would be happy if technical and professional courses equip a young man with good knowledge on the basis of which he would be able to understand details taught to him during training following recruitment.

The importance of post-recruitment training to provide necessary specialization is thus apparent. It is a matter of vital consequence to the country. It is sometimes difficult to distinguish between training and education. What is training for some years, for example, industrial management can become education. I think, a practical distinction will serve our purpose, namely, what is taught before a person is thrown into the job market is education, what is taught by an employer, including the state, after recruitment, whether with regular salary or, with a stipend, is training. If this pragmatic line of division is accepted, then, the first problem of coordination is how to ensure that what has just been defined as education serves the objective of producing a specialist-needed by society. This can be dealt with by associating possible employers with the policy-making bodies connected with the relevant educational institutions. This is ensured in some cases by the educational institution itself being run by the organization which provides the major avenues of employment, for example, training of undergraduate teachers to man elementary schools which in Rajasthan are mostly state-managed or diploma courses for para-medic staff who, in this state generally get employed in government hospitals. There are however many educational courses on completion of which a person has many alternative avenues of employment. The most common example are degrees in technical subjects like engineering, mining, agriculture, veterinary science, commerce etc. The question is whether prospective employers have adequate say in the formulation of these courses and determining the methods of teaching. No doubt, highly qualified experts in the subject, already holding some high academic positions, are deeply involved in these matters. But is that sufficient? In the Central government there is the Board of Technical Education, meeting once or twice a year, and in the case of the Indian Institute of Technology (IIT) there is a board which meets quite frequently. The IIMs have management boards which are broad-based to include some 'laymen'. This is also true about the IISC, Bangalore. As already mentioned, in medical education teaching is closely connected with actual application of knowledge. The matter worth discussion is whether, within our state there should be some machinery for continuing dialogue between universities, Directorate of Technical Education, Board of Secondary Education and similar bodies on one band and the employing government departments, public sector and private sector on the other. Is mere membership of policy making bodies, like Senate, sufficient? Or, should there be advisory committees consisting of all interested organizations?

Having stated the issue relating to coordination in the area which I have tried to define as 'education', let me now come to what is more commonly known as 'training', which I have already defined as the instruction etc. given after recruitment, with pay or with stipend. In view of the employment situation in our country, I have explained how the raw recruit usually has theoretical education of wide applicability, but to prepare him to work competently on a specialized job he requires training. At this state I would like to draw a distinction between jobs which require a technical or professional academic qualification and those which can be handled by a person with general education in Arts or Science. There are border-line examples like persons with degrees in Commerce or Law.

Well, as for jobs of the first category, that is those requiring persons with specialized academic background, in Rajasthan as well as elsewhere in India the general attitude is that they need no, or very little, training. It is assumed that their specialized education will enable them to "Learn while they Earn". 'On-the-job' experience is felt to be sufficient for a

Junior Engineer, Assistant Engineer, Agriculture Extension Officer, Veterinary Surgeon, School Teacher, Draftsman, LDC, and so on. Is this a realistic approach? Are there not variations in duties sufficient to justify an initial period of training? For example, mechanical engineering problems in Buildings and Roads, Irrigation, Power Generation and Supply, Public Health Engineering, Ground Water and production of goods in factories and mines are widely different. Similarly, accounts-keeping in treasuries, cooperative bodies, industrial and commercial undertakings vary very much. Then, if a B. Com. or M. Com. who has done papers on Accountancy deserves to go through an initial training course, can we say that similar training is not required by holders of a degree or diploma in mechanical engineering? The variations in job requirement may determine the duration of this training but, depending on the extent of specialization expected in an organization compared to the nature of the academic course, there should be training courses for this type of recruitments much greater in number than what exists today.

Coming to the second category of jobs, namely, those which can be handled by persons with general education in Arts or Science, and sometimes in Commerce, institutional training, exists in Rajasthan as well as in many other states. The Harish Chandra Mathur State Institute of Public Administration (HCM SIPA) takes care of the administrative services, accounts services, and commercial tax services. There is also the Police Academy. The cooperative services too receive initial training. The matter which deserves attention is whether initial training arrangements for a number of other services are adequate, for example, Naib Tehsildars, excise officers, jail and correctional services, labour and employment services, and, quite important, education services at the stage when they begin to shoulder administrative responsibilities. It is presumed that this matter receives attention of government at the levels of Head of Department, Secretary and Minister. But I feel that this is not adequate. There has to be a coordinated approach. For a study of the adequacy of existing arrangements, to consider views of all affected departments and suggest changes, if any, there should be some organization using the expertise available in the HCM SIPA as well as in any other institution.

Lastly, I would like to mention one aspect of coordination which is assuming growing importance, namely, multidisciplinary approach. As has been pointed out by me earlier, specialization is growing and, to the extent the education system is not able to turn out highly specialized persons due to uncertainties of securing jobs, initial training after education has to take care of this need. The result, highly desirable by itself, is that there is less and less of common ground among the wide variety of specialists. Many sectors of socio-economic development, however, require a multi-disciplinary approach. A dam, an immense canal system, large industry etc. can be constructed and operated by highly specialized persons, either educated or trained as such. But utilization of these assets for public good would require land reforms, land shaping, popularizing use of new varieties of seed, new methods, credit lines, marketing and so on. The need for an area development approach is now generally appreciated. This type of development requires joint effort by a wide variety of specialists. To work together they have to learn basic lessons about one another's work, know about one another's problems and, giving up the convenient method of putting the blame on others, feel the joint nature of their responsibilities. This will require reorientation of outlook as well as adding interdisciplinary knowledge. There is thus an obvious need for a new kind of training of specialists, technical and non-technical, who have already sonic service experience. Special courses, seminars, field attachments and other forms of training are to be undertaken. This will require considerable amount of coordination among various cadre controlling authorities as well as among the existing separate training organizations. The lead organization to apply a phrase used in banking, for such coordination should obviously be the HCM SIPA.

I would like to conclude with expressing my concept of suitable faculty for training institutions since this will always be an important aspect of coordination. The faculty has to be from two sources—academic life and those having good record of service in the field. Among the latter there are often persons who had good academic record and have retained academic interests. What I feel lacking today is that the former type of faculty are not asked to gain the experience of actually working in a government or public sector organization on a tenure basis. If this is done we will have faculty who can combine academic excellence with valuable field experience. Our cadre rules may make such arrangements difficult, but if the idea is acceptable, rules can always be amended.

In our vast country with the state accepting large social and economic responsibilities, the common citizen is often put to a lot of difficulty due to lack of coordination among the various organs of state and central governments and their public sectors. The functioning of government is dependent upon the attitude of public servants and this, in turn, is largely determined by training and by the example of the senior persons.

5

Issues in In-service Training

R.G. SOOD

Once the rationale of in-service training is accepted, the sheer number of government employees makes the problem of training all of them – a gigantic one. And, these numbers are ever growing.

Yet numbers may be a misleading indicator of the problem at hand. In our excessive zeal to make coverage of training comprehensive, formal in-service classroom training is being given to all categories and classes of employees, whereas training needs of different categories may be quite different. It has to be recognized that in-service training is not a magic wand which will cure all organizational ills. A pre-requisite for the success of in-service training is the matching of in-service training to precise needs of an organization or category of employees. Total coverage of each and every employee may not be a feasible proposition in the near future because of limited resources that we are able to allocate for training. If we still insist on covering all employees, in-service training may just remain a fad with no post-training results to show.

It will be, therefore, better to adopt selective approach to in-service training. It shall be necessary to pre-identify key result areas in every government organization and key individuals, capable of achieving results in these areas. These individuals, when trained, can best contribute to improve performance level on going back to their workplace. Expectation also will be that these trained individuals will be able to sufficiently motivate their subordinates to achieve higher levels of performance thus leading to some sort of a 'multiplier' or 'filtering down' effect. A related question whether in-service training is provided to encourage organizational effectiveness or purely individual excellence/self-development will also have to be sorted out.

The basic object of in-service training is to expose the trainees to newer techniques of more efficient functioning involving less economic, social and human cost. Heightened concern for environment and ecology which reduces social costs, techniques of job enrichment, job redesign and human engineering which reduce human costs and ever more efficient machines which reduce economic costs what with computers of the speeds in nanoseconds and piccoseconds—are all means to these ends. New entrants to government service can be more easily convinced of the need to adopt these techniques. However, it is quite likely that in-service trainees, who have been very long on any particular job, might develop an emotional interest in continuing their time tested, established procedures and methods of working. They may look upon such training with an attitude of scorn and cynicism, as an attack of novices on proven methods of functioning, who know nothing about the real world. In-service trainees may also adopt a 'know all' attitude towards trainers. Now, the initial task of a trainer in such situations would be to persuade trainees to abandon this cynical attitude and open up their minds. Importance of this initial task can hardly be over emphasized. Unless this is successfully done, trainees will deliberately refuse to learn. We may consider whether it will be worth while to depute key individuals in key result areas for in-service training programmes regularly after specified intervals to fill gaps in their knowledge, skills and attitudes.

This initial task may not be found to be an easy one at all. Appeals purely on rational plane may not bear fruit. A person, who has built in, deeply ingrained faith in the quack' next door would hardly be influenced by the statistical evidence in favour of the modern medicine man. May be the modern medicine man would have to put on the garb of a quack' to convince him of his usefulness. For example computers would cease to be culture shock, in the last analysis, only when trade unions themselves see their utility in accurately maintaining employees' service records, salary records, leave accounts, provident fund accounts etc.

The Training Division of the Government of India has brought out some indigenous literature on problems of administration in government. But, owing to the lack of adequate publicity, even within government, government functionaries generally do not know about these monographs, training volumes etc. May be it would be worthwhile for the Departments of Personnel in State Governments or State Training Institutes to take up the task of making government servants at district and lower levels aware of the existence of these publications. These publications, concise and relevant to specific problems/techniques as they are, could become excellent media of self study and home refreshers.

Subordinate staff's attitudes and effectiveness primarily depend upon their work relationship with the supervisory and management personnel. It has also been observed "jobs which are relatively simple, involving repetitive tasks which require limited discretion, and no special tools, benefit minimally from formal class room training". Therefore, these categories of employees should be given training within the organization by the supervisory personal in "work-flow interdependence and the acquiring of positive work attitudes". Their requirements do not necessitate formal class-room training.

Effectiveness of any in-service training programme can, in the ultimate analysis, be measured only by the extent of post-training utilization of training. Therefore, some uniform methods of measuring training effectiveness in the post-training actual work situations may have to be devised and applied.

Greater stress should be laid on the training for trainers. It may prove positively dangerous not to train those beforehand whom the job of training others is entrusted.

6

Evolution and Growth of Training

K. K. PARNAMI

As man invented tools, weapons, clothing, shelter, and language, the need for training became an essential ingredient in the march of civilizations. Only a few years ago, training was considered to be a major peacetime function of the military services for inculcating discipline in the fighting forces. But, recently, the term 'training' has acquired a wider connotation. Both the government and the private sector have now embraced enthusiastically the training idea as an essential element to help in developing the competence of an officer as well as to inculcate in him a set of values which may desirable in a particular socio-administrative system.

The emergence of training idea in the civil service is not accidental. In this age of all-round economic development, conditioned by an environment of continuous change and growing society, it reflects the efforts to develop in individuals an attitude of improved performance, both now and in the future.

II

The rapid expansion of training activities in many countries soon after Second World War was accompanied by a good deal of organized thinking, in which the United Nations played the role of both stimulator and moderator. The first opportunity for an extended examination on an international scale of personnel problems was offered in the UN Seminar on Public Personnel Management, convened in 1950-51. This was the first of the training seminars. It was thought of at the time as the beginning the international centre for training in public administration contemplated by the General Assembly in its resolution of 1948. Instead of furthering the development of centralized training, the seminar made recommendations on training as a national undertaking. The seminar advocated a practical kind of training for civil servants, closely related to the job to be performed. It saw the objectives of such training as the increase in efficiency and the maintenance of the employee's interest in his job.[1]

This seminar was characterized as something less than a complete success.[2] However, the formulation of doctrine was carried farther, and with greater authority, in the report of Special Committee on Public Administration Problems, published in 1951.[3] The report in question was in many respects a summary statement of a programme for the improvement of public administration. It served for years as a guide to workers in technical assistance on the elements of a programme of reform that they might, on the practical plane, hope to accomplish.

It cannot be said that the committee report of 1951 put training in the first rank of desirable reform in public administration. It did, however, put problems of personnel in the first rank, and in doing so, it placed great emphasis upon training as a means of improving the resources of personnel available to a country in the process of modernization. The committee made numerous suggestions as to what a country might do with some assurance of good results in improving its administrative system. On a few matters related to training, the committee spoke strongly, stating views, which clearly intended as guidelines. The committee recorded its faith in training as a means of discovering and developing managerial talent.

The next occasion for the collective formulation of opinions on training in the public service came in the Seminar on Public Administration, held at Montevideo, Uruguay, in October 1955.[4] This seminar was much interested in the things which received no attention in the earlier report.

By 1957, the United Nations had assisted in a number of training projects in as many countries. In the belief that a time for stock-taking had come, a score of experts of many nationalities were assembled at Geneva for a week's intensive study of the experience to that date in the operation of training institutions. The group limited its study to the United Nations projects that were concerned with the establishment and operation of institutes of public administration.[5]

In 1961, a "Handbook of Public Administration: Current Concepts and Practice with Special Reference of Developing Countries" was published by the United Nations. This handbook followed earlier publication in assigning the highest priority in administrative reform to personnel matters, and in expressing the faith in training as a means of improving public personnel. Although it had little to say on training in the specialties of public administration, it directed attention to the great need for training in the techniques of national planning.

The brief review of efforts at the UN level to formulate standard and norms in public administration reveals that the various committees and group of experts, which were active from time to time, were engaged in an elusive task. The variety of opinion, practices, and experimentation is so great in all branches of public administration that it is exceedingly difficult to make observations of general validity. In no branch of public administration is this more evident than in training, which lacks even a terminology of general acceptance.

The relatively importance of training has thus been steadily enhanced through the years. A former Director of the

Division of Public Administration of the United Nations wrote: "It is now generally recognized that training is the cornerstone and most important element in technical assistance in public administration. The experience of the United Nations supports this general consensus."[6]

Presently, there is no UN agency, which is not involved in some training activity or the other. Training is an important preoccupation of practically all of them. The World Bank, the international organization most concerned with development, took some initiatives to start training on a systematic basis. Apart from the World Bank, other agencies which are concerned with the training include DTCD, ILO, FAO, UNESCO, UNICEF, UNIDO, and WHO. Then, several training institutions have sprung up directly under the aegis of the UN agencies. Among such institutes are UNITAR, New York; EDI, Washington; NUCRD, Nagoya; ICPE, Lubjliyana, UNAPDC, Kualalumpur etc.

III

During the past three decades, government and international donors devoted considerable resources to the task of stimulating development in the Third World. Though the public services specially designed for poor largely remain well beyond their reach, the Third World countries have taken several new initiatives in recent years. Training to prepare the government officials for their enlarged role as development administrators has received considerable attention everywhere.[7] This interest In training arises from the realization that lack of trained manpower poses obstacles to development as formidable as those of scarce resources. inadequate capital and insufficient technology.[8]

As a means of casing constraints to development by a lack of trained manpower, with a view to improving the overall administrative capability for development, training has witnessed a phenomenal growth in recent years. The number of institutes and the number of participants have all rapidly gone up. There is no gainsaying that what development needs of all is trained manpower.

IV

In India, the training of administrators has a long tradition. From all available accounts it is clear that the value of training for administrators was recognized in the very initial states of the bygone colonial era.[9] The need for imparting, especially to new entrants to the civil service who came from England, had become well established for the reason that they were being inducted into the service for work in a different environment.

The concept of training underwent a radical transformation when the counter become independent. The civil services today have a completely different role what they had in the pre-independence era. Then, they played a rather marginal role in nation-building affairs. Collection of taxes and maintenance of law and order were the two major goals they pursued. They kept themselves aloof from the people.

But things have since changed vastly. From a wholistic perspective, the philosophy of India's development can easily be reflected in the goal of a welfare state. Welfare state stands for protection of fundamental democratic rights of the people, the principle of subsistence-cum-universality, mixed economy and an active and positive state which aims at achieving the broader social goals set for the system as a whole.[10] Translated in terms of Indian planning, the major developmental goals of India as a nation relate to increasing production. minimizing differences in income and wealth distribution, ending unemployment and raising the overall standard of living of the people.

But much of the success of planning depends upon its effective implementation at the field level. Here, the role of personnel of the administrative system per se assumes significance. A sound personnel policy in a country such as our needs to take into account the requirements of personnel who are competent and committed to goals of national development, who can understand intricacies involved in socio-economic progress, who are able to evoke people's participation in development programmes and it is only through training that cadres of such bureaucrats can be built up at all levels of development administration. In fact, it is only through training that the conventional, colonial rule-oriented attitudes of bureaucrats can be transformed into progressive and goal-oriented values and attitudes.

Necessity of training of civil servants was even greater in Rajasthan since the services in the newly formed state of Rajasthan were manned by officers coming from different integrating units which till integration had been working under different patterns of administration. With the formation of state an attempt was made to introduce a uniform system of administration. This obviously required organized training of at least all new entrants in the new pattern of administration. Because of the diversity of patterns prevailing before the formation of Rajasthan, the training to new entrants by the traditional on-the-job method was found to be difficult. The new system was yet in the process of evolution.

These factors and the fact that for many years to come we shall be having year by year new entrants in large numbers to replace those due for superannuation, made it necessary to start administrative training in India.

Notes

1. The documentation of the seminar of 1950-51 is to be found in the official report, issued one year after its adjournment and the collection of papers published in *Personnel Administration,* Vol. XIV No. 4, July 195 1, Washington.
2. F.J. Tickner, "The Improvement of Public Administration", *United Nations Review,* Vol. II No. 3, September 155, pp. 47-52.

3. Standards and Techniques of Public Administration with Special Reference to Technical Assistance for Underdeveloped Countries (UN Publications, Sale No. 51.II.B.7).
4. Its report was published as *Training and Administration of Personnel in the Public Service* (UN Publications, Sale No. 56 II H.2).
5. The documentation of the *Geneva Group* is to be found in the collection of working papers prepared before the meeting and the published report *Training in Public Administration* (UN Publications, Sale No. 58.II.H.1).
6. Hamzah Merghani, "Public Administration in Developing Countries: The Multilateral Approach", *Public Administration: A Key to Development,* Jump-Mckillop Memorial Lectures, 1963, Washington: The Graduate School, US Department of Agriculture, 1964, p. 36.
7. Irving Swerdlow and Marcus Ingle (Eds.), *Public Administration Training for the Less Developed Countries,* Syracuse: Maxwell School of Citizenship and Public Affairs, 1974.
8. In this connection, see, Charless V. Kidd, *Manpower Policies for the Use of Science and Technology in Development,* New York: Pergamon Press, 1980.
9. Bernard S. Cohn, "Recruitment and Training of British Civil Servants in India, 1960-1800" in Ralph Braibanti (Ed.), *Asian Bureaucratic System Emergent form the British Tradition* (Durham: Duke University Press, 1966), pp. 87-140.
10. K.N. Bhargava, "Training System in India: Some Issues" in Arora and Kukar (Eds.), *Training and Administrative Development,* Jaipur: HCM RIPA, 1979, p. 64.

7

Networking Training Institutes in Rajasthan

B.K. KHUNTETA

Training is a planned process to modify attitudes, knowledge and skill behaviour through learning experience so as to achieve effective performance in an activity or range of activities. It not only develops the abilities of the individuals but also satisfies current and future manpower needs of the government. It is the most cost-effective method of improving competencies amongst civil servants so as to measure up expectations of citizens in the context of rapid technological changes as well as economic, political and social transformation taking place in the society. Training has, therefore, been recognized as a very potent tool for human resource development. The focus of training, therefore, is on action, on doing specified things, besides acquiring knowledge about them. The mission of training, thus, is to develop competent, committed, efficient and creative civil servants of all cadres so that administration becomes citizen-friendly.

Training Objectives

The above goals of the training are to be spelt out in terms of specific objectives to be achieved. Training objectives could be summarized as follows:

(1) keeping up-to-date and enhancing professional knowledge, skill and competence of civil servants;

(2) sensitizing civil servants to socio-economic, political and professional environment;

(3) improving actual performance of individuals in all spheres; and

(4) bringing about right and desired attitudinal changes.

Training programmes organized for any of the cadres of civil servants should be substantially conditioned by responsiveness, commitment, awareness, accountability, etc., of civil servants.

Training in Rajasthan

Recognizing the need and significance of training as a very potent tool and integral part of human resource development process, the Government of Rajasthan took appropriate measures fairly early to create training facilities which have expanded moderately over time. Although a lot still remains to be done to improve training facilities in the state, it is satisfying to note that Rajasthan is way ahead of many states in the country in this field.

Until 1957 members of the IAS and even RAS (service came into existence in 1954) had to be sent for their induction as well as refresher training to Uttar Pradesh. A true remarkable step in Rajasthan was taken up in 1957 by establishing Officers Training School (OTS) at Jodhpur where training of RAS, and two years later, IAS, began to be conducted. In 1963, the OTS shifted from Jodhpur to Jaipur and started functioning in a rental building till it moved in 1966 to its present campus. In 1969, the OTS was renamed as Harish Chandra Mathur

Rajasthan State Institute of Public Administration (HCM RIPA) to commemorate the memory of a distinguished administrator and parliamentarian of the state. HCM RIPA saw a devastating havoc of floods in 1981 when more than half of its infrastructural facilities were washed away. Continuous and untiring efforts and support of the government have revamped and revitalized the Institute to bring it to its present position. Today, HCM RIPA is an apex level training institution and is imparting different kinds of training to officers belonging to various State Services and contributing towards continuous improvement in state administration through training and research. Besides, many training programmes, sponsored by Department of Personnel and Training, Government of India, national level training institutions, other state governments and public sector undertakings, are regularly conducted by HCM RIPA.

Departmental Training Institutions

In view of the rapidly increasing number of government servants and specialized job requirements many departmental training institutions in the state were set up from time to time to impart job-specific training, primarily to middle and lower level officers and functionaries. Some of the important departmental training institutions are listed in Table 1.

Moderate infrastructure and faculty do exist in some of these departmental training institutions but others are fairly weak in terms of faculty, finance support and infrastructure. Because of such a large number of departmental training institutions, the number of training courses has rapidly increased and also the number of officers attending training courses has sharply gone up. Job-specific courses are being organized today by these institutions which otherwise would not have been organized so frequently and successfully. Through these institutions budgetary resources for training are also increasing constantly. Concerned departments are authorized and are

Table 1

Departmental Training Institutions in Rajasthan

	Department	*Year of establishment*	*Institute*
1.	Agriculture	1993	State Institute of Agriculture Management, Jaipur and Agriculture Extension Training Centres
2.	Board of Revenue	1995	Revenue Research and Training Institute, Ajmer and All Purpose Revenue Training Centre, Tonk
3.	CD&PR	-	Indira Gandhi Panchayati Raj Sansthan, Jaipur
4.	Cooperative	1994	Rajasthan Institute of Cooperative Education and Management, Jaipur
5.	Police	1975	Rajasthan Police Academy, Jaipur and Police Training Centres
6.	Education	1978	State Institute of Educational Research and Training, Udaipur and District Institutes of Educational Training
7.	Forest	1986	Forest Training Institute, Jaipur
8.	Medical & Health	1995	State Institute of Health and Family Welfare, Jaipur and HFWTC/DTC/ANMTC
9.	PWD/PHED/ Irrigation	1986	Engineers Staff Training Institute, Jaipur
10.	Prisons	-	Jail Training Institute, Ajmer
11.	Sheep & Wool	1954	Sheep & Wool Training Institute, Jaipur
12.	TAD	1964	MLV Tribal Research Institute, Udaipur
13.	Irrigation	1984	Irrigation Management Training Centre, Kota
14.	Fisheries	-	Fisheries Training, Centre, Udaipur
15.	Soil Conservation	-	Soil Conservation Training Centre, Jodhpur

accountable for the smooth functioning of these training institutions, hence keen interest is taken with some exceptions because these institutions work entirely under the control of heads of department.

Though such a large number of institutions exist in the state, but in the absence of a holistic, pragmatic, effective and coordinated training policy, optimum use of these institutions is not being made at present. Also, there is no uniformity in the training facilities available in these institutions. Avoidable duplication of training courses, lack of need-based training, less than optimum use of faculty and facilities, underutilized resources, and less than desired level of quality of faculty are the strong drawbacks of the existing system. These institutions function virtually oblivious of what the others are doing. Between training institutions and departments also, there is not the required degree of cohesion which should exist if training is to serve a useful purpose. Some of the institutions remain totally idle for a specific period for want of nominations for training since officers are too busy due to seasonal nature of their job; for example, officers belonging to GWD or PHED cannot be spared for training during April-June months. Sufficient attention is not being paid for quality training and faculty development. Uninterested, undeserving and unsuitable officers are posted as trainers and are also sent for training. In common parlance it is said that separable officers are posted as trainers and also are sent for training. In common parlance it is said that spareables get training by spareables.

In view of the above, immediate action needs to be taken to develop proper coordination and strong linkages amongst departmental training institutions in the interest of getting the best returns from the total investment in training so that induction training at the time of entry into service and inservice training at suitable intervals in the career to all categories of civil servants is imparted. The following suggestions may be considered for strong linkages and networking amongst departmental training institutions:

State Training Policy

A comprehensive, effective, holistic, pragmatic and long-term training Policy should be adopted and implemented by the government. This policy should provide clear directions to various departments in regard to training and linkages amongst training institutions for best returns from the total investment made in these institutions.

Creation of a Department of Training

Although, the post of Principal Secretary to the Government, along with the post of Deputy Secretary (Training), do exist in the government but in practice these are held ex-officially by the Director and the Additional Director of HCM RIPA respectively. The responsibilities, nature of activities and organizational structure of HCM RIPA is such that these consume the entire time and energy of these two officers leaving almost no time for policy and guidance work for other training institutions. The Principal Secretary (Training) does not have any support of some senior officer with experience, vision, authority and interest in the field of training. Even if the Director, HCM RIPA tries to keep himself free from his routine work, he cannot work out because of the nature of the activities, courses and workload of the Institute.

It is, therefore, suggested that an independent and separate Department of Training, headed by the Principal Secretary (Training), be set up at the state level with full authority and powers. He may also be designated as Director General. Besides, a senior officer from IAS cadre with experience, vision and interest in the field of training may be posted as Additional Director General, HCM RIPA to discharge day-to-day routine functions which are being performed by the Director at present. This kind of arrangement does exist in some other states at present. The Principal Secretary (Training) may also perform the work of Secretary, Administrative Reforms and also training functions of Secretary, Manpower Planning, thereby, keeping extra financial burden of creating a new post nil. This will rid of the Director, HCM RIPA from day-to-day routine and housekeeping functions of the Institute leaving him free to devote time to policy issues, pedagogy of 'training and establishing a vibrant network amongst training institutions by coordinating their activities and providing them much required leadership.

Some of the functions of the Department of Training (DoT) could be as fallows:

(a) To supervise, monitor and evaluate all trainings within the state.

(b) To coordinate training programmes of all departmental training institutions.

(c) To provide advice, direction and guidance to all departmental training institutions.

(d) To help in proper assessment of training needs of government departments.

(e) To create and maintain State Level Training Resource Centre where information and data base regarding training in the state, country and abroad will be collected and maintained for use of all training institutions and to act as a clearing house for training material and case studies.

(f) To work as 'think-tank' for the government.

(g) To report to the government on all matters relating to training and also to suggest measures for improvement in government administration through training.

(h) To prepare short and long-term training plans.

(i) To prepare Annual Training Report of the state.

(j) To work as catalyst in the area of training.

(k) To establish linkages with Government of India, national training institutions, other state governments and funding agencies in regard to training.

(l) To develop Distance Learning Packages.

The DoT should be provided with basic minimum infrastructural facilities which may be independent of HCM RIPA infrastructure.

Planning Cells

Each training institution should have a powerful Training Committee or Planning Cell on which head of the concerned department, Director of Training and Training Manager should be represented.

State Training Council

At present, a State Training Advisory Committee exists for deciding policy matters regarding training. It should be made more broad and strong and rechristened as State Training Council. The Council may be headed by the Minister-in-Charge of Department of Personnel. It will advise the government in matters related of training policy, training strategy and the thrust areas as well issues concerning their implementation. The Council will be assisted by a Steering Committee, headed by Principal Secretary (Training), to oversee the operationalization of the State Training Policy. It will also take decisions on all issues relating to quality the quantity of training in consonance with National Training Policy and State Training Policy. It will meet every two months to review the progress and take further necessary steps as per directions of the State Training Council.

Trainers Development Programme

Various general and job-specific courses on Training of Trainers for the faculty of all departmental training institutions should be organized by HCM RIPA regularly. It should be a pre-condition for placement of an officer as trainer in any training institution.

Faculty Exchange Programme

HCM RIPA faculty should visit departmental training institutions for short durations and likewise faculty of the departmental training institutions should visit HCM RIPA for short duration for getting experience and exposure in the field of training.

Infrastructure Building

HCM RIPA should provide guidance to departmental training institutions in their research, selection of books, preparation of training modules, getting the guest faculty, creating infrastructure, developing software and evaluation of programmes. This should become a regular feature. This should ultimately result into networking with apex training institutes of other states periodically.

Meetings

All heads of departmental training institutions, led by concerned beads of departments, should meet periodically to review the progress and plan future strategy. HCM RIPA should play elder brotherly role in these meetings. The State Level Steering Committee should be involved actively in these meetings.

Training Managers

It should he mandatory for every head of the department to nominate one of its senior officers as Training Manager who will he fully authorized and responsible for coordinating training of all categories of employees of the concerned department. He will help in assessing the training needs of the department and for preparing short and long-term training plans of the department. He should have full authority for nominating officers for training. This will ensure fullest possible use of resources of departmental training institutions.

New Training Institutions

Since, at present, HCM RIPA is not a position to impart training to rapidly proliferating number of government employees, larger departments should make their own training arrangements for the training of their subordinate and ministerial staff, since the behaviour and action of these employees largely influence public thinking concerning the government and specially the concerned department.

Distance Learning Training

Training through distance learning should be seriously considered and its responsibility for implementation may be given to DoT or HCM RIPA.

Some of other very important matters such as selection of trainers, incentives to trainers, earmarking about 1.5 per cent of total salary budget for training, linking of training with career, planning and promotion of trainees and bringing out a compendium of training and other such matters should be considered seriously while preparing a draft training policy for the state.

Initiatives by HCM RIPA

Being an apex training institute of the state, HCM RIPA has taken lead in this direction. HCM RIPA has been conducting many training programmes for the development of the skills of trainers imparting training in the departmental training institutes. These include Direct Trainer Skills, Design of Training. Management of Training and Training of Trainers. Workshops for networking and preparing State Training Policy have also been organized by HCM RIPA. In such a workshop held recently, not only the existing training scenario was discussed but very useful and important recommendations for the State Training Policy were also made. The workshop suggested for universalization of training, standardization of quality of training and mechanism for the implementation of the training policy.

The Eleventh Finance Commission, set up by the Government of India, also recommended for financial assistance to Administrative Training Institutes (ATIs) and departmental training institutions for development and upgradation of infrastructure. HCM RIPA took steps in this direction. On the basis of demand of the departmental training institutions and Regional Training Centres, HCM RIPA prepared proposals for Rs. 91.08 crores (Rs. 26.21 crores for HCM RIPA and Rs. 54.87 crores for departmental training institutions) and submitted to the Finance Commission through the Association of State Training Institutions in India (ASTI) and also to the Finance Department of the State Government (for inclusion in the memorandum submitted by the Government of Rajasthan) and to the Department of Personnel and Training, Government of India (for inclusion in the memorandum submitted by DoPT for all ATIs and departmental training institutions). These are some of the initial steps taken by HCM RIPA but a lot still remains to be done.

8

Decentralized Training in Support of Urban Development

A.N. KRISHNAMURTHY AND HARRY A. MENGERS

Comparing the census figures in India between 1981 and 1991, it is clear that urban centres grow in number, size and density. The urban population is, at present, 27 per cent of the total population and will increase further to 34 per cent in the 2000. While the average annual population growth is 2.2 per cent, the rural growth is only 1 per cent, the urban growth 4 per cent and the growth of slum population a staggering 9 per cent.

Although these figures may be alarming, anti-urban policies are not favoured as cities contribute about 40 per cent to the Gross National Product (GNP). Cities are, thus, rather seen as opportunities to further economic development.

Governments at different levels do their utmost to cope with the tremendous need for housing, infrastructure networks and services to allow the residents an acceptable living and livelihood. It also shows that government is determined to have control over the urban dynamics of growth. That this seems a herculean task manifests itself by the cries over housing shortages, deficiencies in infrastructure, the inadequate services and the deterioration of existing infrastructure without sufficient maintenance.

Of particular concern is the growing number of slums, housing a population of an average of 21 per cent (or 51 million) of the total urban population. In the metropolitan areas, such as Delhi, the slum population starts to reach 50 per cent. These settlements are unplanned, lack proper access and configuration, and also minimum infrastructure facilities and basic services. This cry has been heard for many years and there seems to be no improvement or change. There is as yet no adequate answer to this global phenomenon. Instead, there is a sort of continuous tug-of-war between the officials, city level authorities and the so-called invaders/encroachers/slum dwellers and the battle line is continuously redrawn in the form of regularization of unauthorized colonies with less and less age, as stated by Chakrabarty (1993). Urban planning on-the-ground is more determined by the slum dwellers than by officers in the buildings of the urban local governments.

The on-the-ground and actual planning features could be described as follows:

— it satisfies an immediate need on the short-term, without a medium or long-term perspective;

— it is limited to the scale of a plot;

— it responds to housing market opportunities among the poor in a minimal fashion; and

— it accepts minimum (even sub-human) environmental standards.

These planning features are quite contrary to what urban planners have in mind, still we consider it as planned and also unstoppable urban development. Would it be possible to take this rationale to manage cities? Would it be possible to change the conventional planning paradigm, which do not and probably will not succeed.

Would it be possible to launch a campaign addressing slum dwellers (to be) and give a set of standards, e.g., by a large bill-board at every access road to the city, having messages as given in the following box:

> Welcome to our city. In order to serve you better, keep the following rules in mind:
>
> 1. Build your house away from large drains and flooded areas.
> 2. Keep a safe distance of 5m to the front and back of your house.
> 3. Build in a linear manner, so that water, drains and electricity can be provided and maintained more easily.
> 4. Make sure an access road of at least 5m is within 25m of your house for safety reasons.
> 5. Make sure that you can dispose of your waste in a dustbin within loom.
>
> Have a nice stay! — The *Municipal Corporation*

Another bill-board may list the earmarked areas to put up their shelter. It has been argued (Chakrabarty, 1993) that these so-called 'land banks for the shelterless' may prove to be more cost-effective than improvement and upgradation of existing and spontaneous emerged slums.

The above may seem an unusual proposition, but useful answers to large problems do require sometimes such unexpected ideas. The work-floor, where administrators, planners and engineers are too busy, may not provide the necessary environment to take a certain distance from the day-to-day routines and duties and reflect on larger problems, constraints, opportunities and to develop useful ideas. A seminar or workshop would rather provide the necessary circumstances and ingredients for such ideas and feedback from fellow-professionals.

This example may illustrate that training could be a medium to address urban planning problems and trigger off the much needed creative and effective approaches and solutions.

Objectives of Training

Training has broadly three stages:

1. The first stage starts at primary school with the aim to make a pupil a useful, social and responsible citizen. The primary education invests in transfer of knowledge, certain skills and desirable values, attitudes and social behaviour. For any society this foundation is crucial for its functioning.
2. Later, this knowledge is expanded and analytic skills are strengthened, while the students are exposed to concepts, ideas and various systems of thought and logic. This training aims to make them useful, basically equipped human beings (professionals) in one of the sectors of our society, whether it is health care, construction, literature, art or public administration.
3. The third stage of training, on which we like to concentrate, takes off from the earlier stages and also relates to urban development. Training here aims for two things:
    a. to enhance skills of professionals to do their current tasks better; and
    b. to equip professionals with the capacity to adopt to change and to find the right ways to administer, manage and govern the process of change and to build the skills to execute tasks that derive from change.

The first goal relates to existing urban development schemes (IDSMT, NRY, etc.) and their proper implementation and maintenance. The current implementation of the 74th amendment to the Indian Constitution (Nagar Palika Act) relates more to the latter.

Further, there is a need to encourage learning through the process of visually inspecting and analyzing work or projects in operation. Secondly, training to be meaningful and for the desired changes to happen in reality, creation of a conducive working environment that facilitates absorption and assimilation of the propagated changes is to be brought about. In essence, training should not be confined to only classroom session, Thirdly, training should not be delinked from the realities of the environment in which the enhanced knowledge and insight should be applied and make a contribution to make that environment more conducive through its organizational and administrative channels.

This paper mainly focuses on making a movement towards this change in the urban development sector in which training is visualized as a catalyst in the process.

Current Developments Influencing Training

A number of developments in the urban development sector are important to take note of here.

Since independence, the metropolitan cities had a lead in their efforts to developing the infrastructure with the creation of the development authorities, and the various special function boards, such as the water supply and sewerage boards, the slum clearance/improvement boards, the housing boards, and the like.

Since the early seventies, similar boards were created on a state-wide basis to cater to the needs of the non-metropolitan urban communities, i.e., the City Municipal Corporations, the City Municipal Council, the Town Municipal Council and other lower administrative units. Increasingly, the medium and small-sized towns became dependent on these and other agencies of the state for the provision of infrastructure. While local government of the town or city continued in its traditional role, the superordinate state agencies have been developed and promoted with strong bureaucracies with administrative, financial and technical capabilities. The genesis of state level agencies was accompanied by the decline of responsibilities and powers at local level in favour of state agencies. This development evolved in a changed balance of roles in Karnataka as indicated in Figure 1; e.g., in Karnataka, urban local bodies (ULBs) are allowed to spend a mere Rs. 50,000 on water supply in a single year without the permission of the Karnataka Water Supply and Drainage Board.

Figure 1

Present Role of Institutions in Urban Development in Karnataka

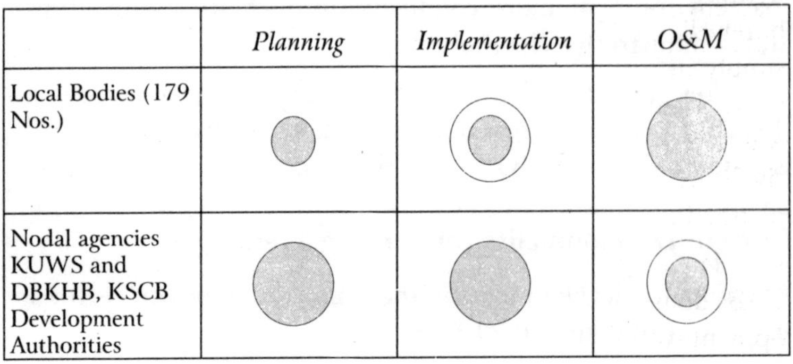

Source: A.N. Krishnamurthy, 1993.

In addition, the financial basis of municipalities has been drastically reduced, i.e., with the abolishment of octroi. Octroi contributed sometimes more than 50 per cent of the municipal revenue. The octroi compensation that came did not compensate for the earlier income for most municipalities. The reduction in receipts had its impact on the staff strength which had to be reduced accordingly.

With regard to urban planning, development plans are made by the state agencies and technical departments in charge of planning efforts (e.g., Department of Town and Country Planning, the State Urban Water Supply and Drainage Board, and the like), and supposedly implemented in collaboration with the local government. The standards, norms and specifications of the plans are, however, solely set by these state agencies on universal basis. It proved that these plans are often found not implementable due to local conditions, left unassessed by the planners, the non-availability of universally assumed resources, and means to maintain the schemes. As a result of these, local implementation takes place in a skewed and uncoordinated manner, with reduced ends, reduced norms, or unsuitable and inadvertent specifications. Frequent examples are found in new layouts and sub-divisions of residential land uses being sanctioned and developed without adherence to basic standards regarding water supply, drainage and sewerage systems, neighbourhood amenities, or even paved streets with lighting and other public utilities. Other examples such as borewells programme are implemented for drinking water supply in semi-urban communities without customary precautions about contamination and without the development of the water resources below ground. These are implemented exclusively by agencies, which are charged with these tasks as per planned investment under the annual or five-year plans.

The current legal, financial and staffing position of these ULBs do hardly allows them to take up any planning and development work. Without such articulation of needs through preparation of plans and self-determination through formulation and execution of projects, the dependency on state level agency increases further. The increased subordinance leaves local administration and council with frustration and little hope for self-reliance, local self-governance and needed development. The local administration and political representation is discredited because of lack of powers to act. This can hardly be commensurate with the democratic principles and spirit in which India fought its freedom and begot its democracy.

The state level agencies responsible for housing and infrastructure have developed mostly into a straightforward engineering and works oriented institutions. Plans and designs are prepared, however, without much participation from the ULBs.

The project funding is mostly a matter between the state level agency, state or central government and the financial institutions. ULBs are too often kept in the dark about their supposed financial contribution, the repayment and cost recovery modalities.

State level agencies tend to neglect the involvement of ULBs when it comes to deciding on the implementation of execution. Local opportunities of contracting, community involvement and transfer of project funds through local channels are hardly explored.

Cost recovery from beneficiaries has a low priority and they are informed, at best, during or after implementation and, at worst, not at all. This strengthens the widespread belief that everything that comes from government is free.

The performance of state level agencies in project planning, monitoring, reporting and administrative and financial vigilance is rather poor. Financial institutions, which borrow to government institutions only, have too often to compromise beyond what is considered minimally acceptable, particularly when compared to project funding routines by commercial banks. This itself triggers of casual repayment discipline.

A large number of government schemes (IDSMT, UBSP, NRY, EIUS, etc.) exist, which provide ample opportunities for providing basic amenities to the poor, alleviate urban poverty, build basic economic infrastructure, provide shelter, and stimulate enterprises. The sad situation is that most of these schemes are underutilized and available funds lay idle and crores of rupees lapse every year without even being touched.

It should also be noted that the current political environment at local level and the weak administration and staffing position generate short-term thinking, ad-hoc decisions and development work, without much consideration of overall development goals, strategies and commensurative activities. The cry for more financial resources for at least payment of salaries to their staff is not only a reflection of the financially weak position, but also the lack of tuning between the available resources and what is actually needed.

As a result, the level of services and the maintenance of infrastructure facilities are deplorable in many towns and cities. It is realized at central government level that the strong centralization of responsibilities and resources needs to be reversed to pave the way for the decentralization of powers and equal economic development. The Government of India, following the suggestions of the National Commission of Urbanization, aims to gear urban development policies to stimulate a balanced regional development and less stressful urbanization process. Small and medium-sized towns should get a more prominent place in economic development.

In this context, the 74th amendment to the Indian Constitution (Nagar Palika Bill) has emerged. It aims to allow for development of activities in a decentralized framework, by adopting participatory strategies. The Act is a framework which needs to be further detailed by the state government, as many functions (housing and urban development) are indeed a state responsibility. Particularly relevant in this context is the adoption of the twelfth schedule, which would give back major development and planning responsibilities to local bodies. It would basically imply that development authorities would be abolished and merged with the ULBs, while the state level sectoral agencies (the Finance Commission in Nagarpalika Act terms) would voluntarily transfer responsibilities and resources in favour of local government.

Challenges, Opportunities and Pitfalls of Training

The above observations provide a number of challenges for training for urban development:

1. Training could strengthen local bodies to utilize existing resources in a more planned, integrated and rational manner.

2. Training could equip ULBs to take up the new tasks for planning and development that will emerge from the implementation of the Nagar Palika Act.
3. Training could sensitize state level agencies to make use of the ULBs in decision-making and to explore local opportunities for project implementation through participatory strategies.
4. Training could assist state level agencies and ULBs to build routines that improve project administration, planning, design, monitoring, reporting, documentation and management.
5. Training could assist in building routines for better community involvement, public-private partnerships and cost recovery.
6. Training could assist in dissemination of government programme opportunities and assist in project application, formulation and implementation.
7. Training could assist in building routines for improved maintenance and rehabilitation of infrastructure facilities.

To achieve such goals, the training programmes and the implementing institutions need to have the following features:

(a) be flexible in order to adopt to emerging needs for training and be able to accommodate training even within one calendar year;

(b) to address in different forms of training the various levels of officials and elected representatives;

(c) to keep a good feeling with the developments on the ground (ULB) and at the state level in order to anticipate certain developments and adjust the training programme where necessary;

(d) to build a good rapport with state level officials at local level and maintain that well;

(e) to make clear that training is a necessary part and possibly positive factor of urban development, which is responsive to the existing needs for support;

(f) a certain level of self-criticism about the ongoing programmes which means regular feedback is necessary from participants during and after the course and from important officials at state level;

(g) to have staff having good knowledge of the urban development sector;

(h) to conduct applied and relevant research to support training;

(i) to design and schedule training programmes that are considered important and supported by relevant housing and infrastructure departments and financial institutions; and

(j) to work continuously on strategies to make the working environment of participants more conducive for reception, absorption and assimilation of change, enhanced knowledge and insights.

There is no shortage of training institutions, programmes or participants. On the contrary, as compared to other countries, the efforts in India going into human resource development are considerable. The priority that is given to training is also high. How come that training is felt so often of little use, making hardly any dent in existing operations of agencies and seen as a waste of money by many? There are a number of pitfalls in which training programmes can fall, which may contribute to this negative image:

— When training programmes are designed and a particular institution is constituted, independently or as part of a department, and is entrusted with the designing and organization of training programmes, a certain reluctance may creep in to reflect on the reasons of their existence (the mission) and their goals. Its shear existence becomes almost a justification for its operation, whatever it is doing.

— Training institutions may also loose the necessary self-critical attitude and become easy on getting post-course feedback or at least at-the-end of the course evaluations, and may be afraid of facing negative messages.

— In the attempt to improve the organization by bureaucratization of routines, by elaboration of decision lines and by refinement of the organizational structure, an inertia may develop at the same time. This inertia will hamper quick response to emerging needs and flexibility to adjust the programme. "We will include your request in next year's programme", may become a standard reply.

— The result of growing inflexibility is that training gets slowly de-linked from the developments in the urban development sector or its parental organization's operations. Pre-casted and rigid training schedules and curricula reinforce inflexibility. Instead of riding on the wave of development or change, the institutions float more and more behind.

— Performance of training programmes and training institutions is considered equal to the number of training days or the number of participants trained. 'Output' instead of 'outcome', and 'quantity' instead of 'quality' have become the measurement stick.

— In this fashion, training calendars are adopted that are packed with courses. Programme directors are forced to confine their tasks to preparation of schedules, to invitation of guest faculty and to arrange for boarding, lodging and other logistic arrangements. They become 'training machines' rather than a professional making a substantial contribution to the subject matter during the course. Quality of programmes may also decline as there is no time for thorough preparation of courses. With such pressure there is also no time to do research, build expertise in a particular field and to reflect on the goal and purpose of training. In addition and over time they may loose the feeling with the workfloor and become shallow and outdated professionals.

— Training institutions forget to further build the expertise of their staff in the sector by allowing research and field training or internship in the parental organization. The deployment of new staff is assessed too much on their training capacities than on their knowledge or experience in the sector of the parental organization.

— Where programme directors are weak professionals in the subject of training, training schedules become a compilation of guest speakers. Such training only builds knowledge and hardly any skills. The ultimate training objectives and processes are lost out of sight and cannot be achieved.

— Training institutions, which are part of state government, may also become part of the circuit of transferable officers with of-and-on little motivated officers. Some may see it as a punishment posting, rather than an opportunity. The training institutions these days have become dumping grounds for unwanted and unwilling officers. Their low interest and efforts result in de-crediting the image of the institutions, the value of training, and deterioration of the working spirit.

The pitfalls do not only apply to training programmes and their implementing institutions but to other institutions as well. They are almost natural phenomena and very human. No doubt, there are many training institutions that have avoided these pitfalls as management and staff have been alert and changed the course of direction.

The decentralized training programme in Karnataka may provide an interesting case that aims to support urban development and avoiding the pitfalls. It is not pretending to do everything better, but a number of elements are worth studying.

Decentralized Training Approach in Karnataka

Objective and Approach

The overall objective of the decentralized training programme is to contribute to the development and strengthening of small and medium towns in Karnataka as a tool to bring about balanced urban development.

HUDCO, together with its training wing—the Human Settlement Management Institute—is approaching this challenge with a two-pronged strategy:

1. financing viable projects in small and medium towns; and
2. capacity building in the local bodies and other nodal agencies to formulate viable projects for funding.

The second strategy is supported under an Indo-Dutch collaboration, called the Indian Human Settlement Programme (IHSP).

Scope of Training

Taking into consideration the limited resources that can be mobilized for training and at the same time make an effective impact in bringing about the desired change, training efforts have been concentrated on two types of training:

1. *Action planning for integrated urban development: This* training is structured to equip officers and staff of ULBs to prepare an action plan for their town which has a clear content about the needs assessment and prioritized goals and objectives. The plans address immediate and short-term as

well as medium-term needs and their financial implications and viability. The course was structured as a sandwich course of one-plus-one week with an interim period of two months for field preparations and follow-up. The document provides a useful starting point for discussion with the council and nodal agencies for obtaining project and financial support. Officers and staff from the District Town Planning Office and other state level nodal agencies like the Karnataka Water Supply and Drainage Board (KUWSDB), the Karnataka Slum Clearance Board (KSCB), etc., participated in this course. In 1993, four municipalities have on a pilot basis participated in this form of training. The prepared plans are now further translated into viable projects for funding. Support for project formulation is being explored through HUDCO and the Government of Karnataka.

2. *Project formulation courses:* This training aims at providing the necessary support to make better use of existing urban development schemes, particularly IPLCS, NRY, IDSMT, EIUS and UBSP. Aspects of project preparation, project justification and application for financial support from state level agencies and financial institutions are addressed. In addition, modalities and requirements of implementation and operation and maintenance are given equal emphasis. In 1993, infrastructure formulation courses were conducted on low-cost sanitation, settlement upgradation and economic support and water supply.

   The framework of this training is given in Figure 2.

Features of the Strategy for Implementation

The following strategies have been adopted to avoid the common pitfalls of training programme and to sustain the efforts after the initial support under IHSP:

Figure 2
Training Framework
(Capacity Building of Local Bodies and Nodal Agencies)

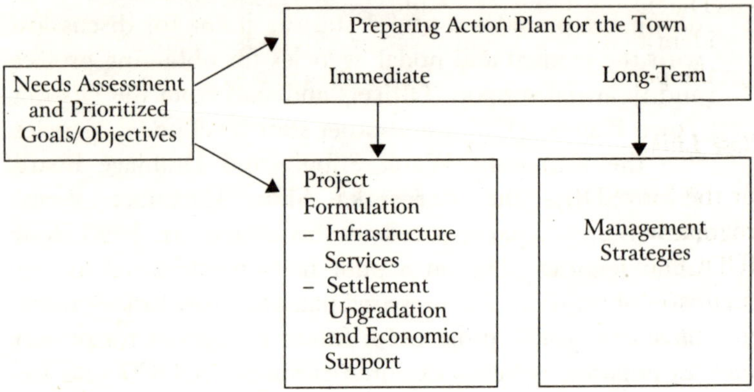

Source: A.N. Krishnamurthy, 1993.

Memorandum of Understanding between HUDCO and Karnataka Government

A close collaboration has been established between HUDCO/ HSMI, Karnataka government and the Administrative Training Institute (ATI), Mysore, the initial counterpart training organization for the execution of the decentralized training programme, A Memorandum of Understanding between HUDCO and Karnataka government (Secretary for Housing and Urban Development) had been drafted and was signed in September 1993. It includes the following points:

— HUDCO will provide financially support for the creation of faculty at ATI for the Eighth Five-Year Plan period (1992-97). It will enable the implementation of the decentralized training programme.

— ATI will support the development and execution of the decentralized training programme, include the proposed training activities in its annual training calendar and provide the existing infrastructure.

— Karnataka government will financially support ATI to run the decentralized training, i.e., will bear course fees, accommodation and material costs.

— The Department of Municipal Administration has been identified as the nodal agency and will nominate and invite the participants for the respective courses.

Close Link of HUDCO's Operations

For the formulation, preparation and execution of the training programme, support has been sought from the regional office of HUDCO in Bangalore. It is ensured that the conducted training remains close to HUDCO's operations and interests, remain relevant and that training outcomes feed in the operations as much as possible. The training programme has also benefited HUDCO otherwise, by addressing the requirements of HUDCO supported schemes to urban local bodies by which better sense of ownership, maintenance and most importantly

Figure 3

Training and Project Funding Support in Karnataka

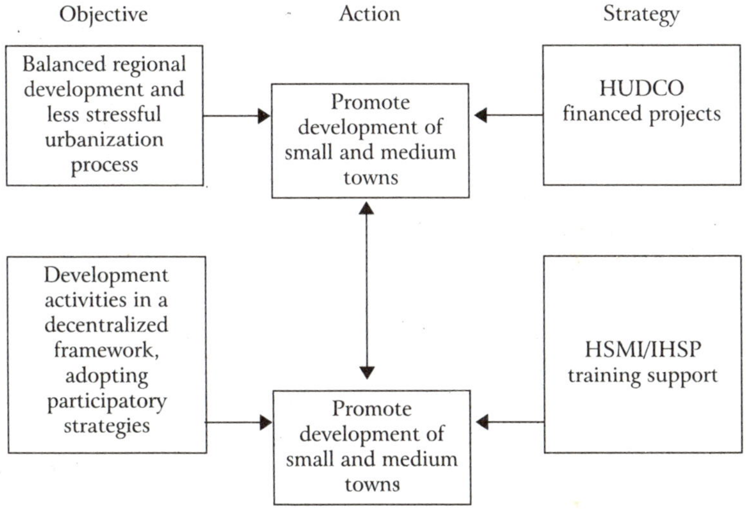

Source: A.N. Krishnamurthy, 1993.

cost recovery could be achieved. The linkage between training and project funding support is shown in Figure 3.

Building Close Rapport with State Level Agencies

The involvement of state level agencies is ensured during the following stages:

- formulation of training activities;
- preparation of the course curriculum;
- nomination of participating municipalities; and
- execution of the courses.

Increasing the Role of Municipalities in Infrastructure Development

The programme would also contribute to increase the role of municipalities in planning, programming and formulating of infrastructure projects. The participation of state level agencies has brought about a certain sensitization to the needs and aspirations of ULBs. Recommendations that are the result of final sessions during the training are forwarded to the respective departments for consideration and necessary follow-up. On the short term it is not possible to assess the impact.

Responding to Immediate Training Needs

In order to establish early credibility and support for this training programme, some expressed needs for training have been addressed. The initial expressed need for training was in practical skill-oriented training courses, which enable them to implement and maintain infrastructure, e.g., to better implement sanitation project, to improve the performance of water supply systems by reducing leakages, to improve maintenance schedules for their infrastructure, and to improve billing and collection of water charges. This strategy was adopted for the first activity, i.e., the course on low-cost sanitation schemes, held in April 1993. The overall positive response from the participants and from state level representatives indicates that this was a successful approach.

Select Dynamic Towns/Cities to Provide an Example

There are number of towns where more clear developmental concepts and plans exist, but these are not materialized due to the dominance and ignorance of state level agencies. As a strategy, these towns should become the first target groups for training in order to:

- show that town-based development planning and project formulation is possible, which may serve as an example and stimulus to other towns. It has been suggested to take these towns as a case study and disseminate these descriptions of such examples;
- show that development of infrastructure is more effective when projects are concerted and coordinated at local level; and
- sensitize state-level agencies and borrowers to local ideas and concepts and to integrate them in new projects, i.e., to come to a more participatory development planning.

This strategy has been adhered to Mandya, Ramnagaram, Chikmagalur and Hassan, which attended the action planning course in 1993, all have a potential to be a show-case. The impact of most of the training of 1993 can only be assessed in 1994.

Building on Local and Existing Training Capacity in Karnataka

Building on and further developing training capacity of existing institutions is crucial in the training programme strategy. This strategy has gained good support from both HUDCO and the Government of Karnataka. ATI has been the nodal training counterpart institution. It was realized that without additional staff strength, ATI would not to be able to be an effective partner. HUDCO has taken the wise decision to create two posts and one secretarial post to implement the decentralized training programme. The articulation of their roles in development and execution of training and research will need further attention in 1994. It is considered to establish a training centre that will focus on human settlements, urban poverty alleviation and urban management. Besides conducting training, it will develop research and build strong links with other programmes in the state, such as UBSP. It is also envisaged to further decentralize training to the district training institutes to increase the reach of training.

Use of Local Language (Kannada) during Training

The experience in Karnataka indicates that the use of the local language in training and the development of reading material is an important approach to increase the effectiveness and participation in training. English proved not to be a common language among the target group. The programme has so far succeeded to conduct training bilingually, which worked out quite satisfactory. The first steps have already been undertaken to translate the material for the second round of course in 1994.

Strong Emphasis on Supportive Research and Documentation

Strong emphasis has been given to undertake action research and documentation that is of direct support to the development of training curriculum and training material. Better understanding of the urban development issues is crucial for making training meaningful and to bring about the necessary change.

Concluding Remarks

Adopting these strategies of implementation, the decentralized training programme in Karnataka aims to be a catalyst agent in support of the process of change in the urban development sector.

The overall response has been very positive so far and it is felt that in particular the training programmes are providing a good support and incentive to the urban local governments to articulate the problems and needs to initiate projects and programmes that are responding to their needs, and are affordable and manageable. Secondly, the programme provides a good insight into the requirement of existing urban development scheme, presents a unique opportunity to exchange project level experiences, offers a forum to discuss these issues with state level agencies, and suggests practical ways and means to overcome day-to-day management problems of implementation and maintenance.

An important phase now is building the training cell within ATI into a dynamic, sustainable and respected unit, keeping close links with HUDCO, the state agencies and the ULBs, aiming to become a positive factor in the development of small and medium towns through training, research and professional support.

References

Indian Haman Settlements Programme, Phase II, *Extension Proposal* 1991-1994, November 1990.

Krishnamurthy, A.N., *Training support for integrated urban development and formulation of viable projects for institutional funding,* paper presented at the seminar on "Effective preparation, implementation and management of urban infrastructure in Karnataka and the role of training", IHSP, March 5th, 1993.

Kumar, M.V., K. Mukundan and Chetan Vaidya, *Investment Planning and Financing Model,* paper presented at the one-day seminar on "Effective preparation, implementation and management of urban infrastructure in Karnataka and the role of training" IHSP, March 5th, 1993.

Mengers, H.A., *IHSP Decentralized Training Programme Karnataka, September 1992-December 1993: State-of-the-Art,* December 1993.

Ministry of Urban Development, Government of India, *The Constitution of the Seventy-Fourth Amendment Act, 1992 on Municipalities*, n.d., New Delhi.

Policy level workshop on the 74th Constitutional Amendment and *UBSP, Issues and Recommendations*, 30th August-1st September, 1993.

Prasanna, Subbarayan, *Infrastructure planning problems in small and medium towns*, background paper, seminar on "Effective Development and Management of Urban Infrastructure in Karnataka and the Role and Approach of Training", Indian Human Settlement Programme, March 5th, 1993.

II

Civil Services

9

The Services in Modern Times*

DHARMA VIRA

I am very happy to be here today among you all to exchange a few thoughts. I have been in the administrative service for over forty years, and during this period I have witnessed the transition from the days of the British imperial administration to the democratic administration of today. At the outset, I would like to make it clear that my remarks about the administrative services are very general in character, and it is far from my intention to hurt the feelings of the services anywhere. I hope that what I say will be taken in the spirit in which it is said and that no one here will be offended. I belong to an older generation, and my only interest is to see that the services in our country continue to uphold the glorious traditions built up over a long period, and maintain the high ideals of public service. My talk today is intended mainly for the younger members of the services, who have had no opportunity of witnessing the events connected with the changeover, nearly 25 years ago, from the bureaucratic system to the democratic system of administration.

---

* Text of a talk delivered at the IIPA Maharashtra Regional Branch, Bombay, on the 28th July, 1971.

According to my conception of the tasks of the services in a democracy, and I have said this quite often—the officers will have to shoulder the responsibility of discharging a four-fold task. Their first task, specially amongst the senior ranks of the services, is to assist in the formulation of policies by giving unbiased and objective advice. Then, it is their task to involve themselves in the speedy and effective implementation of those policies decided upon by the political masters. Their third task is to provide a certain amount of stability and continuity to the administration. Their last function is actually the most important, i.e., to provide a clean and efficient administration to the people.

In the twenty-four years that have now passed since independence, the people have come to realize that a system based upon democratic principles cannot function efficiently if it has no effective support from the administrative machinery. But it must be remembered here that the administrative machinery in a democracy is manned not only by the services, but is a cooperative endeavour of the services and their political masters. If we have been seeing a rather alarming increase in inefficiency in the administration of this country, a large part of the blame for this state of affairs should lie at the doors both of our political leaders and the public administrative services. The British had evolved a system of administration to suit their own colonial requirements. The government was there to maintain law and order and to collect the revenues. That was all. But, since independence, the tasks of the government have increased vastly in the context of our pledge to establish a welfare state. In 1947, the administrative machinery in the country, which was in a fairly good working condition, suddenly faced with a number of difficult problems like the depletion amongst their ranks on account of the partition, communal riots, partition of assets, refugee rehabilitation, integration of Indian states and the like. The depleted services, however, were able to devote themselves to these numerous tasks with determination and dedication, because there was the inspiring leadership of stalwarts like Nehru, Patel, Azad and Kidwai. There was full understanding between the services and their political masters and the country registered remarkable progress in the beginning. But this position remained only for a short while. As lesser politicians got firmly in the saddle and the more far-sighted politicians passed away, pressure on the services increased. That was the time when the senior members, in the interest of their true role of the services in democracy, should have given the lead by resisting such pressures. It is however a pity that self-interest and temporary gain got the better of their sense of duty.

In running the administration of a country under the system of parliamentary democracy, the principal parties are the politicians and the civil services. In fact, it is a partnership in the service of the people. The politicians as representatives of the people come to power with a mandate from the electorate and lay down policies that have to be followed by the administrators for implementing the mandate of the people. The services are the principal advisers in policy making, and, thereafter, they have to ensure that the policies laid down, are implemented. Once a policy is laid down, it is not for the services to question it. But, before the policies are settled, it is the duty and obligation of the services to give honest advice regardless of the personal likes and dislikes of the political masters or of the benefits that accrue to the services. Any civil servant who fails to give this advice or gives the type of advice that will please his political boss is certainly not true to himself or to the national cause.

We are not living in the times of imperialism when the officer was somebody removed from the people, and therefore, had to maintain a distance in order to keep the prestige of the imperialist order intact. But, today, we are ruling for the people, with the people and this makes a good deal of difference, for it means an intimate contact between the services and the people. But, strangely enough, the advent of independence has had a contrary result. The little contact that was maintained in the old days between the senior officers and the people has now almost vanished because of the multitude of duties that the officials have to perform these days. As a consequence, administration is getting divorced from the people. The ministers are preoccupied with various matters, senior civil servants with so many functions that neither have any time for the people. An administration divorced from the people can never be a good administration and, therefore, what is needed today is not only technical competence on the part of the officers but a new approach to the performance of their tasks. Officers have to realize that their approach should be not as the masters of the people but servants of the people, and their well-wishers. They should be approachable, they should listen to the people and try to remove their grievances and difficulties. We all know that it is now becoming more and more difficult for the smallest thing to be done at present in our offices. In a democratic administration, there is no reason why anybody should have to run from pillar to post without being given assistance. One of the reasons for this degeneration is the attitude of the smaller officials in the hierarchy. The smaller the official, the more officious and rude he is. If a job is not done, people harbour grievances. They get more and more frustrated and think that everybody is corrupt, because there are a few corrupt people who have not been punished. At a very early stage of their training, our administrators should be instilled with a sense of service, a sense of participation with the people and in their tasks. They should have the feeling that they have been very fortunate to have been placed in a position to serve the people and that it is their duty to serve them whole-heartedly. It is their duty to provide them a clean administration where work is done quickly, cleanly and well, and where there is no corruption. Our young officers in the services have got the necessary training, they have a fine educational background, and they have technical competence. But I must say it is not only the technical competence of the officers that matters. What is most important is an approach to their tasks such as is required in a democracy. If all our officers are imbued with such an attitude towards their tasks, we will have an administration which will be worthy of the glorious traditions of this country. We must shed the idea that we are high and mighty and that God has made us specially to rule over the people and get paid to be rude to them. That is not the purpose of the administration, that is not the purpose of the service and that is not the way that democracy can be worked.

Another point on which I would like to say a few words is about the much-talked of "commitment of the services". I am not at all clear in my mind as to what who talk about commitment really mean. The Prime Minister, in order to clear the air, the other day, gave expression of her ideas on the subject. I found them to be unexceptional. A 'committed civil service' should mean a service committed to secularism, democratic practices, eradication of poverty and totally committed to serve the people. It should also mean a service committed to the upholding of the ethical principles of integrity, honesty and dedication to work. In all free democratic countries the civil service is neutral. In fact, the neutrality of this service is one of its prized attributes. Every intelligent person will regard this neutrality as one of characteristic traits of a truly efficient and dedicated civil service. If, on the other hand, commitment means that the civil servants should implement the policies and ideologies of any political party in power, it would mean the end of good administration. It would be suicidal to the country if we identify the civil service with the political ideologies of the party in power. Public service is the only ideal to be aimed at by the services and public approbation should be their only reward. The most important element of strength in a community is the sense of satisfaction that it can generate in itself. The services as a community should generate this sense of satisfaction in task done for it is this thirst for satisfaction which will stretch the civil servant beyond his everyday self so that he acquires the full stature of his personality. He must understand that the prerequisite to a genuine democratic government is a feeling by the people that "this is our government". It is only thus and through the identification of local ideals and values that truly indigenous democratic institutions can grow up in our country, and not by mere imitations from elsewhere.

Another point I would like to mention is the importance of public relations in official work. In the old days, it was enough for the people to be governed, to live peacefully under a 'Mai-Bap' government assuring to them safety and the freedom to live as they liked, provided they paid the revenues to the government coffers. But, today, the picture in entirely different. Unless the officer takes the trouble to inform the people of all the beneficent activities of the government of which he is also a limb, the people are bound to get disappointed and frustrated. After all, 'public relations' means the maintenance of good relations with the public. An intimate contact with the people will help to strengthen popular appreciation of the policies and actions of the government. Every member of the services should make it a point to devote at least half to one hour of his day to contact the people, enquire into their grievances, and if possible take prompt decisions to alleviate whatever difficulties the people are experiencing. No amount of office work behind closed doors can be a substitute for this personal contact with the people. Each officer should be a Public Relations Officer in himself, and it is only thus that confidence in the services by the people can be established. This is one point on which I would like you all to think deeply and for long. A correct awareness on the part of the public of what exactly government is doing will help greatly in getting their support and in enthusing them to a sense of partnership with the government.

There is just one other point that I would like to refer to and that is the need for change in the present structure of administration in our country.

The British had evolved a system of administration to suit their colonial requirements mainly to maintain law and order and also to realize the revenue. Since independence, the tasks of the government have greatly increased. We are now pledged to establish a welfare state. To achieve this object the country has to be developed rapidly in all directions and the machinery that was very effective for a colonial administration may not be up to the requirements of a developing welfare state. In fact, the stresses and strains are already beginning to be felt. We have, however, continued the old structure practically unmodified to sift the present requirements. A careful look at the present structure of administration with a view to modify or alter to meet our present needs would be worthwhile. For example, it is at all necessary now to have water-tight hierarchies? Why should we not provide an incentive to the lower-paid officials to do better work by opening to them opportunities for rising to the top-most rungs of the ladder, depending of course on careful selection on merits at various stages? Would it not be worthwhile in the process to reduce the market disparity between the minor officials and the so-called clerks and the senior officers, in order to infuse into them a greater sense of responsibility, self-respect and initiative? Is it necessary to have so many tiers in administration? In a Secretariat, beginning from the receiving clerk up to the Secretary, there are as many as eight or at least seven tiers. If a file has to go to the Minister, another tier is added. The file goes up, right up to the Minister in nine stages and then travels backwards through the same stages. If per chance, there is also a horizontal action, viz., consulting another department, the same process has to be repeated in the other department. How can work be disposed of speedily in such an arrangement? Why should not more authority to dispose of cases be given at the lower levels and the officers at each level be encouraged to authority delegated to them and not pass the back on upward? The whole process of decision-making should not in any case take more than two or three stages. Then, there is the question of officer-clerk ratio. In my view, this ratio is far too high in our country, leading to inevitably greater reliance on the clerks or lower officials for disposal of business, and lesser supervision. The ratio should be reduced appreciably. This might make for more expenditure on administration, but the results would more than compensate for the increased expenses. In the long run, from the point of view of the people, the expense would be worthwhile.

Our's is a country that has recently emerged from foreign rule to independence. In such a country the need for a change in the administrative structure would appear to be obvious. Even in the UK, whose administrative and parliamentary practices we have followed, the need for change has been felt as would appear from the following extract from the report of the Fulton Committee. I quote: "Throughout it (the civil service) has to remember that it exists to serve the community, and that imaginative humanity sometimes matters more than tidy efficiency and administrative uniformity. In our (Committee's) view, the structure and practices of the service have not kept up with the changing tasks. The defects we have found can nearly all be attributed to this. We have found no instance where reform has run ahead too rapidly. So, today, the service is in need of fundamental change." These words could, with much greater justification and advantage, be applied to the present administrative conditions in India.

What I have been saying so far is only by way of pinpointing the present defects in our administrative structure which are the main cause of sufferings of people. We should not allow these defects to continue, because once they get stabilized, it will be very difficult to do anything. Our's is a new democracy. The period of adjustment between the politicians, the services and the people has not yet passed. We have very good and efficient people in our services who are extremely patriotic and are anxious to serve their country and the people. I have found it necessary only to highlight some of these disturbing tendencies that are developing in respect of the role of the services in our young democracy before they result in irretrievably damaging the structure of the democratic institutions of our country. After all, I need not repeat that the future is in our hands if we can only adjust ourselves to the requirements of our society. It is only thus that we can ensure progress and good administration.

These are only certain random thoughts of mine. But I have tried to give you the reasons for the present malaise in our administrative structure. It is no possible in a short talk to be exhaustive in regard to these matters. It is for organizations such as the Indian Institute of Public Administration and its branches to go into these matters dispassionately, and with a sense of objectivity. We must rise above self-interest and help in providing the country with an administrative machinery free from petty-mindedness and red tape and which will give our people a clean and efficient administration. The matter is urgent and any delay would be dangerous and at great risk not only to the service, but to the country too. The people will not wait for all time. They cannot continue patiently to suffer. If we do not put an end to the present-day ills ourselves, by imaginative reforms and a sense of dedication in the service of the people, the people are sure to revolt some day or the other and put an end to these ills themselves.

10

The Anatomy of Civil Administration

G.B.K. HOOJA

The Administrative Ethos

As it is, in the Indian policy, it has become a fashion to blame the bureaucracy for all the failures (or excesses) of the government, and the irony is that the learned professors of public administration who should know better also tend to fall a prey to this temptation, and join in the chorus. Let me state at the outset that I am certainly not an apologist for the services. I would not condone at any rate a willful illegality committed by or a serious lapse in the discharge of duty on the part of an erring public servant. I will call him to account for these, but I will refrain from tainting the entire civil service with the same bush.

In the parliamentary form of government which we have adopted after the Westminister model, the role of the bureaucracy or the permanent civil service as distinct from the ministers of the Crown is well defined. The British civil services are drawn on the basis of merit through an open competitive examination (as in India) and their intellectual quality and moral calibre is of a high order. They are no less jealous of their reputation for competence and integrity than the judiciary. On the other land, the ministers, at least initially, are amateurish and have to depend on the permanent services for expert knowledge and trained judgement. It is the recognized duty of the permanent civil services to advise the ministers on matters of state policy, and to implement the same the best of their capacity, once a policy decision has been taken. The civil services are expected to tender honest and sincere advice, fearlessly, and to carry out the orders, even when they are over-ruled, without demur. While the council of ministers is answerable to the nation through the parliament, the responsibility of the civil service is to place at the disposal of the ministers its expert knowledge and ungrudging loyalty. That is why the civil servants, as a matter of healthy convention, are not attacked in the parliament, while the ministers may be ruthlessly dismembered for their lapses, real or imaginary. It was owing to this peculiarity of the British system that Prime Minister, Clement Attlee, happened to administer a bit of a shock to his fellow conferees at the Potsdam Conference when he landed there with almost the same team of experts which had accompanied Winston Churchill earlier at the Yalta Conference. When pointedly asked if he had encountered any trouble from the Tory breed of civil servants, he categorically stated that he found them loyal. In consequence of traditions, well-established and fully accepted, the commitment of the services is to the nation as distinct from the party in power for the time-being. Is it any wonder that the day-to-day work of the nation is carried out without any serious jolts, irrespective of whichever party may be in the saddle?

Prof. Harold Laski laid down the ethos of the British civil service when he enjoined upon young entrants to the service to take three vows: poverty, obedience and anonymity. The inference is clear.

Here, in India, however, the recent trends are seriously disquieting. For every ministerial sin of omission and commission, the Indian bureaucracy offers itself as the obvious scapegoat.

Let us not forget, however strongly we may feel about it, that we cannot just wish away the bureaucracy, even as we cannot wish away the government. The administration of a modern state set on the course of development and growth with justice calls for a cadre of men who possess not only trained judgement and expert knowledge, but are also imbued with transparent integrity and unquestionable incorruptibility. Good government does not simply descend on a people by enshrining high-sounding 'mantras' in the constitution, which may as easily be snuffed out, as was sadly realized during the trauma of emergency lately experienced by an unprepared nation.

It is universally acknowledged that the Indian bureaucracy, under sound leadership, has played a notable role in the matter of rehabilitating millions of refugees from Pakistan, in the matter of quelling communal riots which seemed at one time to consume the entire social fabric, in the matter of integration of 560 states, in providing civil support to the armed forces in the three major wars, thrust upon independent India since its inception, in extending the researches of science and technology for and wide, thus leading to the green revolution which has more than doubled India's foodgrain production in a generation and above all, in organizing six fair and free general elections. By any standard, this is a record of which any service can be legitimately proud, but oddly enough, day in and day out, we exult in denigrating our services for the failures and lapses which may, in fact, be seeded elsewhere.

Here one's thoughts naturally turn to the atrocities committed during the dark days of the emergency, but may one pertinently ask what about those who blotted out civil liberties by the stroke of a pen. What about those who, without as much as a gesture, allowed the dubious rule of merit, and therefore of political patronage, to prevail over the time-tested rule of seniority in making high-ranking appointments? And, what about the barons of the press and the knight-schevalier of the

Tribune whose specific function was to protect the plebeian citizen from the arbitrary action of the patrician magistracy?

Civil service is an instrument of state policy. You may cut your own nose with it, if you please, or you may use it to cut the throat of a thug. Keep it sharp, even as you would, your armed forces, ever at the pitch of professional efficiency.

The pertinent question is how to ensure this, how to evoke the afore-mentioned qualities of integrity, incorruptibility, trained judgement and loyalty in the services.

Unquestionably, Sardar Patel was one of the foremost political leaders who realized the importance of a competent and devoted civil service in the fulfilment of the arduous tasks facing the country soon after the attainment of independence.

Apart from other faculties, he was endowed with a Nelsonian eye. The story is told of a senior officer who happened to take a decision which was not palatable to Sardar, and was eventually questioned in the cabinet. Instead of letting him down, Sardar owned it up and thus earned the lasting respect of this officer. To quote the testimony of V.P. Menon: "It is remarkable how the services reacted to his touch. It became a question of honour with them to live upto the Sardar's expectations."

As we know, at the time of independence, India was threatened with balkanization. The British bureaucrats who had been made to quit India were yet itching to stage a come back. They fervently hoped that Indians would becknon them to return even as their ancestors, 2,000 years ago, had petitioned their Roman masters to stay back. Millions of displaced persons were emitting fire and fury; millions others were enveloped in the deepest despair. The country was consumed by communal conflagration. At such a juncture India was lucky to have men of vision and sagacity at the helm of her affairs. They had the knack of eliciting the best from the members of the steel-frame.

History is evidence that they were not let down. Under their leadership the civil services made an herculean effort to rise to the occasion and in the endeavour displayed remarkable initiative, drive and loyalty.

Political Will

Allow me to cite another instance of the influence of political will, for good or evil, on the administrative apparatus. When 20 years ago, the Congress Party assumed the reins of government in Rajasthan, it proceeded to ameliorate the condition of the tenantry in a business-like way, committed as it was to the cause of the uplift of the toiling masses, A beginning was made with the Rajasthan Protection of Tenants Ordinance. It was followed in quick succession by legislation ordaining the Abolition of Jagirs, Rajasthan Tenancy Act, Rajasthan Land Revenue Act and the Ceilings Act. The government also adopted the community development programme, subsequently converted into panchayati raj with great enthusiasm. Result: the administrative apparatus though assembled from 22 integrating units, with varying degrees of administrative skill, did not fail the government and carried out its tasks in a manner which elicited approbation from far and wide.

It would, however, appear that by the middle of the sixties, the political engine had exhausted its steam. As a result, the process of deceleration ensued. As is well known, panchayat elections were, time and again, postponed on one pretext or the other, and action under the ceilings law was halted from time to time.

As long ago as in 1970, Jaya Prakash Narayan had to say this on the subject of rural change: "If the reform laws already enacted come to be fully and truly implemented, it would amount to a minor social revolution... I had instanced the laws concerning homesteads, share-cropping, land ceiling, minimum wages, money-lending etc. The benefit of these laws will not accrue to those for whom they are meant unless .... the village community comes to be organized more democratically, so that the balance of power .... comes to be held evenly by all the interests in the village."[1]

The following observations from the report of the economic and social survey of Asia and the Pacific for the year 1975 also support the above thesis:

> "Although governments are committed to such programmes their effectiveness has been limited (by) the lack of political will... the economic, social and political power of the landlords... the lack of bargaining power of the rural poor, the loopholes in the law, the lack of administrative machinery for enforcement.... the absence of land record indicating who is cultivating what land and the lack of supporting services, such as legal service, credit and input... of overriding importance in a successful land reforms programme, is the political factor... A meaningful land reforms programme will envitably destroy or limit the power base of many persons,... This is the basic cause which .... accounts for the lack of will on the part of the governments to pursue reforms .... A second factor in making the reforms effective is the development of the beneficiaries as a political force in order to ensure that implementation does take place (by) harnessing the beneficiaries together into some form of rural organization to ensure their representation in the process of decision-making and implementation."[2]

Lamenting on the disinclination of the powers that be to share responsibility and authority at the grassroots level with the local beneficiaries, Jaya Prakash Narayan remarked in the context of the situation then obtaining in Bihar.

"The Zila Parishad and Panchayat Samitis Act provides for development work to be placed under the Zila Parishad with the District Development Officer as Secretary. The Act thus aims at separation of general and development administration.

It is now several years since the passage of this Act, but Zila Parishads have so' far been formed only in three districts. The intention to enforce the Act in all the other districts is no doubt (.) there, but nobody knows how long its enforcement would take. Nobody knows how many years it would take to reconstitute a Zila Parishad when for some reason it happens to be dissolved.... Finally, I should like to say that irrespective of whether or not Zila Parishads are constituted, the decentralization of district administration .... is essential for the promotion of development activities."[3]

Can there be a severer indictment of the forces which are holding back the march of the nation towards justice, liberty, equality and fraternity?

This then is the rationale for autonomous local, self-government, based on adult franchise so as to ensure government of the people, for the people and by the people.

Here, permit me to say that notwithstanding political constraints, instances are not wanting where dedicated officers have kept the torch burning, and carried on with their administrative responsibilities as best as they could.

May I, in this context, seek your indulgence to mention the good work done by my erstwhile colleagues on the Rajasthan Board of Revenue and several Collectors, young and old, who cheerfully accepted the lead of the Board. It was realized that though there was a lot of nebulous talk of land reforms from various platforms, the cadres on whom depended the task of implementing the programme were not fully aware of the contents, nor of the methodology of land reforms. In short, there was lack of communication along the transmission line and there was hardly any feedback. To meet this serious gap, it was decided to run a quarterly journal, called the *Raaviraa* (by Rajasva Vibhag, Rajasthan) with a view to disseminating information regarding revenue matters in general and land reforms in particular. Free copies were sent to revenue officials numbering about 10,000 in the state. It was started on

2 October 1969, and fulfilled a great need, so long as it lasted. Besides, drives were mounted to liquidate old cases, both in the Board and the lower courts, to expedite disposal of pending mutation cases, to regularize unauthorized occupations fall in within the revised government policy, to update the land records, to collect revenue dues etc. It is on record that in certain fields, almost all-time high figures were touched.

Special mention may be made here of the distribution of passbooks to *khatedars,* which enabled them to go to the loaning authorities such as the commercial and cooperative banks directly, without having to wait in the patwari and other revenue officials: this indeed provided a great boon to the *khatedars* as was recently acknowledged by the bankers and representatives of non-governmental organizations assembled at Delhi in a Seminar on Rural Development: Focus on the Weakest, organized jointly by the PAD (I) and AFFRO.

The aforesaid exercise conducted by the Board of Revenue emphasized the importance of training and constant dialogue between the various echelons of the administrative machinery, as also the necessity of concurrent evaluation and performance audit.

Of course, what did not take off was the Panchayati Raj. It was stifled by the apprehensions and fear of being dismounted, sensed by the persons who had come to occupy positions of power and authority in the wake of the first flush of freedom Let it be said to the credit of the present regime in Rajasthan that in holding the panchayat elections after a lapse of 13 years, it has exhibited its faith in the democratic process. The next logical step, of course, would be to demarcate the necessary financial resources to be handed over to the local authorities, so that they can function autonomously and without constraints. I would allot the entire land revenue accruing from a village to the village panchayat, leaving it to the village body to exercise its power of exemption or of levying a surcharge, as it pleases. I would also hand over control over the necessary administrative staff to the local administration to enable it to discharge its responsibility to city corporation. This will bring self-government to the doorstep of the farmer and the weaker sections of society and to the extent, we support this programme it will be a testimony to !or much proclaimed concern for the common man.

Administrative Paralysis

I fully share the anxiety of B.G. Verghese that "the current upheavals in the various parts of the country must cause deep disquiet to anyone who pauses to think of the consequence of this unfortunate show of insensate violence, anger and unreason. The tendency once more to take to the street or to seek the settlement of grievances, some of them wholly imagined by strong-arm methods cannot be to strongly deplored."[4]

For the past several months (in fact, since I was obliged to close sine die the main campus of the Shraddhanand Gurukula Kangri Vishwavidhyalaya, in August 1977), I have been watching the situation in the universities rather closely, and not without sorrow and anguish. I have often posed the question, why is it that the authorities who are paid to maintain law and order prevaricate and fail to discharge their duty by the academic community. The law, the Code of Criminal Procedure, saddles them with a responsibility and arms them with powers to discharge the same. Then why is it that they fumble? In the first place, they do not act. They go on watching and watching, bemused spectators of an escalating drama, in which the unruly elements gradually gain the upper hand. When, finally, they decide to act, they find that the situation has become explosive; and now they overact, and find themselves caught In the maze of their earlier indecision, as it were. Follow shootings, unwarranted deaths, judicial probes, accusations and counter-accusations, demoralization, leading to further inaction.

Is it small wonder that those officers who can manage to avoid district postings and prefer to be ensconced in sheltered secretariat jobs?

Admittedly, only a dare-devil may now-a-days accept the post of a Vice Chancellor. In his amusing and yet not so amusing essay, *Looking for VC's*[5] Mohamed Pulikkal make the barber slip out and get into the first train to Rishikesh to escape the fate of being adorned with the crown of a VC. It is indeed a tragedy of our times that the exalted office of the VC has come to such a low pass. If the chorus in the press and the popular forums of thought were any indication, the students are responsible for much of the mischief at a university campus. If, however, an X-ray were made of the U-corpus it will be observed that the disease, in fact, lies elsewhere, and the students are more of ten than not pawns in the game, more sinned against than sinning. When at the end of the game, an assessment is made of the gains and losses, it will be noted that the worst sufferers have been the students, and their parents who had hopefully sent their wards to these temples of learning to acquire knowledge and skills ta equip them for the battle of life. The teachers, the employees, the politicians, all emerge unscathed, even fattened out of the fracas. Amongst the casualties lie littered the work-days of the students, library hours, lab practicals (assuming that the libraries and laboratories have escaped vandalism), and, of course, discipline and peace, not to mention respect for law, or *dharma.*

It was equally cynical of the Education Minister to declare, with all the complacency at his command, that in 1977 there were only 7,000 cases of student violence as against 11,000 cases in 1974. He is reported to have said that the situation is not so bad as made out.

One is tempted to echo the waring raised by the *Indian Express* editorially (in a different context, though) that involved here is a formidable challenge which of hand before the authorities bestir themselves?

An Administrative Formula

Amongst others it was Sardar Narinder Singh who initiated me into the art of administration. "A District Magistrate who does not know what is cooking in whose house might as well seek a secretariat job. He cannot run a district" he used to say. Such was the emphasis on intelligence, and, therefore, on anticipation placed by seasoned administrators in days gone by. As in tennis, so in administration, you may score a point against your adversary if you are able to be anticipated, if you fail to act, it is your doom. That is the law in tennis, but in public administration, the law takes a greater toll. The District Magistrate may avoid his doom, but the innocent citizen who solely depends on the authority, invariably pays for his gullibility.

In the educational field, we have been hearing of the formula 10+2+3 for a long time, which now seems to be yielding place to 8+4+3 (lest one good custom should corrupt the world) but in the field of administration, the formula is 10+20+70. In every society, in every group of humans, you will find 10 percent people who are disgruntled, alienated, out to break the law, and to upset the social order, 20 percent who are sitting on the fence, waiting to fish in the troubled waters and 70 percent who want peace to prevail, so that they can go about their lawful business, unhindered by lawless elements. It is the duty of the guardians of the law to provide an umbrella to these 70 percent to keep in check the elements prone to break the law, in short, to hinder the hindrances. Surely, a District Magistrate or a Superintendent of Police, worth his salt, knows or has on his file the names of persons falling in the first two categories. (The experience of the emergency has, at any rate, brought out the efficiency and the capacity for knowledge of the forces of law and order.) The question which arises and puzzles remainder 70 percent is why the district authorities fail to act in time to prevent a situation from deteriorating and going out of hands. From all indications, it would appear that this indecision, paralysis if you please, stems from political source. Given the political will, there is no reason why the guardians of law and order, the paid servants of the public, should not act, well in time.

Did they not provide an ample proof of their anxiety to please their political bosses during the traumatic days of the emergency? Then, why this hesitation now? All they need is clear orders and an occasional pat.

Let me confess that I have not been able to swallow the advice if so non-chalantly and pontifically given by a responsible minister of state to a deputation of senior citizens who had waited on him to seek effective police protection, that they might as well use counter-force to evict the intruders from their property.

More recently, I heard a member of the Planning Commission stating at a national seminar that nothing moves in this country unless there is an agitation. He, therefore, thought nothing of organized marches. Let us not forget that marches may lead to counter-marches engulfing the country in an orgy of lawlessness all around, in which not only the marchers but also the standers-by may be submerged. And suppose, the states started marching on the Planning Commission. Will the brains gathered there yield before mobocracy? Or, will they also catch the first train to Rishikesh.

While on the subject may I in all seriousness invite the attention of the learned experts in the field of public administration to the disinclination allegedly exhibited by the Home Minister, Government of India, to visit Pant Nagar and Sambhal on the tenuous plea that law and order was a state subject. One may be permitted the audacity to ask whether the Government of India would offer the same alibi if locust invaded India?

As stated by J.N. Khosla, "Thirty years ago, our nation seemed much more united, and the problems of our development much more simple .... Since then, however, our social, economic and political contradictions have assumed serious proportions. New contradictions have emerged to aggravate the situation. By now we are a 'soft state' par excellence of Gunnar Myrdal. While we are equipped with a facade of political super-structure of a modern democratic state and every aspect of our life is politicized, we have shown utter incapacity to develop viable political sub-systems for promoting a responsive and sensitive administration, a responsible citizenship, clear party politics, a sense of social justice, tolerance and fair play, and above all for accelerating social transformation and development.[6]

Manu on Administration

It does not require much convincing to say that no worthwhile change is possible without an appreciation of the cultural foundations of a country.

Swami Dayananda, the founder of the Arya Samaj, was the first amongst the leaders of Indian renaissance, who drew the attention of the learned scholars, the native rulers and the common folk to the wisdom enshrined in the Vedas and the relevance of the teachings of Manu to modern times. Contrary to popular belief, the Swami was not merely a religious guru. He was also a political guru. In his magnum opus, the *Satyartha Prakasha*, he has devoted a whole chapter, the sixth, to the art of government (Raj Dharma).

Amongst others, Maharana Sajjan Singh of Udaipur was a disciple of the Swami. At his request, the Swami drew up for the benefit of the Maharana, a set of 51 instructions, based on the Shastric injunctions, as to how a king should conduct himself. Besides these, the Swami enjoined upon his princely disciples the study of the seventh, the eighth and the ninth chapters of *Manu Smriti*. He also recommended the study of the Shukra Niti, the Vidur Prajagar and Shanti Parva of the *Mahabharata*. In the chapter on Raj Dharma, the Swami quotes extensively from the *Manu Smriti*.

According to the law of Manu, which is as hoary as the Vedas, the authority of the king, the cabinet and the civil service to rule flows from their responsibility to protect and serve the people. The king should not forget that he, too, is subject to *dharma,* the rule of law. It is enjoined upon all the three wings of the government mentioned above that they should be men of integrity, wise, firm, honest in collecting taxes of the state, well-tried. They should be skillful, clever, alert, brave and honest, free from the corrupting influences of office.

Similarly, the judiciary is placed on a high pedestal by Manu. Justice is one of the chief functions of the state. Where justice, wounded by injustice, approaches, the judge must extract the dart, otherwise he becomes a partner in the crime, and where justice is destroyed by injustice and truth by falsehood, the judges shall be destroyed. According to Manu, punishment should fit each case individually. The higher the status of the individual, the more is his responsibility to uphold the *dharma* and, therefore, his liability in case of a transgression or lapse. Thus, where an ordinary individual may be fined a trifle, the king should be fined a thousand fold, says Manu.

Besides the two main duties of the state viz., preservation of internal peace and protection from external danger, there are several other duties which the state has to discharge, as for instance, price control, adjudication of disputes between guilds and families, to ensure that the Vaisya attends to his trade, banking and agriculture, and the Sudra, likewise attends to his duties.

Further, the state had a prominent role to play in the field of education. Teachers belonged to an honoured class and the support given to them was the richest treasure of the state. According to Manu, the state should levy no taxes from the teachers. They are the custodians of wisdom, and they should be encouraged to spread it abroad.

The state had paternal responsibilities towards the hermits, ascetics, widows, pregnant or childless women, the blind, the crippled and the old.

The state must punish those who take bribes, cheats, rogues, gamblers, fortune-tellers, officials and physicians who act wrongly, and harlots. These persons and others who behave like non-Aryans should be considered as thorns in the body of the state.

Thus, in the state of Manu's conception, the politicians serve disinterestedly and the enlightened ruler supported by an efficient and loyal cabinet, a competent and incorruptible civil service, and intelligent judiciary dedicates his life according to the dictates of *dharma* to the protections and service of the people who are the ultimate repositories of sovereignty. In Manu's state, education is free, the teachers are respected, the poor and the needy are well-looked after, Here internal order is accompanied by independence of external control.[7]

Dayananda closes his chapter on Raj Dharma with the Vedic injuction, *vayam prajaapateh prajaa abhum* (Yajur Veda). We are the subjects of the God. He is our ruler. May he make us worthy of our station and guide us in the path of truth and justice.[8]

As is known, 'Rama Rajya' was the India of Gandhi's dreams. Understandably, it caused titters in certain quarters, but the following description of 'Rama Rajya' by Will Durant should set all a thinking:

> And'tis told by ancient sages, during Rama's happy reign
> Death untimely, dire diseases, came not to his subject men
> Widows wept not in their sorrow for their lords untimely lost
> Mothers wailed not in their anguish for their babes by Yama crost
> Robbers, cheats and gay deceivers tempted not with lying word
> Neighbour loved his righteous neighbour, and the
> People loved their lord

Trees their ample produce yielded as returning seasons want
And the earth in grateful gladness never-failing harvest letn
Rains descended in their seasons, never came the blighting gale
Rich in crop and rich in pasture was each soft and smiling vale
Loom and anvil gave their produce, and the tilled
and fertile soil
And the nation lived rejoicing in their old ancestral toil.[9]

As Jawaharlal Nehru said: "The service of India means the service of the millions who suffer. It means the ending of poverty and grievance and disease and inequality of opportunity. The ambition of the greatest man of our generation has been to wipe every tear from every eye. That may be beyond us but as long as there are tears and suffering, so long our work will not be over."

The rulers (servants) of modern India would do well to pause and think if they may be depended upon to carry on this task.

Notes

1. *Face to Face.*
2. *ESCAP Report*, 1975.
3. *India and Her Problems.*
4. *India Today* (May 1-5, 1978).
5. *Indian Express,* 25 April 1978.
6. *Inaugural Address: Seminar: Political Science in Transition.*
7. Motwani, K., *Manu Dharma Shastra.*
8. Dayananda, *Salyartha Prakasha.*
9. *The Story of Civilization: Our Oriental Heritage,* Vol. 1.

11

National Civil Service System in India: A Critical Overview

R.K. MISHRA

The Indian civil service has a long history. During the Mauryan era, in ancient India, the civil servants performed the role of personal servants. During the medieval period, they were acting as state servants. In the British period they became public servants, and the civil service became a protected service. Over the five decades of Indian independence, 1947-2000, the Indian civil service has more or less followed the British model, but the pressures emanating from within and outside are now forcing the Indian civil service to professionalize itself.

The Indian civil service system is composed of the central and the provincial civil service system. The central civil service system comprises the three all-India and many other civil services. The provincial civil services follow the same pattern. The candidates for the civil services are selected on the basis of a three-tier examination. The Indian civil service system is rank-based, where generalists are preferred to specialists, and lifetime employment is provided to its incumbents. The pay and perks received by the civil servants are many more times higher than the per capita income of the common man in the country. However, these perks and perquisites have been definitely on the lower side as compared to what are being received by the private sector managers and employees of multinationals in India.

The civil services are dominated by the urban middle class. A handful of universities have been able to send a large number of their English and Hindi-speaking students to the civil services. The representation of women has been very meagre, and despite the provisions of reservation of 50 percent seats for scheduled tribes and scheduled castes, their number has been very inadequate. Interestingly, the powerful sections of society in different provinces are well represented in the Indian civil service system. About half of the civil service entrants have their parents employed in the central or provincial governments.

The Indian civil service system has followed the classical Weberian model. In the process of cooperating with the politicians very often they tend to be conformists. The public opinion about the Indian civil service system is that it lacks innovativeness, initiative, empathy, and drive for change. The civil servants hold exactly a different view of themselves. The Government of India and its 25 provincial governments spend about 3.5 percent of the GDP on their civil servants. They employ about eight million in the civil services which is 50 percent of the employment provided in the organized sector.

The civil service system is the backbone of the administrative machinery of the Indian nation. India, which is a union of states, has a democratic system. The political system of the country is pluralistic, having three tiers of administration, namely, central, provincial and local. The federal parliament is bicameral. The lower house known as the Lok Sabha constitutes elected members. The members of the upper house, known as the Rajya Sabha, are elected by the various provinces on the basis of an assigned strength. Together, the two houses constitute parliament and the members of these houses are called members of parliament. A more or less similar structure also exists at the provincial or state level. At the local level, the villages have panchayats (council of villagers). Several villages constitute a block and the block-level councils are headed by Pradhans. These Pradhans constitute a district council which is headed by a district chief. The elections are governed by the principle of majority vote, which simply means that the elections are decided on the basis of highest votes polled by a person.

India is a multireligious country. Its Constitution adopted in 1950 declared the country as a secular state. The Constitution also recognized the special rights of minorities. Some of the religious communities follow the system of castes and sub-castes. The country's Constitution recognizes English as the link, and Hindi as the national language, and bestows upon 13 more the status of official languages. The 24 provinces and two union territories of the country, besides having some of these languages as their official languages, are inhabited by masses having a number of dialects and sub-dialects. The social system of the country is characterized by inequities. As per the 1997 estimates indicated in the Draft Ninth Five-Year Plan finalized in January 1997, about 50 percent of the people are below the poverty line. The unemployment in the country is rampant.

India is a mixed economy, where both the public and private sectors are accorded a place of importance. In the public-private sector mix, the balance is now shifting in favour of the private sector. The monopoly and controls are fading away. The government is seriously engaged in the task of infrastructure and social sector development. Both the public and private sectors are striving for gaining the competitive edge. Both the federal and provincial budgets are plagued by huge fiscal deficits. In 1996-97 the fiscal deficit was 5 percent of the gross domestic product (GDP) in the case of the central government, and the various provincial governments also registered a similar level of deficit in relation to their state domestic product. Inflation has been a constant problem for the country. On an average, the rate of inflation has been about 10 percent per annum. The country's balance of trade and balance of payments have always remained in negative. One of the perennial features of the economic management of the country has been its deficit financing.

The Fifth Pay Commission, in its report submitted in January 1997, had suggested sweeping reforms and a 30 percent downsizing of the civil service across the board. The civil service reforms worldwide have in part forced the policy makers to make the Indian civil service system people-oriented, productive and yield the value for money. In terms of the Ferrel Heady configuration the Indian civil service system has a majority-party responsiveness and is mixed corporatist. The qualifications for entrance into, earning promotions, and retentions in the civil service, are professional and performance based. The sense of mission held by civil servants is a mixed bag of compliance, cooperation, policy responsiveness, constitutional responsiveness and guidance. In terms of the configuration of Philip Morgan, the Indian civil service system acts as the principal agent of the state. In saying this, it has to be kept in mind that some of the characteristics of the patrimonial state still pervade the country and to that extent also its civil service system.

Historically, the country had a great past. The ancient Indian state was prosperous where art and music greatly thrived. The medieval period belonged to the Moghuls who introduced a number of administrative measures, including a land revenue tax collection system, local manufacturing of industrial goods, and exports of arts and crafts to the other nation-states. The decline of the Moghul era saw the rise of the East India Company in the 16th century, which ruled the country for more than 250 years. The British government took over the reigns of the country from the East India Company. During its 200-year rule it created an Indian state, introduced an education system, laid down foundations of very strong administrative and bureaucratic structure, and interconnected the various parts of its administration through a vast network of road and rail transport. In 1947, the country gained independence. In 1950, the Planning Commission was set up to initiate a system of economic planning and the First Five-Year Plan was launched in 1951.

Today, India is a country of over 880 million people. Though its rate of growth has touched a mark of 6.7 percent in 1996-97, the average annual rate of growth has been about 3 percent per annum during the 50 years of its independence. The rate of growth of population has, however, been about 2 percent per annum, leaving only 1 percent as the net rate of growth per annum for the country. The standards of living enjoyed by the masses are significantly lower as compared to many countries in Asia and elsewhere on the globe. Unquestionably, the country faces a daunting task of lifting itself above the barriers to its growth, and assuring its people a quality of life of which they could be proud. The country also has to free itself of its past where it used to only look inwards. The main challenge before it is to integrate itself with the rest of the world and achieve the global benchmarks of the levels of efficiency.

The main purpose of this paper is to discuss the development of the civil service, delineate on its internal labour market, and analyse its representativeness. The issues such as the politicization of the civil service, the perception of the civil servants about themselves, and the views that different sections of society have about them, are also discussed in the paper. The paper also outlines the various measures introduced for reforming the civil service in India and the extent of their diffusion. Finally, in the concluding section, the paper sums up the salient features pertaining to the various issues discussed about the civil service, and suggests a scheme for the revamping of the Indian civil service system, which specifically centres round the Indian Administrative Service (IAS) that acts as the hub of the administrative machinery of the country.

Development of the Civil Service

There is no account of the organization of the civil service pertaining to the ancient Indian state (200 BC-1000 AD). However, in the Mauryan period (313 BC), Vishnugupta (also called Kautilya) authored the treatise known as Kautilya's *Arthashastra*. Kautilya laid down the qualifications of the civil servants for appointment to the court. He described the views of various experts on this issue. In his view, loyalty and sincerity were to be the two main qualifications in a person to be appointed as a civil servant. Kautilya also suggested some checks and balances on the appointment of civil servants. He prescribed a clearance by the vigilance department of the states for the appointment of civil servants. He recommended a continuous watch on the functioning of the civil servants on a regular basis. He talked of the various heads of the different branches of the civil service. The superintendent of trade (Panyadhyaksha) was to head the commercial service, including internal and external trade, and in that capacity, was expected to organize an array of functionaries engaged in such service. The superintendent of agriculture (Sitadhyaksha) was the head of the department of agriculture, in which capacity he had to look after the state farms, government lands and regulation of the lands belonging to individuals. His primary job was that of formulating the agriculture policy and ensuring its implementation. The superintendent of chariots (Rathadhyaksha) was the head of the defence department. Besides ensuring the security of the people from foreign aggression and preserving the safety of the borders, he was responsible for the matters related to defence production, which invariably had to take place in the defence factories owned by the state. He had to deal with the matters relating to the army and appointments of the heads of the defence factories. The superintendent of mines (Swarnadhyaksha) was head of the department of mines, dealing with the mining of various minerals such as gold, copper, iron, diamonds, etc. Among other things, he had to appoint efficient mining engineers on the basis of a test which would invariably help an examination of their knowledge about the inner and upper crusts of the earth. The superintendent of forests (Vanyadhyaksha) was head of the department of forestry. He had to ensure the protection and conservation of forests and be in charge of the formulation of policies concerning the growth of forests. The superintendent of weights (Bharadhyaksha) was head of the weights and measures department. He was assisted by trained inspectors who were responsible for conduction of surprise checks to ensure the correctness of the various weights and measures. He was also competent to prescribe punishments to errants not complying with the state provisions of transacting the business with specific kinds of weights and measures. The superintendent of textiles (Sutradhyaksha) was responsible for formulating the textile policy of the state, running of the textile factories, and providing employment to socially discarded people and those living in abject poverty. The superintendent of audit (Lokadhyaksha) was the chief of the audit. He had a cadre of officials supporting him in the task of auditing the state accounts and examining the state budgets. Kautilya also laid down a code of conduct for the civil servants which prescribed swift promotions for efficient and effective officials, and severe punishment for those who were corrupt. The severest punishment suggested by Kautilya was beheading such corrupt civil servants. Kautilya talked of the responsiveness of the civil servants since he believed in the view that the power of the state came from its subjects.

During the medieval period (1000-1600 AD), Akbar the Great founded and nurtured the civil service. During his period, he initiated land reforms (1457 AD), and established the land revenue system which later became a major constituent of the Indian taxation system. His civil service had a welfare and a regulatory orientation. The East India Company had a civil service responsible for carrying out commercial functions. They were far away from the common people, as they never tried to mix with and impress upon them that they had been there to bring about a transformation in Indian society. The British civil service came on the Indian scene after the takeover of the East India Company in the 1860s. Initially, the British civil service was a part of a police state, where its major task was that of carrying out law and order functions. It was disjointed as the different provinces had different civil services. There was no code of conduct developed by any of the British Indian provinces. The functionaries of the different provinces were free to appoint people of their choice. Officials were handpicked both from the army and non-army fields. Their pay and allowances were subject to the discretion of the government. However, these used to be very high by the standards prevailing then. The term 'civil service' is an Indian contribution to the discipline of public administration. To distinguish the government officials from the army officials, the term 'civil service' was used by the British government in undivided Punjab in the later part of the 18th century.

The British government set up the Indian civil service in 1911, primarily with the objective of strengthening the British administration in the UK. However, it could not succeed in that, but very usefully retained the idea for strengthening the administration of its colonial base in India. Initially, the recruitment to the Indian Civil Service (ICS) was confined only to the Britishers. The minimum age of entry was kept at 19 years and the maximum age was prescribed as 21 years. The language of examination was English. The only centre for conducting the examination was London. However, due to pressures and demands raised by the Indian National Congress in 1921, Indians were allowed to take part in the examination. In 1922, one Indian passed the ICS examination. Later, on the basis of the recommendations of the Aitchison Committee, the minimum and maximum ages were increased from 19 and 21 years to 20 and 22 years respectively. The candidates were allowed to appear in the examination both at London and India. A ratio of 50:50 was decided for the British and the Indian citizens for intake in the ICS. In 1935, the British government decided to establish interim rule in various provinces of India, which resulted in an exodus of the British subjects as civil servants and, as a result, the number of Indian subjects in the ICS increased tremendously. Though initially the British government set up only the ICS, later on they added a statutory civil service and central civil services. In the course of time the statutory civil service was weeded out and there remained on the scene only the remaining two services, namely, the ICS and the central civil services. At the time of independence, besides the ICS there were nine central civil services in the country. The independence of the country posed new challenges to the civil servants. They were no more expected to perform the role of a police state. The welfare of the Indian people was viewed as the central task to be performed by the Indian state, and hence they were to be an instrument of carrying out welfare functions which, among other things, included the settlement of refugees and providing minimum conditions for their day-to-day living, safeguarding the national borders from external aggression, and promoting conditions responsible for internal peace.

The civil service system in post-independence India was reorganized. At the central level, the civil services included the all-India services, the Indian Police Service and the central services. The central services are grouped into four categories in order of their importance, namely, Group A, B, C, and D services. The union territories were to be served by both the all-India and the central services. The various states of the country had to have their own civil services.

The onset of economic planning in India in 1951, with the launch of its First Five-Year Plan, enjoined on the ICS the role of development administration. In this new mould, they were expected to participate in the administration of public enterprises, regulation of the private sector, formulation of socio-economic and political policies, elimination of poverty, development of rural areas, combating inflation, effective monetary management, reduction of gender gap, elimination of social inequity, etc. In the early 1980s the Indian state had its first experience with the severe resource crunch, which deepened by the end of the 1980s. This led to the emergence of a new economic policy in 1991, which saw a rollback of the state in economic activities both at the macro and micro levels, meaning thereby formulation of such macro-economic policies which spurred a favourable environment for private sector participation, and reforms at the macro level leading to the contraction of the public enterprise system, and the existence of only healthy public sector units. In other words, service in the 1990s and beyond would have to don this new role for itself, which means the Indian Administrative Service (IAS), the Indian Foreign Service (IFS), and the Indian Police Service (IPS), as the three all-India services, and 29 other central services in the country, will have to have a new orientation. The state civil services will have to follow suit.

To sum up the above discussion, it is clear that in ancient India, the civil servants acted as personal servants of the rulers, in the medieval age, they became state servants as they were in the state employment, and in British India they acquired the complexion of public servants. During this period, the civil service also became a protected service, as in 1861 the first Indian Civil Service Act was passed which contained provisions regarding recruitment, promotion, termination, pension, payment of salaries, etc., of civil servants. The ethos of the civil service in independent India changed from welfare-orientation in the late 1940s to development-orientation between the 1960s and 1980s and finally to the facilitator's challenges, collective choice mechanisms reflected in the manifestoes issued by the various political parties during the 1996 general elections, and the challenge of meeting the democratic needs of the teeming millions.

Internal Labour Market

As already stated, the civil service in India is composed of the central and the state civil services. The central government has constituted three all-India services and several other services categorized as Group A, B, C and D services. As noted earlier, the three major civil services at the central level comprise the

IAS, the IFS, and the IPS. Each state government has constituted 10-20 services, depending on its historical background and size of the province. Besides the three top Group A civil services mentioned above, the other important services include the Indian Audit and Accounts Service, Indian Customs and Central Excise Service, etc. In all the states the civil services mostly include the state civil services, education service, judicial service, medical service, engineering service, agricultural service, and forest service. The central civil services have about 4,00,000 employees presently on its rolls, and the state civil services employ an equal number of people.

The civil service system, both in the states and at the centre, are rigid in nature. They have many grades/ranks. The Indian civil service system is rank-based and does not follow the tenets of the position-based civil services. Between 1986 and 1997 the central civil services of Group A had 53 grades, which have been reduced to 33 by the Fifth Pay Commission. It has the domination of generalists, as the basic philosophy guiding its initial setting up and later its continuation, advocates the belief that as the civil servants have to face any challenge posed to them, they should have general skills to exploit and manoeuvre for problem-solving. Within this generalist approach, there has been an effort to allow civil servants in the central government to specialize in certain areas. However, more frequently than never, the civil servants are shifted to assignments without having regard to their specialization. The state civil service system has had no regard to the question of specialization, and hence the state civil service cadres have by and large been generalists.

The Indian civil service system, both at the central and state levels, has provided very short tenures to civil servants. Many officers have made a vivid note of this in their writings, mentioning that their lives have been one of packing and unpacking. A study of the IAS movement patterns shows that the percentage of officers serving for less than one year has been more than 50 for the country as a whole (see Table 1). The

Table 1
IAS Movement Patterns

Strength of IAS Cadre		*Length of Time in Post (percentage of IAS)*			
Year (as on Jan.)	*Number*	*Less than 1 year*	*1-2 years*	*2-3 years*	*Over 3 years*
1977	2901	54	28	11	7
1978	3084	58	26	10	6
1979	3236	55	30	10	5
1980	3404	49	32	13	6
1981	3373	60	22	11	7
1982	3239	52	31	9	8
1983	3734	51	29	13	7
1984	3797	56	26	12	7
1985	3910	51	31	11	7
1986	3970	58	25	12	6
1991	4497	58	25	10	6
1992	3951	56	27	11	6
1993	3991	49	13	13	8

Sources: Potter David C., "IAS Mobility Patterns", *Indian Journal of Public Administration*, New Delhi, October-December 1987.
Also see Potter, David C., *India's Political Administrators: From ICS to IAS*, Oxford India Paperbacks, Oxford University Press, Oxford, 1996.

officers putting in one to two years of service are about 25 percent of the total strength of the IAS in the country, and the number of officers putting in two to three years of service has been, on an average, about 10 percent of their total number. The percentage of officers serving over three years has been less than one digit, on an average, taken as a whole for the country. The officers of the Indian civil service system work both at the centre, and on deputation in the various states of the Indian union. What emerges is an interesting fact that the short tenures of less than one year for 50 percent of the officers is a phenomenon common to both the central and the states governments. However, when a study of tenures enjoyed by the IAS officers in the various states is taken, it is found that some states such as Gujarat, Maharashtra and West Bengal have allowed a greater proportion of the IAS officers on deputation to these services a tenure longer than one year, but states such as Haryana, Andhra Pradesh and Rajasthan represent the other extreme, where a majority of the officers were not allowed to continue in their positions for more than a year, and the percentage represented by these states turns out to be higher as compared to the percentage of IAS officers working in the central government in this regard (see Table 2).

Table 2

Number of Officers in Position in the IAS

Name of the State	*1988*	*1996*
1. Andhra Pradesh	320	326
2. Arunachal Pradesh-Goa–Mizoram-Union Territories	388	242*
3. Assam and Meghalaya	186	211
4. Bihar	363	370
5. Gujarat	230	232
6. Haryana	182	198
7. Himachal Pradesh	115	130
8. Jammu & Kashmir	95	130
9. Karnataka	235	260
10. Kerala	155	162
11. Madhya Pradesh	372	391
12. Maharashtra	328	364
13. Manipur and Tripura	114	159
14. Nagaland	39	44
15. Orissa	203	202
16. Punjab	180	196
17. Rajasthan	231	248
18. Sikkim	41	41
19. Tamil Nadu	293	314
20. Uttar Pradesh	504	540
21. West Bengal	283	301
22. Union Territories	193	—
Total	5050	5061

* The number has declined due to the statehood given to Goa.

Source: Government of India, New Delhi, Civil Service List for 1988 and 1996

The British government in the early 1930s suggested the recruitment of the civil service through the Public Service Commissions both at the central and provincial levels. Such Commissions, however, could be constituted only after the post-independence era. For the recruitment of Group A central services, the Union Public Service Commission (UPSC) was set up, whereas State Public Service Commissions have been created for recruiting civil servants at the state level by the various state governments. For Group B services, a Staff Selection Commission has been established. The terms and conditions of the appointment and work of the central civil servants were first specified in the Civil Service Act, 1861. These were later detailed in the All India Services Act, 1951, as sought under Articles 308-314 of the Indian Constitution. The ladder of promotion in the case of the central government for Group A services starts from Under Secretary and ends at the Secretary's position. The Cabinet Secretary is the head of all the civil services of the central government. Between the Under Secretary and Cabinet Secretary, there are ranks of Deputy Secretary, Director, Joint Secretary, Additional Secretary and Secretary. In the state governments, in their Group A services, the lowest rank is that of Assistant Collector and the highest rank is Chief Secretary. The functionaries in between include the ranks of Deputy Secretary, Joint Secretary, Secretary, Commissioner-cum-Secretary, Principal Secretary Member of the Board of Revenue and Chief Secretary. The civil service officers belonging to the IAS start with a junior scale and move upwards to senior scale, selection scale, supertime scale, Additional Secretary, Secretary and Cabinet Secretary. The maximum period between which an IAS officer is promoted to the senior scale is six years. The supertime scale is given by the time of the 17th year of their service. These officers face the problem of upward movement from the rank of Additional Secretary onwards. The central government empanels the IAS officers for the post of Additional Secretary. About 20 percent of the recruits in the IAS are empanelled to the post of

Additional Secretary. About 10 percent of the recruits become Additional Secretaries. Only 5 percent reach the top position of Secretary.

For the top three IAS cadres, the strength is fixed by the Department of Personnel and Training (DoPT) in consideration with various ministries at the centre and the Chief Secretaries of the respective state governments. The Establishment Officer in the DoPT manages the IAS. He is accountable for his actions and receives guidance from the DoPT. The IAS cadre for the different states is composed of direct recruits and promotes. The promotees in the case of the IAS are about one-fourth of the total cadre strength. Recently, a suggestion has been made to increase this to one-third.

The UPSC holds a three-tier examination for the selection of the officers of the IAS and other central services. The first rung of examination is called the preliminary examination, which contains objective-type questions of three hours' duration. About 1,00,000 candidates appear annually for the preliminary examination. The cut-off point is set in such a way that 10 percent of the examinees are eligible for appearing in the main examination. It is here that the candidates have to give their option in priority for selection to the various services. About 15 percent of the candidates appearing in the main examination are declared eligible to appear for the personal interview. Half of these are declared successful for recruitment to the various services. Amongst these the top tens are given an option to opt for the Indian Foreign Service (IFS). The preliminary examination tests the numerical ability, awareness of current events, and the state of mind of the candidate to grapple with administrative issues. The main examination tests his/her grip on the language, general knowledge, and expertise on subjects which he/she takes as option, which normally have two papers each of three hours' duration. The candidates also have to write an essay. The personal interview is conducted by the boards constituted by the UPSC and composed of the chairman, subject experts, psychologists and reputed civil servants. Such a system was introduced in 1979. The Fifth Pay Commission, in its report submitted in January 1997, has suggested switching over to the pre-1979 system, which did not have the first rung of the present testing scheme, namely, preliminary examination, and made it obligatory on those seeking selection to the all-India services to take two extra papers. The introduction of the preliminary examination was suggested to weed out non-serious contenders.

The promotees from the state civil services to the central civil services are officers who have put in eight to nine years of service in their respective state services and have performed commendably. In certain cases, officers who have put in 17-20 years of service are sometimes recommended for inclusion in the IAS. There is virtually no lateral entry in the central civil services. However, from the rank of Joint Secretary onwards, empanelment of candidates is done by the DoPT of the central government. Barring a few exceptions, most of the positions in the IAS are occupied through vertical mobility. This had led to inbreeding in toto and deprived the central civil services, and even the Group B services, of freshness which could come via the inclusion of members through lateral entry.

The foundation of the British civil service was based on aristocracy. The Indian civil service system has made a number of compromises to accommodate consideration of region, caste, creed, etc. The civil service system at the centre provides for induction training to probationers. The probationers, irrespective of their service, have to go undergo a foundation course which is conducted at the LBS National Academy of Administration, Mussoorie. However, separate academies have been established for the institutional training of the of various services; for example, probationers of IPS are trained at SPV National Police Academy in Hyderabad whereas probationers of IFS are trained at Indian Institute of Foreign Service in New Delhi. The probation is of two years' duration, which comprises exposure to a foundation course, visit to several states in India, field work, and working as a probationers with the officers of the cadre of the concerned state to which he/she has been assigned. In 1985, the then Prime Minister, Mr. Rajiv Gandhi, brought a revolution in the training system for the officers of the IAS. The vertical programme was conceived to bring to the classroom officers of different lengths of service and the develop a camaraderie among them. An eight-week programme, shortened to six, four, and finally to three weeks, was suggested for officers of 10-16 years' seniority with the objective to equip them with management and decision-making concepts. For officers having put in 18-30 years of service, a four-week programme in policy management, which was later shortened to three weeks, was suggested. The training institutes were asked to devise need-based programmes in fundamental areas or topics of contemporary significance for the officers of various seniorities. The scheme enlisted in 1985 the support of six institutions. This number shot up to 43 in 1989, and later to 83 in the early 1990s. The participation of the officers in such programmes was made mandatory. However, with a new government coming to power in 1991, though belonging to the same party, this scheme of training was made optional, and it suffered a setback. In the present form, the identified institutions offer training programmes designed in consultation with the DoPT. However, the number of training programmes conducted has sharply declined, and so has the participation at these programmes. The Government of India, after several years of effort, has prepared a training policy for the civil servants in 1996 which envisages, among other things, a foreign training component. The officers of the civil service in Group A are seconded for training to the various countries for a period ranging from six weeks to a year. Some civil servants also go for their master's/PhD/post-doctoral courses under the bilateral fellowship programmes between India and several other countries.

A study of the feedback received from the participants of the training programme for the officers of the IAS points out that the benefits received are substantially high. The participants appreciated the training programme both in terms of contents and application. However, the training institutes echoed their disfavour with the fee fixed for conducting such training programmes, and the faculty competence. The participants of the training programme made several suggestions about improvement in accommodations and local hospitality. One of the criticisms of the foundation training is that the officers find the real world is much different from what is painted in the academies where they are trained. The training has to become realistic, application-oriented, and lead the participants to meet the challenges of an effective and responsive administration. The plans for continuing education did not inspire much hope and the expenditure incurred on training is very petty by world standards. Together the central and state civil services have about eight million employees, and about 60 percent of this strength constitute attenders and peons. Thus, the Indian civil service system does not have an officer-orientation. Further, the strength at the top of the IAS has not changed significantly between 1988 (5,050) and 1996 (5,061) (see Table 2). Several state governments have complained about the top-heavy structure of the IAS in their states. The central government, as a part of the new economic policy, decided in 1991 to surrender 10 percent of the posts of the level of Joint Secretary and above. The Fifth Pay Commission has also suggested the rightsizing of the Indian bureaucracy to the extent of at least one-third of its present strength. Today, the central government spends Rs.15,000 crore per annum as the pay and perquisites. Related to the GDP, this amount comes to 1.5 percent of the GDP. The state governments too spend an equal amount. Thus, the country spends 3 percent of its GDP on the pay and perquisites of its civil servants. To facilitate this, a generous voluntary retirement scheme is planned to be offered to the employees. One of the limitations of taking a drastic step to cut down the size of the bureaucracy is that the members of the various civil services have been accorded a special protection under an Act, and

Table 3

Comparative Perceptions of IAS Officers by Police, Politicians, Technocrats and Academicians

	IPS (n=118)			Politicians (n=106)			Technocrats (n=166)			Academicians (n=138)		
	F	%	RK	F	%	RK	F	%	RK	F	%	RK
Projects self as an expert on most things	102	86.4	1	80	75.5	1	108	65.1	1	106	76.0	1
Concern for and focus on own career	106	89.8	2	8	64.2	2	108	65.1	1	82	59.4	4
Self-opinionated	100	84.7	3	62	64.2	2	108	65.1	1	82	59.4	4
Power-hungry	88	74.6	5	68	64.2	2	86	51.8	4	66	47.8	6
Shrewd and manipulative	91	79.7	4	54	50.9	4	90	54.2	3	61	44.9	7
Procedure and rule-focused	88	74.6	5	40	37.7	6	76	45.8	5	82	59.4	4
Arrogant	84	71.2	6	62	58.5	3	60	39.8	9	72	52.2	5
Inaccessible	68	57.6	7	62	58.5	3	74	44.6	6	50	36.2	9
Judgemental and critical	30	25.4	8	36	34.0	7	68	41.0	8	86	62.3	3
Action and result focused	16	13.6	11	46	43.4	5	68	41.0	8	48	34.8	10
Concern for minor details	16	13.6	11	32	30.2	8	70	42.2	7	44	31.9	11
Committed to organisation/institution	22	18.6	9	22	20.8	12	60	36.1	9	28	20.3	12
Intellectually of high calibre	8	6.8	15	26	24.5	11	30	18.1	12	56	40.6	8

Contd...

Contd...

Understanding and helpful	18	15.3	10	30	28.3	9	44	26.5	10	22	15.9	13
Respects others competence and capability	12	10.2	13	30	28.3	9	44	26.5	10	22	15.9	13
Conscientious	14	11.9	12	18	17.0	14	32	19.3	11	28	20.3	12
Trustworthy	14	11.9	12	28	36.0	10	32	19.3	11	8	5.8	17
Risk-taker	9	8.5	14	20	18.9	13	26	15.7	13	12	8.7	15
Treats others with dignity	14	11.9	12	4	3.8	17	20	12.0	15	8	5.8	17
Visionary and transformational	2	1.7	16	10	9.4	15	22	13.3	14	10	7.2	16

F: Frequency; RK: Rank

Source: Singh, P. and Bhandarkar, Asha, *IAS Profile: Myths and Realities*, Wiley, 1994, pp. 21-22.

unless a new legislation is brought about withdrawing a number of privileges and perquisites, or the present Act is scrapped, nothing much can be done. One of the solutions suggested is to reduce the number of permanent posts to the bare minimum and incorporate a provision for contract posts. The figures presently point out that contract posts almost do not exist anywhere in the Indian civil service system. The posts of the advisors to the different ministries/departments can be cited only as one exception to this generalization. The reward structure for the civil service personnel is rigid. Their salaries are determined by the Pay Commissions. Five such Commissions have been set up in independent India so far. The recommendations of the Fourth Pay Commission covered a period of ten years between 1986 and 1996. The Fifth Pay Commission covers the period of 1996-2006. A study of the recommendations of the Fourth and Fifth Pay Commissions points out that in each revision the basic salary has been multiplied by a factor varying between three and four. The perquisites have been liberalized Commission after Commission. A comparison of the public and private sector emoluments in India reveals that the private sector salaries are about two to three times higher than that of the public sector. In fact, in certain categories, the salary differential is very large. For instance, the chief executive of a private sector bank gets a salary five times higher than that of the Secretary of the Department of Banking in the Government of India. With multinationals coming into the country, these differentials have greatly widened. It is interesting to note that a management graduate from a premier management institute of India is offered in the very first year a salary two to three times higher compared to the salary of the Cabinet Secretary, the highest civil service position in the country, drawn at the fag end of his career. The pay increases are mostly determined on the basis of seniority-cum-time in service. The concept of pay-for-performance does not exist in the Indian civil service system. The public sector enterprises in the country have partly introduced this concept. The private sector enterprises have put this into practice as far as possible. It is said that the incumbents in the Indian civil service are underworked and underpaid, and hence they underperform. While this may be true of the members of the all-India services and Group A services, this is not true of the members of the Group B, C and D services who are said to receive two to three times the emoluments of their counterparts in the private sector.

The promotions in the Indian civil service system are dual-track-based following a ratio of 66.67: 33.33 up to junior level. Beyond this, most of the posts are filled up by internal promotions of the officers manning the state or central cadres and by departmental promotion committees set up by various central and state civil services. Promotions to senior posts are based to the extent of 50 percent on the recommendations of the departmental promotion committees constituted as per the guidelines given in the service rules concerning the various civil services.

Representativeness

The Indian civil service system reflects the characteristic of representativeness in multifarious ways. There is no bar on persons belonging to different regions, castes, and creed to join the civil services. There is no gender discrimination too. There is no bias for people with a particular educational background which could facilitate their entry into the civil services. However, to enter the Indian civil service, one has to have a minimum age of 21 years and a maximum age of 28 years. One cannot make more than three attempts. The Indian society is composed of different castes, some of which are scheduled in the Indian Constitution. The rich and powerful section of the Indian society deprived them of their due share for a very long period in the past. India is also inhabited by a large number of tribal people who have yet to join the mainstream of the society. The modern culture has not made inroads among the tribes. These have also been given a privilege in terms of reservations of seats for entering into the civil services. Then, there is another category of people known as OBCs or other backward castes, who have for one or the other reason have not shared the fruits of development, and to bring them on equal footing they have also been accorded the privilege of reservations with regard to their entry into the civil services. There are also reservations for handicapped and migrants from neighbouring countries who are economically and socially depressed. All together, 50 percent of the total seats for the recruitment to the IAS and the central services are reserved for these sections of the society. In the case of the various states of the Indian union, this figure comes to 74 percent as suggested the Mandal Commission which submitted its report in 1980.

The state cadre for the civil service is determined on the basis of the population of each state of the country. For instance, Uttar Pradesh which was of late the biggest state in terms of population, had a strength of 540 officers in the IAS as compared to 41 in the case of Sikkim—a state which is the least populated among the 21 state cadres of the administrative services in existence in India today (see Table 2). Interestingly, each state has certain forward castes which have had the benefit of strengthening themselves in terms of education, professionalization, and claim on economic resources, including the ownership of the land. It has been found that across the country such forward caste people have dominated the selections in the Indian civil services (Subramaniam, 1971). This is equally true of tribes. For instance, in Meghalaya, the Khasi tribe has had the upper hand over the other tribes. In terms of religion, Hindus have dominated the selection, may be because of their overall dominance in terms of proportion of the total population in the country. In so far as language is concerned, it is English which has taken the lead in the sense that English-speaking inhabitants have succeeded in much larger proportion as compared to candidates not proficient in English. Educationally, entrants with science background have taken precedence over arts and commerce backgrounds. Of late, even engineering, medicine and management graduates have started participating in the Indian civil service examinations and they have been able to wrest about 50 percent of the total entrants. However, this number is on the increase as more and more women candidates have started appearing both for the Groups A and B of the all-India and state civil service recruitments. A study of the financial background of the candidates shows that most of them come from the upper-middle income group families. Further, a majority of the candidates selected had parents working in government.

The Indian civil service is patterned after the administrative structure of the country. It is both centralized and decentralized. It has centralized in the sense that the recruitments to the Indian civil service, and in particular to the IAS and the central services, are made by the UPSC and the Staff Selection Commission. Once the candidates are recruited to the IAS, they are allotted the state cadres and it is the responsibility of the respective state governments to manage their cadres. However, various state governments cannot take disciplinary action on the members of the IAS without permission of the Government of India. As explained earlier, though·the officials of the IAS are allotted to the various state cadres, 40 percent of such officials are deputed to the central government and thus they get an opportunity to have a wider experience. This pattern of the Indian civil service is a colonial heritage where initially the various sponsors of the Indian government had their own civil services, and later on central law was passed for bringing in uniformity relating to appointment, promotion, and terms and conditions of services. The various states of the Indian union also maintain their own civil services. Recruitments to state civil services are mostly done through the State Public Service Commissions. Each ministry of a state government maintains its own cadre. Thus, it can be said that the pattern of the Indian civil service system has nothing to do with its political structure as selections are not based on regime type or party system. The tenures of the officers of the civil services are invariably very long. A civil servant normally puts in 30-35 years of service and, therefore, enjoys a great deal of stability. Though there have been social dissensions in the country, these have never marred the stability of the civil servants.

Politicization

A number of constructs with regard to civil service systems have been presented, of which the classical one known as the Weberian construct dominates the Indian civil service system. According to this concept, a civil servant has to be of steel frame, following an impersonal style of work. Rules, regulations and procedures govern the day-to-day working of the Indian civil service system. Manuals are prepared to resolve conflicts. Innovativeness is a casualty, and takes precedence over creativity. Seniority is regarded more important than merit. Hierarchy acts as the backbone of the system. Buckpassing is a common phenomenon. Result-orientation is not the goal; procedural accountability takes a lead over performance; faithful execution of orders is done single-mindedly without giving any regard to the final outcomes. Decisions do not emerge out of discussions and consensus. Orders flow from top-down to bottom. There is no communication channel conveying the mind of functionaries at the bottom. The post-independence Indian civil service system has turned out to be different from what it used to be in British India, where an ICS officer used to be a member of the Council of Administrators headed by the Governor-General. The ICS officer, besides acting as a minister, had also to take the responsibility of implementing the policy. In post-independent India this privilege of the civil servants was taken away. The scope of the functioning of the civil service was limited only to implementation of the policy as conveyed by the politicians. Thus, the civil servants, both at the central and state levels, are charged with the responsibility of faithful execution of political programmes. They have to pledge their sincerity not to a particular political party but to the political regime in power at any point of time. This often necessitates changing colour like a chameleon with the change in political regime. For instance, the present coalition government in power at the centre is backed by thirteen political parties which have developed a common minimum needs programme. This is very different from the programmes and policies of the previous regimes in power which represented a single-party government. The civil servants at the centre have no other option but to switch over their loyalty to the implementation of the common minimum needs programme. This does not mean that they are now sold to the members of the political parties which are a part of the present coalition government and that they have become powerful earlier. They function in such a way that they become indifferent to the personal whims and choices of the members of the various political parties and the political programmes which were to be implemented by political parties not currently in power. Their commitment is to the governmental programmes which happen to cater to the political and economic agenda of the party in power.

The Indian civil service system is well organized and considerably independent. The civil servants continue in the civil service for very long periods and wield a great degree of influence as they act as a buffer between the political bosses and the masses of the country. In a lighter vein, it is said that the civil service system in India has become another caste, which means that civil servants from one part of the country gain the sympathy and support of civil servants from other parts of the country as and when they are in need of it. The Indian civil service lacks professionalization too. As noted earlier, civil servants act more as generalists and much less as specialists. The induction training has been designed in such a way that hardly any scope is left for giving a non-generalist orientation. Once they join the civil service, they are shuffled for short trainings from one to the other department, so much so that they hardly get an opportunity to develop an understanding of technical aspects of a problem or acquire a technical expertise. The inputs coming from civil servants can lead to a much higher value addition in certain areas if they could have an understanding of practical aspects related to them. For instance, professionalism of a high degree is required to handle/complete tasks at the Ministry of Finance, Petroleum, Commerce, Power, Transport, Food and Agriculture, Irrigation, Communications, Atomic Energy, etc.

The political and administrative systems have to work together to achieve the socio-economic goals. Though V. Kamath, a member of the Constituent Assembly, observed that the political ambition of the country could not be achieved without support from the Indian civil service, and hence continuation of the British legacy of the Indian civil service was necessary in independent India, it may be noted that there is no love lost between the civil servants and politicians, as the perceptions of both the groups are not homogeneous. Things have come to such a head that the civil servants have blamed politicians for asking them to get involved in undesirable tasks and help them in non-ethical, illegal and un-social pursuits for the personal benefits of the politicians. On the other hand, the politicians feel that the civil servants do not act as change agents, believe in status quo, and lack transformational leadership qualities. Fortunately, the appointments of civil servants at the entry level do not vest in the hands of politicians as they come through a competitive examination conducted by the UPSC, as the case may be. However, once they are inducted, then only upto a certain level their promotions are governed mostly by non-political considerations. Once the process of empanelment starts, the political whims and fancies come into the picture, super-sessions become a routine matter and the merit may often go ignored.

The civil servants are not expected to participate in political activity, especially elections. They are not expected to take up a job for a period of two years immediately following their retirement. Permission from the government is required for taking up assignments in India or abroad.

The impact of the civil servants on policy-making depends on the expertize of the civil servants in a particular area, and in that area the mind of the minister and his approach to conduct the work of the ministry. The fact of the matter is that civil servants are in a privileged position of having access to all possible information necessary for evolving a policy. They also have at their disposal the manpower support. Over a period of time they develop their own network. At times they continue longer than the minister and, therefore, have become the spokesmen of the ministry and get very closely associated with the formulation and implementation of the policy. Further, the civil service system is blessed with continuity as compared to political regimes which change much more frequently, or at least once in five years. That the civil service system and the political system are seen as two different things established by the fact that a negligible percentage of civil servants have become politicians, unlike France where the present President keeps his lien on the civil service. In India, a civil servant can not act as a politician and continue to be a part of the civil service.

Public Opinion

Public opinion acts as a mirror about the effectiveness or otherwise of the civil service system in any society. What once used to be said about the British times and the civil service seems to stand true even today. For the Indian civil servants during the British period it was said that they were neither Indian, nor civil, nor public servants. It was expected that with independence they would be Indian in thinking as well as in action. The general perception is that the Indian civil service has hardly changed a bit in terms of attitudes, mores and culture. A study of the overall perception of the officers of the IAS by members of the IPS, politicians, technocrats and academicians points out that they project themselves as experts on everything. Their concern for, and focus on, their own career is very high. They are self-opinionated, power-hungry, shrewd and manipulative, procedure and rule-focused, arrogant, inaccessible, judgemental and critical, and having concern for minor details. They have been rated very low on positive traits such as commitment to organization, trustworthiness, risk-taking, conscientiousness, innovativeness and creativity. Most of the studies have rated them lowest as visionaries and transformational leaders. They are considered to be no-change agents (see Table 4). The self-perception of these officers (of the IAS) is exactly opposite (see Table 5). The thrust of the criticism of the Indian civil service system is on overstaffing. Wastefulness, cautiousness, unfairness and non-responsiveness, the last one being the most important of all, which could be seen from the fact that as per a recent decision of the government, discussions are being conducted on effectiveness and responsiveness of the Indian administration in the different parts of the country. Rajkrishna, an eminent economist, once observed that if the size of the Indian bureaucracy could not be reduced, the least that the government could do would be to keep its officers open only three days a week. At each and every level there is overstaffing. A High-Power Committee set up by the Government of Andhra Pradesh has mentioned in its report that 40 percent of the 6,00,000 people working in the state government is in excess of the requirements. This is more or less the case with the other state governments in the country, and with the central government as well. The manpower required for the government—central/state—is not reviewed at fixed-time intervals. Unfortunately, this work is done by the Pay Commissions both at the centre and state levels which in no way have expertise in ergonomics, time and motion studies, and work study. Recently, the Indian civil service system has come in a very poor light on the charges of corruption. In Uttar Pradesh, which till some time back was the largest state in terms of population, the Civil Service Association of the IAS Officers

Table 4
Self-Perception of IAS Officers

	F	%	*RK*
Projects self as an expert on most things	51	17.65	18
Concern for and focus on own career	62	21.45	16
Self-opinionated	25	8.65	19
Power-hungry	13	4.50	22
Shrewd and manipulative	23	7.96	21
Procedure and rule-focused	31	10.73	20
Arrogant	55	19.03	17
Inaccessible	65	22.49	15
Judgemental and critical	74	25.61	14
Action and result-focus	178	61.59	3
Concern for minor details	89	30.80	13
Rational and logical	172	59.52	4
Committed to organization/institution	210	72.66	2
Intellectually of high calibre	222	66.82	1
Understanding and helpful	104	35.99	10
Respects others competence and capability	98	33.91	11
Conscientious	166	57.44	5
Trustworthy	140	48.44	8
Risk-taker	160	55.36	6
Treats others with dignity	93	32.18	12
Innovative and creative	151	52.25	7
Visionary and transformational	130	44.98	9

Source: Singh, P. and Bhandarkar, Asha, *IAS Profile: Myths and Realities*, Wiley, 1994, p. 27.

named the top three most corrupt civil servants. The vigilance and income tax departments conducted raids on the houses of a number of bureaucrats in the state and seized property/assets many more times disproportionate to their incomes. One of the officials dealing with intelligence was caught trading secrets for monetary considerations. There are many more such cases. One

Table 5
IAS Location, 1993

Name of the State	District Administration	State Government	State or Central Public Enterprises	Govt. of India	Other	Total
1. Andhra Pradesh	87	127	39	48	15	213
2. Arunachal Pradesh, Goa, Mizoram, Union Territories	38	119	12	36	8	213
3. Assam and Meghalaya	41	77	14	41	19	192
4. Bihar	114	131	35	56	16	352
5. Gujarat	62	95	45	26	18	246
6. Haryana	48	88	28	27	12	203
7. Himachal Pradesh	29	54	10	17	21	131
8. Jammu & Kashmir	15	58	6	19	6	104
9. Karnataka	59	99	37	49	14	258
10. Kerala	34	67	22	25	13	161
11. Madhya Pradesh	129	142	25	56	21	373
12. Maharashtra	107	103	52	54	26	342
13. Manipur and Tripura	35	57	9	26	10	137
14. Nagaland	8	32	1	3	2	46
15. Orissa	44	104	19	39	9	215
16. Punjab	29	90	16	17	18	170
17. Rajasthan	58	105	20	33	7	223
18. Sikkim	5	32	1	3	2	43
19. Tamil Nadu	73	139	56	26	16	310
20. Uttar Pradesh	—	—	—	—	—	—

Source: Civil Service List, Government of India, New Delhi, 1993.

of the reasons for this corruption lies in the inception of the Indian civil service which had its origin during the East India Company time. The commercial origin of the Indian government, colonial status of our country, and the ecological factors which existed then saw the germination of the seeds of corruption. It was expected that the civil servants who were to perform commercial functions could be paid nominal salaries as they would make the rest good by taking extraneous considerations for the jobs they had to do for the people at large. The earliest civil servants of the East India Company got well-drenched in commercial traditions and had "graduated in chicanery and grown grey in fraud and corruption". The colonial status bestowed on the civil servants created a hiatus between them and the people and developed a feeling among them as aristocrats which kept them apart from the Indian people. Environmentally, the Indian society was one with a low level of equilibrium on the economic, social and political fronts which did not put the civil servants under pressure to take up developmental work and act as a facilitator. The Indian civil service in its present form is no different though there are pressures on it to don the caps of developmental administrator and facilitator.

Civil servants in this country generally feel that they do not have freedom to work and are exploited politically to undertake jobs for which they are not answerable. For instance, a very senior civil servant in Karnataka was jailed by the Supreme Court in 1996 on the charge that he did not carry out the orders of the apex court to promote a government servant. The explanation given by the civil servant was that he was prevented from implementing the court orders by the political bosses. There are charges that the civil servants have been vociferously complaining about the judicial activism in India which has made it difficult for them to function in their offices and face the verdicts from the courts, sentencing them to imprisonment. The relationship between the politicians and civil servants has undergone a great change. A resolution passed by the Council of Ministers was not implemented by the Secretary in the Home Ministry on the ground that he had opinion of difference during the early years of independence, and the minister hailed the right of the civil servant to have his own opinion on such matters and went to the extent of withdrawing the proposal. Today, not many civil servants would air their disagreement to the minister. The poor opinion of the civil service held by the Indian masses thrives on the fact that the nation has failed to give a decent life to its people. This is reinforced by the fact that the educated masses of India prefer to go abroad and settle down. The demands on the passport offices to issue passports has gone up to such an extent that they have to work for more hours and give notifications about issuing the passports to people from time to time in the daily newspapers. The community attachment is low in the case of urbanites and high in the case of villagers. It is the urban system which has developed much faster during the post-independence era. The urban rural population ratio is 20:80. This shows that the civil service as a system does not have a strong grip.

Reform and Diffusion

Civil service reforms have become a buzzword of today. The central and state governments have started thinking in terms of reforms due to internal and external pressures. Internally, both the central and state governments, irrespective of the fact as to which party/parties are in power, want to present an image of effective institutions. They intend to have become leaner and fitter organizations. They also aspire to have quick reflexes. Instead of bureaucratic orientation they propose to have a customer orientation. In India, civil service reforms have mostly come at the initiative of the elected representatives forming the government of the day. In 1996, the Administrative Reforms Commission submitted its report appraising the effectiveness and efficiency of the systems and procedures of the various parts of the central government. The different state governments have also set up administrative reforms departments and appointed committees to look into their functioning. The whole effort has been to make the government efficient and effective by rationalizing different laws, manuals, rules, and methods of functioning. What has lacked is the attempt to corporatise the government systems both at the central and state levels. The business and professional orientation has not been initiated nor the practice of questioning the value for the money. There is a general feeling regarding the need to overhaul the civil service system in India. The main reason behind this has been the resource crunch faced by the governments at the various levels and shift in the thinking of the political parties with regard to the state ownership. The idea of privatization is gradually gaining ground and has become a driving force to classify the government activities as core and non-core. There is wide agreement about the fact that the non-core, non-essential activities of the government could be given up to private parties. For instance, some major municipalities in the country have privatized the cleaning of garbage, sewerage work, and installation of electric poles and extension of electricity network. The public enterprises in the country are also being forced to categorise their activities as core and non-core, and concentrate on the area of their business competence. A number of local government institutions/public enterprises are approaching the capital markets for funding. Even the central and state governments are approaching the national and international institutions for funding their deficits and infrastructure projects in place of depending on the support of the central bank which could collaborate with the governments in deficit financing. The most important budgetary and financial reform that has taken place at the centre is sticking to the fiscal deficit of not exceeding 5 percent. In the second stage of economic reforms, the state governments would also be expected to arrest their financial deficits. Both the central and the state governments attempted to introduce zero-based budgeting in the 1980s. Attempts have also been made to imbibe the concepts of programme-cum-performance and performance budgeting. Even, both the central and state governments have stopped recruitments. All these reforms have been effected under the dispensation of the new economic policy adopted by the central government in 1991.

The policy makers and administrators have been talking for quite some time about a performance-oriented civil service and linking rewards with output and efficiency. The private sector in the country has been able to implement these ideas as they have a work cadre different from the Indian civil service and their ethos also happens to be different. They have been able to enmesh the concept of performance measurement and performance appraisal. In the case of the Indian civil service system there has been only an annual appraisal by the senior of his subordinate and such an appraisal is always kept confidential. There is no goal congruity as the communications of the government do not traverse from top-down to the bottom. In the private sector the idea of performance appraisal goes far beyond its mechanical application. The private sector enterprises do even performance counselling and there is no question of keeping the performance appraisal records confidential. They also practise management by objectives (MBO) system.

One source of reform in the government, both at the central and at state levels, as well as in their various organs, has been competition of the private sector enterprises, and it has been found that wherever such possibilities have existed, the government control systems have either reformed themselves or are under pressure to do so. For instance, the Steel Authority of India Limited (SAIL), a corporate major owned and managed by the central government, is in competition with the Tata Iron and Steel Company, a corporate major in the private sector in India, and corporate majors in the steel sector located abroad. The central government has allowed SAIL to formulate performance-related pay packages, raise funds from abroad, redesign the capital structure, and restructure its internal operations.

The economic reforms in India have come about not all on their own. It is often commented that the global institutions, such as the World Bank and the International Monetary Fund (IMF), have been behind such reforms. While this may be true, it should be said that India has adopted the general concept of reforms but redesigned it to suit its own needs. It may be very fair to say that the country has largely succeeded in introducing the economic reforms. However, the administrative machinery has not been able to respond to the needs of time and has failed to make the full-scale changes so necessary to absorb the impact of the implementation of the economic reforms.

Configurations

The configurations in the Indian civil service system can be discussed in terms of Ferrel Heady and Philip Morgan constructs. India is a democratic society. The civil service system has to be there for accountability and answerable to the political system as for quite a long number of years both at the central and state levels one-party rule was the order of the day. However, right from the mid-1970s, the trend of one-party government came to an abrupt end and the era of coalition governments started. Thus, there has been a very painful transition in the relationship of the civil servants with the politicians, from single-party representativeness to majority-party representativeness. The concept of loyalty which earlier meant loyalty not only to the programme of the single-party but also to the party itself, has undergone a change, meaning now loyalty to the programmes of the parties/party in power but not to the party itself. The civil service system in India developed its roots in the post-independence period in the context of a planned economy. Though it was not a centrally planned system, it was also not following an indicated plan and was thus far out from the French economic system. The state intervention started finding its place in every walk of economic and political life. Public enterprises were chosen as instruments of policy in the economic field, whereas a raft of institutions put in place at the local, state and central levels started acting as policy instruments in the political arena. The civil service system has a great role to play in the above context. Over a period of time many of these institutions and instruments have developed morbidity. This has been mainly because they have not been able to read the pulse of the market. This change is not going to lead India to become a free market. Nevertheless, the market will play a significant role in the social, economic and political systems in India in future. This would present a new context for the functioning of the civil service system in India and they would adopt themselves to this change, one of the ramifications of which could be a shift from traditional government-oriented bureaucracy to managerial-oriented bureaucracy striving to achieve professionalism of a very high order. As mentioned earlier, the civil service system in the central government is managed by an Establishment Officer in the DoPT who allocates, in consultation with the Chief Secretaries of the states, the officers of the IAS and other central services to states. The deputation of these officers to the centre is again done through this same consultative process. The central ministry places indents of their demand on the Establishment Officer and signals their broad choices which may or may not be accepted by the Establishment Officer. The disciplinary action, promotion/demotion and pension-related issues are settled by the DoPT. In case the officials of the central civil services intend to have a legal recourse to the decisions of the department, they could approach the Central Administrative Tribunal whose decision is binding excepting for appeals in exceptional circumstances to the Supreme Court. In the case of the various state governments, a similar system has been adopted.

For entry into the civil services, both at the central and state levels, candidates have to possess a Bachelor's degree, and a certain minimum and maximum age that goes on varying as per the decision of the government, which gets influenced by the suggestions of the political parties and the unemployed youth. In no case has the minimum age been less than 21 years. The maximum age has not exceeded 28 years. A concession of five years is normally provided to the members of the backward classes, scheduled tribes, migrants from some neighbouring countries, handicapped persons and women candidates. The performance of the civil servants is commented upon by the controlling authority, which normally is the head of the department, on several parameters such as competence, punctuality, efficiency, capability, ability to work with the team, leadership qualities, etc. This is not to suggest that the Indian civil service system has been able to evolve a professional performance appraisal system as it squarely fails to measure technical competence and their capability to carry out neutrally and impartially the policy directives of political decision-makers though this should be the spirit which guides their functioning. It is said that each profession should develop its own code of conduct and performance appraisal system. By this reckoning, the civil service system in India should also respond to the need for developing its own system of performance appraisal and code of conduct. No law can offer an all-time solution in these regards. Most of the Indian laws in their present form are adopted versions of their British editions. A perusal of such laws clearly reveals that they were never intended to prescribe a code of conduct or a performance appraisal system. They only contained the powers and privileges, the service benefits, and the accountability mechanism which had to be followed by the civil servants. Thus, the Indian civil service system has to do a lot of heart-searching to answer the question as to why it has not responded to the need for developing a code of conduct of its own and also a system of performance appraisal. A study of the sense of mission held by civil servants leads us to arrive at mixed conclusions, though for most of the areas of the governmental work policies have been laid down, and the Indian Constitution contains elaborate provisions of the do's and don'ts for the civil servants. There have not been many cases where they have departed from compliance and cooperation. However, the recent incidents of the civil servants being dragged to the courts of law, and their scathing criticism of conformance, have made them cautious and objective. In the Indian Constitution, in Article 356, there is a provision to impose presidential rule in the states of the Indian union. The Governors make such recommendations when they feel that the democratic machinery cannot function under the normal circumstances. In such a case, the officers of the IAS work with a guidance mission and it entitles them to assume and carry out a leadership role in the political system to the maximum extent that circumstances permit. Similarly, in the case of local governments, when the elected representatives are dismissed or not reappointed on the expiry of their term, the civil servants get command of the administration and work with the guidance mission.

Configuration of Philip Morgan

There has been a transformation of the Indian society during the 50 years of its independence. In the early years of the independence era, the state assumed the responsibility of an entrepreneur, a producer, and a resource allocator. It assumed the charge of setting up a machinery for economic development and operating it. Though it had the legacy of receiving a political state, it had to take action to bring about emotional integration. However, over the years, the state has lost some of its command on the socio-economic-politico system due to the emergence of centres of power extraneous to it. The political bosses have been influenced in many a case by these extra-constitutional centres of power, and consequently the civil service system in India has been badly bruised in terms of power. On the other hand, to insulate itself from such an environment, the party in power guiding the state machinery, i.e., the civil service, gave a slogan of loyalty and committed civil service. This slogan, in turn, has broken the backbone of the civil service system as it has acted as a roadblock in the professionalization of the civil service and allowing it to act as the custodial state. The masses have been unhappy with this development. If they are not anti-state, they are certainly not also pro-state, and thus the Indian polity has reached a point where both the political bosses and the civil service system have to work hard to re-establish its credibility. In order to enable the civil service system to accept this challenge, the political system will have to allow a high level of independence and make it outcome-oriented.

Suggestions

The revamping of the Indian civil service system has become a must. We give below some suggestions to make the civil service system yield the desired goals for the socio-economic development of India and their unison with the Indian political system:

- India needs a leaner and fitter civil service system. The Indian civil service system has in all about eight million members. The recommendations made in a number of reports suggest that the civil service could shed its weight to the extent of one-third of its present strength. This is true not only of the lower classes of the civil service but also of the three all-India services, namely, the Indian Administrative Service, the Indian Foreign Service and the Indian Police Service.
- The manning of the civil services should be done on the basis of positions and not on the basis of ranks. Further, for the lower levels of the civil service it is necessary that time and motion studies/work studies are carried out when the strength of the various services is fixed. For all-India services, the Establishment Officer in the DoPT of the central government should have a continuous dialogue with the Chief Secretaries of the various state governments. The strength of the various services should be continuously examined and the fact which grows from time to time should be removed immediately.
- A generous scheme of voluntary retirement should be offered, which may encourage the civil servants to quit the government. An attempt should be made to privatize some of the non-core activities. They could be contracted out or privatized permanently.
- There is also need to restructure the systems and procedures as well as the style of functioning. The Indian civil service should modernize itself. The professionalizing of its

various activities is very essential. This will bring need, cut down red tape, reduce paper work, and trim down cost of its maintenance.

- An extensive training in office administration and administrative methods needs to be imparted to the officers other than of the all-India services. The officers of the all-India administrative services and the top grade services of the state governments should be encouraged to acquire computer literacy and get intensively trained in database, etc.
- The Indian civil service system should become more representative. At present, 80 percent of the Indians living in villages have only 15 percent of representation in the civil service. The urban upper-middle class has a dominance, with 75 percent of the positions in various civil services. This leads to alienation of the civil service from the masses. There is a need to increase the representation of women too. It is suggested that special pre-entry training schemes may be devised to remove this bottleneck.
- The civil servants develop overconfidence in their career as they are assured of a permanent job for a period of 30-35 years. For all civil services, especially all-India services, lateral entry at different levels needs to be encouraged. The other incumbents should be given contract positions. The lateral entry would inspire competition among the civil servants and allow the best talents to come into the civil services. It would also give opportunities to such people who might have either missed it initially or might think of entering the civil service at a later stage after acquiring expertise in a particular area.
- The present scheme of civil service training needs to undergo a complete change. The induction training should follow a new format. Instead of providing a wide sweep of the various subjects, modules should be designed having relevance to the skills and knowledge required for

performing the various jobs during the initial years of the civil service. Some of the modules could include training in behavioural areas and environment of administration. A compulsory annual refresher training should be introduced of a duration of at least one week. This should be an appreciative training in the general developments relating to the civil service environment taking place in India and abroad. Those who have served for a period of ten years should be given a specialized training in district administration which may emphasize training on development administration, maintenance of revenue records, and coordination between the autonomous agencies of the government. Training courses in enterprise administration should be imparted to officers of the knowledge so acquired to the administration of public enterprises. This will also help them in dealing with subjects having a bearing on the government interface with private enterprise. For those who have put in more than 20 years of service, there is a need for exposure to policy administration. They should be familiar with the concept of policy formulation and its implementation.

- There should be a component of foreign training for the officers of the IAS. This will help in integrating them with the rest of the world and redesigning their vision of strengthening the country through their work.
- For other services also, the training systems need to undergo a radical change. Opportunities should be created to provide access to training facilities for the members of the Indian civil service selected by the State Public Service Commissions. In the present form, the training given to Group B,C and D civil servants is completely inadequate. The contents are poor and the frequency is inadequate.
- Action should be taken to remove the grievance of the non-IAS personnel that most of the training opportunities abroad are cornered by the officers of the IAS.

- The organization and functioning of the Indian civil service needs to undergo a change. There is an urgent need to ensure much longer tenures than what is being enjoyed by the officers of the three all-India services and Group A services of the central government. This should apply with the same force in the case of the state governments. Efforts should be made to remove the rift between the Establishment Officer in the DoPT and chief secretaries in the state government. Hasty decisions by the state governments to suspend the officers, or set up enquiries without consulting the central government, is not desirable. By the same token, the cadre management at the centre should also consult the state governments on matters such as posting and foreign deputation of the IAS officers.
- The most important challenge for those managing the cadre is the reorientation of the service along certain specializations. These could include economic administration, financial management, industrial management, management of environment, international trade, law and order, energy and transport, district administration, local government, etc. Efforts should be made to devise schemes to build up an ethos of the Indian civil service. This can be made possible by encouraging the members of various civil services in the country to formulate their own code of conduct and design their own rules, procedures and systems through a wide concurrence of the public. The all-pervading rampant corruption should no more get further oxygen.
- The relationship between the politicians and the civil servants should improve. The politicians should act as the bosses and the civil servants should translate the policies of the government into action, but while doing so they should insulate themselves from personal influence of one or more politicians or political parties. They should aim at winning the trust and confidence of the people through constitutional means.

Concluding Remarks

The Indian civil service system is one of the oldest civil service systems in the world. It had its origin in the Mauryan times. Kautilya's *Arthashastra* lays down the principles of selection and promotion of the civil servants, the conditions of loyalty for appointment to the civil service, the methods of their performance evaluation, and the code of conduct to be followed by them. In medieval India, the Moghuls set up their own civil service system which centred round the management of land revenue, administration of government factories and establishment of the welfare state. The East India Company, which ruled India for about 150 years, did not set up a civil service as its mandate was limited to commercial exploitation. The British rule came to India in the 1850s. However, as the Britishers had a long-term interest to stay in India, they consolidated their power and laid down the foundation for a unified India. This required the setting up of a strong civil service. They enacted a Civil Service Act and included the civil servants on the Council of Administrators, which resulted in the accrual of both political and administrative powers to the civil servants in India. The Britishers constituted the Indian Civil Service (ICS). Initially, the membership of the ICS was confined only to the Britishers, but over a period of time it was thrown open even to the Indians. Upto 1935, the Britishers dominated the ICS in terms of numbers. However, introduction of interim rule in 1935 led to a significant change of the domination of the Indians in the civil service. In 1947, free-India inherited the ICS. After prolonged consideration, its Constituent Assembly decided to continue to run the Indian administration with the help of the ICS. After independence, the civil service in India was reorganized as a two-tier system. The central government controlled the all-India services, namely, the Indian Administrative Service, the Indian Foreign Service and the Indian Police Service, and the central services which were classified as Group A, B, C and D services. The selections to the all-India services and Group A and B services are made by the Union Public

Service Commission (UPSC). The incumbents to Group C and D services are selected by the Staff Selection Commission. The selection of the candidates for various services to man the administrative machinery in the union territories is also done through the same arrangement. The state governments, however, have their own State Public Service Commissions. The recruitment to the state civil services are done by these Commissions. The functioning of these Commissions is regulated by a separate Act.

The Indian civil service system is rank-based and does not follow the tenets of the position-based civil services. This has led to the absence of a specialized civil service system in the country. The basic philosophy of the Indian civil service system has contributed a lot to this phenomenon, as it puts a heavy emphasis on the recruitment of generalists and not specialists. The incumbents of the Indian civil service enjoy very short tenures, usually less than one year. Based on this, one could conclude that this is no way of running the country. Interestingly, some states, such as Gujarat, Maharashtra and West Bengal, have allowed longer tenures to their civil servants.

The members of the all-India services start as Deputy Secretary and normally go up to the level of Joint Secretary, beyond which promotion is granted only after selection. For every post beyond the Joint Secretary level, candidates are empanelled and the selection is done by the Cabinet Committee on Appointments, receiving inputs from the administrative ministry and the DoPT. The Establishment Officer in the DoPT provides the policy inputs. There is no lateral entry in the all-India services. Only at the level of Secretary to the Government of India, specialists are taken. The advisors to the various ministries could also be non-IAS persons. Only 5 percent of the members of the all-India services reach the top position of Secretary. The post of Cabinet Secretary to the Government of India, the highest in the Indian civil service, has remained the privilege only of the officers of the IAS.

The cadre management of the all-India services is done by the Establishment Officer, Government of India. This officer has to transact the business in consultation with the Chief Secretaries of the various states and the secretaries of the central ministries. The Establishment Officer has to ensure that 40 percent of the officers of the all-India services are on deputation with the central government, and the rest work with the concerned state/union territories governments. The strength of the cadre for each state is determined by this officer in consultation with the Chief Secretary of the concerned state. He has to further ensure that 50 percent of the posts are manned by the promotees recommended by the various state governments, and only 50 percent are selected through direct recruitment. Likewise 50 percent of the selection have to be made from the scheduled castes, scheduled tribes, other backward castes, handicapped, and migrants from some neighbouring states. The rest are selected purely on the basis of their merit. In the case of Group A, B, C and D services, the entire management rests in the hands of the central government and the states have no say in the matter. In the case of the civil services of the various state governments, the rules of reservation vary from case to case.

The entry to the Indian civil service, both at the central and state levels, is done through a competitive examination system. For the all-India services of the central government and also for the rest of its services in Group A and B, the UPSC conducts a preliminary examination of objective-type questions. Normally, 1,00,000 candidates appear every year for this examination. Perquisites may be lower as compared to the counterparts in the private sector. However, the members of Group C and D services are said to earn around twice more than their counterparts in the private sector. There is a general criticism that the Indian civil service has become top-heavy. This appears to be true. If pronouncements such as 10 percent reduction across the country of the posts of the rank of Joint Secretary and above, as suggested in 1991, and the recent recommendations of the Fifth Pay Commission to downsize the Indian civil service system at the centre to the tune of 33.33 percent are given due credit, and the modernization of the civil service through computerization, introduction of networks, training and outsourcing work is done, it may go a long way in making the Indian civil service leaner and fitter.

The Indian civil service system has discriminated in favour of males, some select universities, urbanites, and candidates well-versed in English. Though right from the inception of the Indian civil service reservations were made for the scheduled castes and scheduled tribes, these are found to have preponderance in selection only in the case of Group C and D services. The government's efforts of allocating 50 percent of seats to these classes may still take some more time to translate itself into a reality.

The middle and upper-middle income group people have had a greater representation in terms of profession. The wards of salaried people, especially those working in government, have had a greater representation, followed by the wards of lawyers, doctors, engineers and teachers. The representation of the farming class, which was at its peak during the British regime, has come down significantly. All these are now being taken care of, but it may take quite some time to remove these anomalies.

Despite a great influence of the political world, the Indian civil service has so far been able to keep its own identity. In the case of the British days, the politicization was much less. However, with independence bequeathing a new role of development, the Indian civil servants could not hold their flock together. The number of cases of corruption has also increased tremendously. This has been partly due to the political pressure, and also partly on account of an erosion in the values of the civil servants. In recent times, a number of civil servants have been jailed, and the courts of law in India have found them guilty of dereliction of their duties and amassing wealth many more times in proportion to their earnings.

The civil servants have been ranked very low on innovation, transformation, involvement, etc., by politicians, academicians and the police officers. However, their own assessment of their work has been very high. The senior members of the Indian civil service find their work extremely challenging, whereas the civil servants holding middle-level positions do not find their work very interesting.

Worldwide civil service reforms have become a matter of great concern. It was in 1996 that the Administrative Reforms Commission gave its report on the working of the civil service system of the central government and its functioning as relating to the various ministries. Since then, the Fourth Pay Commission in its report in 1986, and the Fifth Pay Commission in its report in January 1997, again went into this issue. The essence of the discussion here has been the introduction of performance-related orientation, professionalization and appraisal of performance of the public servants.

The configuration of the civil service points out that it has acquired the traits of serving a majority-party rule. It is loyal to the programme of the party in power and not to the individuals in the political parties. It can register its disagreement with the government on various issues. However, the tendency has been to tread the path very carefully and avoid any confrontation with the political bosses.

References

Bhattacharya, Ratna, *Administrators in a Developing Society*, Himalaya, Bombay, 1989, pp.16-66.

Constituent Assembly Debates (Government of India, New Delhi), Vol. IX, 1947-50, p.585.

Maheshwari, S.R., *Major Civil Service Systems in the World*, Vikas, New Delhi 1997, p.133.

Singh, P. and Bhandarkar, Asha, *IAS Profile: Myths and Realities*, Wiley, New Delhi, pp.21-27.

Subramaniam, V., *Social Background of India's Administrators*, Publications Division (Ministry of Information and Broadcasting, Government of India), New Delhi, 1971, pp.25-55, 56-68, 87-100, 101-113.

The Hindu, Hyderabad, January 31, 1997, p. 15.

Trivikram, K., Training of Indian Administrative Service Personnel, *Indian Journal of Public Administration*, New Delhi. July-September 1988, p.674.

Tyagi, A.R., *The Civil Service in a Developing Society*, Sterling, Delhi, 1969, pp.21-22.

12

Civil Servants and Civil Service

V. JAGANNADHAM

Overlapping Categories

Dealing with the subject of relations is always a delicate matter because the subjective element predominates. Hardly any worthwhile study with a common focus exists concerning the civil servants' relations with citizens, pressure groups and people's representatives separately or together. Further, the mutual perceptions differ radically for two reasons: the differences in expectations about services and obligations of each other. For example, the civil servants expect the citizens to comply with the rules and wait until their turn reaches for services whereas citizens might be ignorant of or indifferent to the rules or may demand service out of turn or, sometimes, in contravention of rules. So also, the mutual relations between civil servants and pressure groups are subject to officials' professional standards and the groups' influence with the authorities or the clientele. Here too, sometimes, the pressure groups browbeat the administrators occasionally, utilizing the influence of pressure groups for lobbying in favour of more resources for certain mutually desired policies or programmes. The elected representatives come handy for all because they may have pull in the government or persuade the public to follow government policies, laws, rules, leadership etc. We may draw a diagram of the above relationship as under:

The Universe of Civil Servants and the Publics

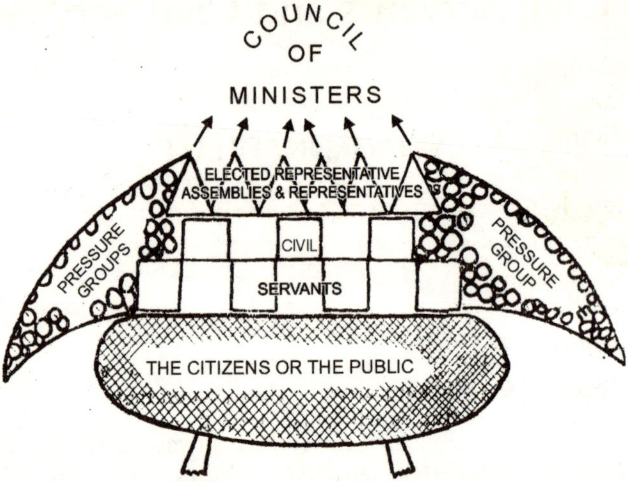

The above diagram should not be understood to consist of watertight isolations but it is a congeries or beehive wherein coalitions and coalescences, contacts and contracts often take place among the groups for gaining mutual advantage to the profit or detriment of different parties at different times. This is a picture of dialectics and dynamics of social life. No disrespect is meant for any but it is necessary to recognize pragmatism.

Coalition of Interests

By way of caution one should remember that the seemingly homogeneous character of the above categories is misleading. Civil servants range from the Secretary to the Lower Division Clerk or the *Chaprasi* who ushers people in and out of the department's rooms. What level of civil servants are we to consider is not clear. Civil servants at different levels come from different socio-economic backgrounds with loyalties ranging from caste and community to language and region with a foreign language intersecting all-through. By and large, the top civil servants at policy making levels and the bottom civil servants directly facing the citizens in providing the service bear a larger brunt of the interactions than the middle layers.

So are the pressure groups ranging in number and variety of interests. Sometimes, each interest, such as labourers or peasants, has more than one competing pressure group with conflicting claims about each one's representative character. Under these circumstances the professional conduct of civil servant is always under test and they may play for safety through pursuing the path of least resistance and delaying tactics. Multiplicity of pressure groups with competing claims of representative capacity is always a source of weakness and confusion.

The citizens, like the common man, are an undefinable inchoate mass, some of whom are enterprising middlemen having contacts with party politicians, elected representatives and senior ministers. But, the bulk are mute, helpless victims of ignorance, confusion and fear of authority.

Often, there may be coalition of interests leading to a consensus among the more articulate and enterprising citizens and civil servants to get things done through elected representatives and pressure groups. Hesitation might not be a virtue in selecting the means with a view to get 'interest' served provided it is possible to evade detection of unscrupulous means by law-enforcers. Law's arms are proverbially short and these are being squeezed, greased or twisted by the enterprising citizens through elected representatives. The pliable civil servants fall an easy prey to the devious ways of diverse groups. The pressure groups play this game with greater finesse than many individual citizens because organizations have varied and greater resources at their command. Consequently, generalizations of any kind about the relations among the four categories could at best be tentative as well as hazardous. But, one statement could be made without fear of dissent, namely, the more the role of government in the regulation and control of public affairs, the greater is the interplay among all the categories referred. The benefit or detriment of the interaction to the public would be determined by the softness or severity of the steel frame or the civil service. A reason for the growing popularity in the study of the personnel policies and individual behaviour of the civil servants could be explained by the increasing role of the state in the modern times.

Ruling Servant and the Serving Ruler

Civil servants in a developing country have a few special problems. The chief among them is the transformation of a ruling service into a serving ruler. With the introduction of adult franchise and parliamentary form of government at the Centre and in the states, the state everywhere is compelled to respond to the mounting demands of the new masters, namely, the illiterate but awakened masses of the people. The excuses and explanations of civil servants for their lapses affect them not so much as their political masters who have to render accounts to the voter citizens every five years or before, if the legislatures are dissolved earlier. Under these circumstances, the ministers, the elected representative and the citizens expect the civil servants to be loyal, responsive and effective. They demand the civil servants to be serving rulers rather than ruling servants. The development planning within the democratic framework has added to the tasks of the civil servants by requiring them to be missionary agents of change and active supporters of the policies and programmes derived from the ideologies of the ruling party of the moment.

A further analysis of the civil servant's role in a developing democracy aspiring to be socialistic (because nothing short of socialist ideology is a current coin in the Third World in the third quarter of the twentieth century) shows that the traditional neutrality of the civil servants (if at all anywhere such a pure concept prevailed because none could be neutral about values which form the core of any government policy) is a square peg in a round hole. The professional ethics lay emphasis on ideological neutrality but programme commitment. In periods of rapid and radical change, the policies and programmes may run counter to the private convictions of individual civil servants. For example, the Untouchability Offences Act or the prohibition policy or the land to the tiller ideology might not be indifferently enforced because the ruling servants might not be intellectually convinced or emotionally elated about them. In enforcing laws which they may consider to be show pieces of radicalism and detrimental to public interest, the civil servants may show slackness in pursuit and sabotage the policy in fact.

Rules: Goals and Roles

Democratic policy and development planning render their multi-varied tasks more difficult of fulfilment by civil servants. Their tasks may be more complex and confused because of politics of flux, economics of scarcity and culture of conflicts. Every civil servant at different levels has to be conscientious as well as loyal in serving the minister as well as in upholding the public interest to the best of his ability. Traditional theories and inherited precedents may be of little avail amidst mounting pressures of organized interest groups and rising demands of diverse citizens. An elected representative does not have the comforting sense of security of regular career service. His interest lies in getting many things done to his benefit and also to the benefit of the citizens in his constituency. When politics is full-time profession, as is the case today, the old ideas of honorary service by elected representative are obsolete. Like lawyers, doctors or consulting engineers and managers and private teachers, politicians look upon their activities as a money-making career.

Necessary changes in ideas should take place in the light of the changing reality of the profession of politics. This is necessary because civil servants have to work with frequent shifts with political office holders. The civil service is 'rule-minded' whereas the politician is 'goal-minded'. How to strike a balance between the two and adapt the democratic system by bending but not breaking it for achieving development, there is no answer. One could point to the need for a high level of intelligence, integrity and devotion to develop the material well-being of the citizens. But, how to operationalize the normative prescription? The ball is thrown into the court of educational institutions, into family and above all into the arena of leadership in all walks of life—business and commerce, industry and agriculture, social reform and social work, law and medicine. If all these spheres of life shine with brilliant leaders, poverty will not be a puzzle and life will not be a quiz. We are in a question begging dilemma or an egg and hen sequence.

Career and Public Interest

A last word about civil servants and civil service. The civil servants could by no means be above the level of morality prevailing at any time in a society. They are part of the ethos and its product. But, the civil servants are a specially recruited and trained group of citizens with an emphasis on service to the public. The service itself should build into the structure some correctives to maximize the leadership potential and minimize the risk of black sheep. Every civil servant looks after his own interest in the career but in the process the ethic and the *esprit de corps* of the team of civil servants at each level should not be thrown overboard. The civil servants are not deemed to be angles nor are they to be black guards. Each civil servant has to search his conscience and decide within the ethos of his professional training, associational activities and individual judgement how he would like to get along with his superiors and subordinates, peers and colleagues, pressure groups and elected representatives and above all towards the inarticulate and helpless citizens. The civil servants take an oath to uphold the Constitution. The preamble to the Constitution of India contains, like the old four-fold *purshartha*—Dharma, Artha, Kama, Moksha—the four goals of justice, liberty, equality and fraternity to be ensured to every citizen—born poor or rich, or a Brahmin or pariah. But what do these mean in operational terms? How many civil servants are capable of understanding the conflicts flowing from each of the goals to each category of citizen population? Liberty and equality are mutually hostile unless homogenized; so are justice according to law and fraternity of scriptures. These have to be reconciled by understanding the imperatives of each category such as equality at the level of need, liberty in the fulfilment of individual wants which do not violate law or ethics, is one possible approach. Justice, according to law, needs to be interpreted in the light of the larger goals of brotherhood of humanity. Laws might have to be tempered with humanism without tampering the system. These few points are given as illustrations to point to the high level of knowledge, skill and integrity necessary among civil servants in the administration of public affairs of a developing democracy in which neither wealth nor power is above abuse. Both are corrupting and tempting. We live in a world which worships wealth and power and discounts wisdom and integrity. The civil servants are called upon to render service while vested with the power of rulers. Each civil servant has to equip himself with the desired degree of wisdom for correct judgement and good conduct.

Individual and the System

One word about how to help individual civil servants to orientate themselves to the new democratic developmental tasks and the demands thereof. This is where the interaction between the individual and the system and systemness of individual development is relevant. No individual could go beyond the system permits him but the system is a creation of the individuals; it is a product of the collectivity of individuals behaving as a system. The renewal or adaptation of the system is a function of individual civil servants. Leadership in administrative system is a product of professional ethics and skills. Is civil service a profession? Apart from the conduct rules, does it have a code of conduct prescribed and enforced by the profession as against the personnel or establishment departments?

What do individual civil servants need to adapt themselves to the new masters and new tasks? Three characteristics could be singled out for emphasis. These do not exhaust but are selected as essential. These are: (1) courtesy at all times, (2) consideration for particular and general interests, and (3) compassion to help the ignorant and the needy within the elastic framework of rules. These three characteristics, namely, courtesy, consideration and compassion are not available for sale and they do not come easily without effort in cultivation. The essential characteristic of government, which is the fortress of civil servants, is the possession of information, which is treasured as a secret and the power to extend or withhold benefits or favours. These two make the civil servants feel their importance as rulers and forget their role as servants. Hence, courtesy, consideration and compassion seldom manifest themselves in the conduct of civil servants towards citizens unless they organize themselves as pressure groups or approach through the 'interfering' or 'meddling' elected representatives. The cause and effect of interference of politician in administration are too complex to deal but there is no doubt that political interference acts as a corrective to the callous administrator who is sheltered and secured in the secretariat fortress. What the civil servants call 'interference' by elected representative is called by the latter as 'involvement' of the policy makers for humanizing administration. We now come back to the old issue of rules and goals. Rules are not an end in themselves. The rules are intended to promote the well-being and serve the interests of the people. If the civil servants fail to adapt the rules to serve the people, the elected representatives see to it that they are adapted. This is their function in a democracy. There may be shortfalls and deficiencies but democracy has an in-built self-corrective mechanism through periodic elections.

References

Eldersveld, S.J., V. Jagannadham and A.P. Barnabas, *Citizen and Administration in a Developing Democracy,* New Delhi: IIPA, 1968.

Hayward, J.E.S., *Private Interests and Public Policy*.

Jagannadham, V. and H.R. Makhija, *Citizen-Administration and Lokpal*, New Delhi: IIPA, 1969.

Jagannadham, V. and N.S. Bakshi, *Citizen and the Municipal Bureaucracy,* New Delhi: IIPA, 1971.

Key, V.O., *Politics, Parties and Pressure Groups*, 3rd edn., 1952.

Kothari, S. and R. Roy, *Relations Between Politicians and Administration*.

Latham, E., *The Group Basis of Politics*, 1952.

Legislator's Administrative Role Perceptions in an Indian State: An Empirical Exploration, *IJPA*, October-December 1971.

Mathur, Kuldeep, *Bureaucratic Response to Development*, New Delhi: National Publishing House, 1973.

Role of Civil Service in Indian Political System, *Indian Journal of Public Administration*, April-June 1971.

Valsan, E.H., Development Bureaucracy: A Tentative Model, *IJPA*, January-March 1972.

13

Career and Cadre Planning for the IAS: Some Reflections

RAKESH HOOJA

Few can doubt that the country needs dedicated and intelligent men, well experienced in different types of jobs and professional fields, having different academic and environmental backgrounds, who can help in the administration of the country. Such men, if they are competent and possess a sense of pride in their work, are required at all levels of government to coordinate activities in all walks of today's complex life. The greater the interaction between such men, more the government, and thus society, is liable to benefit. Thus, it is not surprising that the government has appointed a committee to examine the existing selection procedure for recruitment to India's higher service, viz., IAS. While my reactions to the questionnaire issued by the committee are available elsewhere,* I intend here to examine how to increase the effectivity and

---

* Rakesh Hooja, "Apropos the UPSC Questionnaire on Recruitment and Selection Measures," *Journal of LBS National Academy of Administration,* Vol. XIX, No. 4, Winter 1974, of which this article is a carry forward. Interested people may also refer to that piece.

standards of the IAS, since that appears to be one way of creating a bunch of men most suited to administering the country.

Recruiting the Best

One immediate measure required would be to attempt to weed out all who are incapable of taking quick decisions as also those who cannot, or are not willing, to work long hours on a regular basis. I would not advocate screenings and dismissals for this. Instead, I suggest that the workload of IAS officers be planned in such a way that only the brightest, most hard-working as well as those possessing the maximum initiative, as also technical skills of varied sorts, would feel comfortable in the service. Thus, no newcomers wishing to have an easy time will aspire to join the service; those who find they cannot cope may decide to resign; and those who are most capable (regardless of previous background—academic or otherwise) and have the maximum sense of pride in their work would be attracted more and more to the IAS. If the level of performance of the entire service rises, then the question of increasing their emoluments may also be considered. Thus, if the service acquires the reputation of: (1) being the most difficult job in the country, (2) being the job where doing the most good for the people is possible and rewarded, (3) where only the best men of various professional fields are to be found, (4) where hard work, quick and good decisions and experienced and skilled decisions are most appreciated, and (5) the maximum on-the-job training is available to people already selected for their excellence; then the best men available in private and other government jobs shall also flock to the IAS and help to make it a body of people who are undoubtedly the most suitable in the country to administer it. Not only this, but the service spirit itself would work against the shirkers or less capable in the service. Thus, what I advocate is that the IAS should consist not only of experts in administration as of today, but also of engineer-administrators, scientist-administrators, doctor-administrators, educationist-administrators, lawyer-administrators, managers etc. For this the recruitment pattern has to be changed. I advocate five methods of recruitment to the IAS.

Methods of Recruitment

Method I would be a reformed model of the present system of selecting regular recruitments. Graduates between the age of 21 and 26 would appear in six compulsory subjects (unlike the present three), namely, English, Hindi or Regional Language, Essay, General Knowledge (World Affairs), Indian Affairs, and Logic. For all other central services (including IPS) they would also appear in three lower options, and only candidates for the IAS/IFS would also appear in three higher optionals too. The number of optional papers allowed should be raised (to even more than fifty if need be); the new additions including medicine, engineering and technology, architecture, journalism, banking, accountancy and commerce, management, public administration, agriculture and farm management, and even such options as papers on tourism, hotel management, publishing and military science should be added so that every Indian, no matter what subjects he may have studied, may think of appearing at the examination. Those qualifying in the written examination would have a personality test lasting at least forty-five minutes and having 25 per cent weightage in respect to total marks. Selected candidates would then be sent for basic training (of which more later) which unlike today would also be part of the selection process, at least 20 per cent of selected candidates being either thrown out or offered a lower service (All-India, Central, or State), on the basis of their weak performance in the basic training. Each person would get two attempts at selection through Method I.

Candidates would have to choose between Method I and Method II and would not be allowed to try both. Method II would be for those between 22 and 28 years of age who would prefer not to appear through a syllabus-based examination and the minimum qualification in this case would be a pass in the examination of the first year of a three-year degree course according to the 10+2+3 system. They would appear in the same six compulsories as in Method I, followed by three essays (five for those interested in IAS/IFS) on major developmental, economic, technical, social and cultural problems of India. Following this, selected candidates would be asked to undergo a six month liberal education course before an expert-screening board of teachers and would also be administered a differential aptitude test. Selected candidates would then undergo a personality test and the basic training-cum-screening course as in Method I. Method II would be available only *once* to a candidate.

The only qualifications for Method III and IV would be age: 33-38 being the range for Method III and 30-40 for Method IV. However, Method IV would be reserved only for State, Central or all-India officers recommended for promotion to IAS/IFS by the present screening procedures. Both these methods would be for recruitment to the IAS/IFS only and only *one* attempt would be allowed through either method. Method III would consist of an examination in the same six compulsory subjects as in Method I and II, followed by an evaluation of the candidates' academic record, work experience and previous employers' reports if available, and a personality test as in Method I. Method IV would consist of recommendation to be allowed to appear in the examination by the concerned employing authority, written examination in English, General Knowledge and any one subject related to the service the candidate is already in, and a personality test as in the other three methods. Recruitment through Method III would be made once every two years and through Method IV once in three years. Recruitment through both would be followed by a six-month orientation course.

Method V would consist of direct appointment of eminent Indians like scientists into the IAS/IFS at the level of Secretary to the Government of India by the President and the UPSC.

The ratio of people selected according to various methods should be Method 1—60 per cent, Method II-10 per cent, Method III and IV—20 per cent, and Method V-10 per cent, with the percentage of Method I being increased if necessary.

The Training System

Now to turn to the initial training period, before enumerating my views on postings and on-the-job as well as special post-entry training. The basic training-cum-screening course that I suggest for those recruited under Methods I and II is a modification of the existing IAS training programme. I suggest a foundational course of three months which is held in common with other all-India and central services, and where I also feel that the person standing first in the selection processes of each state's administrative service should also be sent simultaneously. This is partly because (as I have advocated earlier) 20 per cent of those selected according to Method I and II have to be relegated to the central or state services or even thrown out. It would also serve as a reward for the topper in the State Public Service Commission selection. During this foundational course emphasis should be placed on teaching the science graduates more humanities and social sciences and vice versa. This should be followed by seven months of the professional course in three instalments of two months, two months and three months each. The foundational course should be held at the National Academy of Administration at Mussorie, while the professional course at a separate IAS Academy. The present one year of training in one's state of allotment should be increased to 18 months with the following break-up:

1. three months at the State Officers' Training School;
2. nine months in a district for law and order, revenue, development, panchayat etc. training (here it should be kept in mind that while each trainee shall normally be kept in one district for this training, all probationers in the state could be sent temporarily to any other district to work and learn

in the case special conditions such as flood, earthquake, elections, law and order problems, or the conducting of a fair, are to the found only in that district);

3. three months training with the police with a rank equivalent to that of an IPS probationer of the same seniority;
4. two months' attachment to agricultural and industrial institutions in state; and
5. one month at the State Secretariat.

There should also be two periods of four months each, regulated by the National Academy of Administration, of attachments. The first should include attachments with agricultural universities, the armed forces, public sector institutions, municipalities, universities, research institutes, the railways, posts and telegraphs, and some of the central services. The second should consist of one-and-a-half months at the Central Secretariat, one-and-a-half months in a state besides one's state of allotment inside one's zone of allotment (of which more later), and one month's touring in one's zone of allotment.

Rationalizing the Posting Procedure

Thus, the entire training course should last three years. As regards postings, one's postings should normally be in one's state of allotment (with the prevailing criteria of half of a state's vacancies being filled by residents of the state and half by outsiders being continued minus the present special consideration for girls and Scheduled Caste and Scheduled Tribe candidates, the last two already having gained an advantage at the time of the original selection). One's state of allotment should be declared within one week of his joining the foundational course. By virtue of an IAS officer being allotted to a state cadre, he shall automatically be deemed to have been allotted to a zone (the country being divided into four zones). Every IAS officer should be posted for at least one year to a state besides his state of allotment but within his zone of allotment at least once every eight years. This shall help in keeping his mind open to new ideas and new environments.

All officers should spend at least half their careers in field jobs and at least one-fourth in staff jobs, unless they have gone through the IAS Staff College (of which more later) in which case they would get more staff postings. One's postings should also be so planned that in addition to retaining his present generalist nature he also gets an opportunity to specialize in at least one area (e.g., law and order, revenue, commercial taxes, municipal, rural development, industrial management, education, health, finance, personnel, public relations, judicial and planning) of administration. He should be allowed to choose one out of three options given to him by the state of his allotment at the time his initial training ends and should be posted to jobs related to that area at least thrice in his life.

There should be a one month overlap between officers at the time of transfers to avoid any post being manned by an officer not yet fully conversant with the various aspects of his job to be called transfer training. As a corollary, no posting should be of less than four months' duration. Similarly, to avoid stagnation, no posting should last more than three years.

Now, we turn to further training while on the job.

On-the-Job Training

It should be compulsory for every IAS officer to attend at least one special course of a month's duration after every five years of service, with those failing to keep to the required standard at such courses (both theoretical and practical) being liable to demotion. A field job every three years should be made compulsory at least till an officer is 45 years of age and "secretariat allowances" replaced by "hard-duty-field allowances" for extra-tough postings. Each promotion should be referred to the UPSC (seniority becoming less important) and those from a state service to an all-India one should be the resultant of a nation-wide examination held for the purpose according to Method IV.

Something similar to the Army Staff College at Wellington should also be set up. Officers of the age group 30-35 should be allowed to compete once for admission to a two-year field trip-plus-classroom course. All administrative officers of all services should be allowed to compete at this examination which would test a candidate in the fields of his work experience, and men of the IAS and IFS should be selected in the ratio 2:1 to all the other all-India, central and state services (with there being a separate provision for men from other services to appear at an examination for entry into the IAS). Men trained at such a staff college would, upon admission to the college, be asked to specialize in some field of administration, and thereafter be posted at least two-fifth and at the most three-fifth of the rest of their career in very high level jobs in that field. This would ensure both "specialization" as well as "generalization" and also make the course prestigious. (It could also be considered to give a special allowance to those selected for the course provided those not keeping up to the mark could be sent back in mid-course). Thus, through better selection, harder, more frequent training (aimed at developing not only administrative skills but also a spirit of service and a Spartan attitude of life), and well regulated promotions, as well as tougher work conditions and increased "competitiveness" within the service, a new sense of pride in the service and "service culture" could emerge.

In this context, Philip Woodruffs *Men Who Ruled India* is illuminating. Woodruff has described how a sort of *esprit de corps* was formed in the HEICS and its successor the ICS, whose members felt that they were the most able and dedicated of men and tried to live up to that service reputation (exceptions apart). The hard life of an officer was considered more of a status symbol than money, perquisites, or power. I propose that another status symbol shall be added to this as far as the IAS is concerned, that of professional excellence.

Conclusion

Thus, what I am advocating is that career and cadre planning for the IAS should be such that the best Indians from all walks of life are available in the IAS and that they are given appropriate formal as well as informal training and used in such a manner that all state governments as also the Centre have the best possible manpower available to them to undertake the jobs that our administrative system is called upon to perform.

III

Personnel Administration

14

Introducing Change in Bureaucracy: A Framework

UDAI PAREEK

Bureaucracy is an extremely important system in the country, as it determines the major administrative styles and influences a large section of society. 'Bureaucracy' here is used as a descriptive term to denote the government systems which govern most of the country.

Bureaucracy has a vital interface with the political system of the country. The political system consisting of the political party in power, elected representatives in the parliament and state legislatures, exercises a great deal of influence in policies, and in many cases even in the procedures of work. This interface both produces problems as well as provides opportunities for easier introduction of change in the system.

Indian bureaucracy has deep roots in the British administrative system introduced in the last century. It was primarily meant for maintaining law and order in the country and for carrying routine administrative functions. Although Indian bureaucracy has taken long strides in the direction of developmental work, the basic character continues to be oriented towards the maintenance of law and order. This goes against the spirit of experimentation and change.

Bureaucratic system (i.e., various departments of the government) have a transient membership. Excepting the secretarial staff who usually do not move from the place where they live and work, administrative officers are mobile. This is true of those who are selected in the Indian and State Administrative Services. Such officers remain with a department only for some time and are transferred to some other departments, to enable them to have a variety of experiences. This transient membership creates special problems for the introduction of change. An enthusiastic officer who introduces a change in a system may soon leave the system, and somebody else who succeeds him may, in the absence of proper understanding of the experiment, wipe it out.

These characteristics of bureaucracy may be taken into consideration while planning change. Here, three major dimensions of bureaucracy are used to suggest a model for introducing a change.

Major Dimensions of Bureaucratic Change

Various dimensions of bureaucracy are important, when we consider the change to be introduced in it. As already stated, one of the main characteristics of bureaucracy is its vast size. Its system (with the contextual factors) and several dimensions of that system that are important are: the systemic structure of bureaucracy, its systemic dynamics, and the change process which occurs in bureaucracy. Following is a discussion of these factors, their main properties and how they interact.

Systemic Structure

Various aspects of the structure in bureaucracy are important in relation to change. Bureaucracy is divided into several departments or parts of a larger system. At one level, bureaucracy, as an aggregate government machinery, consisting of all the departments of which the government is constituted with its various sub-parts, spread over the whole country, can be considered as a system. At another level, each department is also a system. Usually, a department is regarded as one unit. For example, the Department of Education, in a particular state, may be regarded as a basic unit of bureaucracy. We shall call it the focal system—the system in which change is being introduced. Other departments within the bureaucracy are equally significant for change. These we can call as proximate systems. The third important system is the political system, determining the direction for bureaucracy and the way in which the change will be introduced and implemented. Representatives of the legislative assembly or the parliament constitute a system, because they make policies, and because their representatives as ministers have direct roles in the bureaucracy. The ministers who head the various departments in the government, although not part of bureaucracy, have a legitimate role in determining many things. This system we shall call the political system. These are the three important aspects of the systemic structure. Here, we shall briefly consider each of these.

The Focal System

It is in the focal system that change is implemented. The significant dimension of the internal system can be said to be that of conformity-creativity. If the change is properly implemented, the persons working in the system will be creative, they will use the change effectively, and will also conform to the minimum necessary level required. Both conformity and creativity will be balanced. However, if change is not accepted by them, they may either not conform or passively conform and may cease to be creative. Creativity, therefore, becomes a relevant aspect of the internal structure.

The focal system consists of those who are operating within the system, where the change or experiment is being attempted. These people do not remain with the system for a long time. They are in a particular department or part of bureaucracy for some time, and then they leave that department and go to some other department, so that their commitment to a particular department or sub-unit of bureaucracy is not as high, as it may be in the case of an independent unit, which people may join and where they think they will continue for a fairly long time. Because of this transitory membership of a system, the motivation of the people who live in that system would depend on how much they feel themselves as a part of it. Their conformity and creativity will also depend on this factor. If people within the system are not in favour of the experiment, they can very easily thwart that experiment, by either not adhering to the requirements of the experiment at all, or even if they do what is required, this may be a passive response. They may patiently live out the time in the hope that in due course of time they will have a chance of going to some other department. This may affect the success of the experiment.

The Proximate System

A unit of bureaucracy is a part of a complex network of several ways. A change which is being brought about in one part of the bureaucratic system has implications for the other parts also. If the experiment succeeds, there may be pressures for such change in other parts of the bureaucratic system also. Therefore, the main property of the proximate system is that of diffusion and spread of the change which occurs in one system, depending, of course, on the success achieved in that process of change. If the change threatens the proximate systems, it can again prevent the change from spreading. Not only the boundary systems may attempt to contain it within the focal system (the system in which the experiment is being made), but may even prevent it from growing in the focal system itself.

No change can remain confined to one section of the bureaucracy for a long time. It will have implications for other parts of the bureaucracy. So, the eventual choice for an experiment of change being introduced is, either its diffusion or its ultimate death in the system in which it originates. The proximate systems are significant in influencing this decision. It may be useful, therefore, to consider various factors, which contribute to the attitudes of the proximate systems towards a change being attempted in any department.

The Political System

The political system provides support for any experiment or change. The political system consists of elected representatives, mainly the ministers and members of state legislatures or parliament. They wield power in the bureaucracy and are concerned about policies and general matters. The main role which they can play is to provide necessary support for the experiment to grow. Lack of such support may eventually result in problems for the experiment. If the political system is in favour of change, it can provide opportunities for the experiment to continue and even spread. However, if somehow the political system is not in favour of change, or if the change threatens the political system in some way, it may not provide support for such change and in the absence of that support the change may not take root. The political system may use several ways of providing, withdrawing, or not giving the necessary support for the successful implementation of a programme of change.

These three main systems, which operate in the bureaucratic context are, all equally important for making the change effective. A discussion of the other two dimensions follows.

Systemic Dynamics

The dynamics of bureaucracy revolves around power. And, in that sense, it is power dynamics. There are three main aspects of power dynamics. Power is wielded through influence in decision-making, through the monitoring role (control systems), and through the knowledge and skills relevant to the tasks. The absence of any of these may produce a threat and a fear. If one cannot influence decision, he may feel irrelevant to the system. If one loses control, because of lack of the monitoring mechanism, he may feel impuissant. If one does not have the relevant knowledge and skills, he may feel obsolete. The three fears, therefore, arising out of the three dimensions of power in a system (influence, monitoring, and knowledge), are irrelevance, impuissance, and obsolescence respectively.

The main function of systemic dynamics is to deal with the problem of defensive behaviour (arising out of the fears), when change is introduced. If the proposed change threatens the power or influences members of a system who exercise power, the fear of irrelevance may produce aggressive behaviour, which may result in rejection of the proposed change. If there is a threat to the monitoring of change and to the possibility of knowing what is happening, the fear of impuissance is likely to produce regression, or a going back—a tendency to suggest that the older method was a better one and a feeling that the system should go back to the previous method. If people feel that they do not have enough knowledge and skills which are required to properly understand and go along with the change, the fear of obsolescence, or if a change makes a particular system or members obsolete because of the involvement of new skills, it is likely to result in rationalization of the merits of the previous system, with people giving arguments as to why the previous system was a better one. People do not want to face the realities or obsolescence. One way to deal with the resistance to change is to find proper reasons for not going along with the change. Therefore, to deal with these aspects of the dynamics of change, it is necessary that enough attention should be paid to all the three aspects, so that the various systems continue to have some influence. As they have ways of knowing and monitoring what happens, the necessary knowledge and skills to be able to understand what is involved in the new change and bow this will benefit various aspects of the working of the systems.

Process of Change

The process of change has several stages. Change cannot be introduced all at once. Various stages have been identified in various studies. Most of these are some form of adaptation of the classical explanation which Kurt Lewin gave about the adoption of change. Taking an example from the changing shape of liquid into another shape, he proposed three main stages of the change process: unfreezing, moving and refreezing. The first stage of change is when the current state is disturbed and the system is ready for change. The second stage is the actual adoption of change, and in the third stage the change gets stabilized in the system. Various other authors have proposed more elaborate stages, breaking down the three main stages into several parts. For example, Waston et al have suggested five stages of change. Rogers has also suggested five stages while Pareek and Singh, reviewing various studies in India and critically looking at the conceptual framework of the process of change, have suggested seven stages of change. But, basically, the three-stage model seems to hold well. We can use a three-stage model of change in bureaucracy comprising the stages of acceptance, action and stabilization. All the three stages are important for the final adoption of change in the focal system. Let us take each step and consider what it involves.

Acceptance

In the first stage of change, the change has to be accepted by all the three systems: the political system, the proximate system, as well as the focal system. The acceptance of change is the initial stage of motivation, when there is enough motivation amongst all the three systems in favour of change. Such motivation comes about, when the three main factors which we have considered in power dynamics are not disturbed, viz., when those in power feel that their influence is not (nor will be) affected, that they will have enough monitoring control over what happens in the system, and that the change is not beyond their own knowledge and skills. Acceptance will be more when the need for change is high, and the concerned system sees change as an instrument in increasing the various important dimensions of their own competence and control over it. At the stage of acceptance, if the concerned systems are dissatisfied with the present ways of working and they perceive the experiment as a potential way of improving things, the motivation for change will be high.

Action

After the necessary acceptance and planning, definite action is taken for the implementation of the change being introduced. When the change is actually being implemented, again, all the three systems are involved in some form or the other. Involvement, therefore, is the main process dynamics at this stage. This involvement comes about, because the change is promising in terms of solving sonic problems, as well as the change provides an opportunity for various persons involved in the system to retain their power; and in fact to increase it. When they feel that they are partners in the process of change, their involvement is continued. They watch with interest and continue to get involved in what is happening as a result of change.

Stabilization

This is the stage when the change, which has been introduced and for which action has been taken, becomes a part of the system, and the system is able to internalize it and make it more or less a permanent part of its working. Change does not remain a new thing any more. It is regarded and accepted as a regular part of the system. This is the process of legitimization of change. All the three systems regard the change as a legitimate part of the system; they do not consider it as new, or anything yet to be experimented. The three aspects of dynamics are important in this also, viz., to what extent the power and control is retained or threatened, and to what extent the three systems feel that it is still within their knowledge and skills to be able to contribute to the understanding and implementation of the change.

Bureaucratic Change Cube

Considering the various aspects discussed so far regarding change in bureaucracy, a three-dimensional cube emerges which depicts the different aspects of the change. This appears in the Figure 1 given below. Figure 2 gives the underlying processes.

Three dimensions, along with the key processes, are mentioned in the figure above. The combination of the three dimensions may produce 27 cells in the cube, suggesting 27 elements. Each element can be discussed to know what happens

Figure 1

Dynamics of Change in Bureaucracy

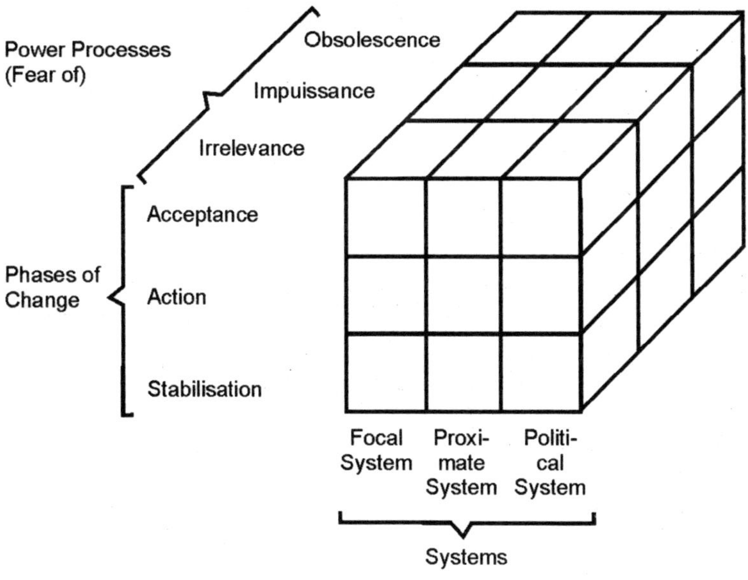

Figure 2
Underlying Processes of the Change Cube

Elements	*Underlying Processes*
Systems	
Focal system	Creativity-conformity
Proximate system	Diffusion
Political system	Support
Power Processes (Fear of)	
Irrelevance	Aggression
Impuissance	Regression
Obsolescence	Rationalisation
Phases of Change	
Acceptance	Motivation
Action	Involvement
Stabilisation	Legitimisation

when the change is introduced in the system. However, instead of discussing them separately, we shall use the three main dimensions of power dynamics, namely, influence, monitoring, and knowledge (the related fears of irrelevance, impuissance and obsolescence), discussing how these operate at different stages of change, in relation to the different systems.

Influence (Fear of Irrelevance)

Political, proximate or focal system all feel it is necessary to have influence in and be relevant to the system. If the system threatens the power which different people have, there will be an aggressive reaction by the people concerned and these can be expressed in several ways. It may, therefore, be assured that power is not threatened.

Let us take the political system first. The political system influences what happens in the focal system in which any experiment or change is being tried out. In the initial stage, therefore, it is necessary to ensure that the external system not only does not feel threatened, but perceives that the influence it has, in fact is enhanced by the new experiment. The perception of power can be in various forms. In the absence of a positive concept of power, the people involved are likely to consider only that aspect which gives them importance in the system.

One way to increase the power of the political system is to involve it in the process of change itself. The various ideas of change can be discussed with the political system, and the political system can be helped to feel, that it is not only approving, but in fact is generating ideas for such experiments. When a prestigious idea is implemented and when such an idea succeeds in a system, the persons who feel that they participated in originating that idea and in giving shape to it, feel very proud of it and quite powerful. Power can therefore be enhanced by involving the political system.

If the idea which is being implemented, relates to an important aspect of the system, the political system can be involved in presenting the arguments in favour of that system, whenever such an opportunity arises either in the Central Government, or when there is a meeting of the experts, where the case is to be presented for such a change. If people in the political system, such as Ministers, are involved in arguing for the experiment and for the change, their involvement and commitment to that change is higher. It also enhances their influence. In the initial stages, if the persons belonging to the political system are able to understand the process of change; know why it is necessary, feel that the change will be a feather in their cap, and have an opportunity to advocate that change and argue for it whenever there are opportunities available, the possibility of getting their support will be high and their motivation to provide that support is ensured.

When that change is being implemented, it is necessary to make sure, that the people in the political system continue to feel powerful in relation to that change. This is possible, in the first place, by providing necessary information to these people. Their continued involvement in the change is necessary. They feel powerful when they continue to own the change which is being introduced, and are able to provide necessary ideas and participate in some aspects of the discussion. Secondly, the political system can be given some feeling of power, when the various difficulties which people come across are discussed with them and they are involved in removing these difficulties. A person also feels powerful when he is able to use his expertize, abilities and skills to contribute to the solution of problems. This is a positive aspect of a person's power. In fact, the political system people have a lot of power in that sense. It may be in the interest of the experiments being tried out, that this aspect of their influence is properly utilized. When we use this power, we are in fact involving them more and more in the change process.

Similarly, the political system can be involved even at the stage of the stabilization of change. After the change has been introduced, has been found to be effective and is becoming a part of the system, the necessary support from the political system for its legitimization is very important. Here, the concerned persons from the political system, can provide a lot of support, by initiating discussion of legitimization with other members of their system. So that change becomes a part of the regular procedure. In this process, not only are the Ministers or the concerned people directly dealing with the department helpful, but also others, who deal with other departments. Persons in the political system dealing with the department may become instrumental in this process. It may, therefore, be useful to continue to involve the political system people in providing such support. Power can also be increased, if the new experiment which is being tried out, is able to solve some problems which the public is facing in relation to a particular department. The possibility of acceptance of the systemic change increases, if the change is seen as a very useful instrument of problem-solving.

As it is important to take care of the power which the political system feels in relation to a particular change; it is equally useful to see that the proximate system's power is not threatened by the experiment, or the change being introduced and tried out. Again, this can be considered in relation to the various stages.

At the stage of acceptance, the power of the proximate system can be threatened, if the experiment is seen as deviating too much from the normal practices followed in the proximate system. In such a case, there may be a complaint that the change does not conform to the norms, which leads to lack of uniformity in the various departments. One way to let the proximate system feel powerful, is to have a committee which is able to discuss various dimensions and raise questions from time to time. If such a monitoring committee can be devised, for looking at the change which is being tried out and seeing what are the different dimensions which require consideration, some people from the proximate system can feel a part of the process. However, this has to be balanced with autonomy. If such a committee is given all the power to intervene and make the necessary adjustments in the experiment, or the change which is being tried out, it can also result in unnecessary interference and subtle ways of preventing the change to assume significance. However, if the people belonging to the proximate systems, are able to raise questions, but do not necessarily go into the details of what is being done, they can serve a useful purpose. In one department in Indonesia, where some change was being introduced in one system, people from the proximate systems, were appointed members of the steering committee and even while the steering committee raised several inconvenient questions from time to time, the collective decision taken helped in making the change more acceptable, although this process slowed down the progress of change. It may be worthwhile to make an initial investment of time, in helping the various agencies to perceive that their power is retained and in fact, increased as a result of the proposed change. The main advantage the proximate systems can derive, is to see that the practices which the change introduces or produces, can also be tried out in their system. This is facilitated, if they are involved in the change programme from the beginning.

The power of the proximate systems can be threatened at the action stage also. If the experiment is proving very effective, they may feel that there will be pressure for similar change in their own system. This feeling may arise mainly, when they do not have sufficient knowledge about the innovation, and what is happening as a result of that change. These threats can be reduced both by their continued involvement, and at the same time by discussion of what is happening with some important members of the proximate systems. Some diffusion of information from time to time amongst the proximate systems may help in reducing such a threat at the action stage. Mostly, threat is produced due to lack of knowledge, and because of some rumours which may float around. To reduce these rumours, it may be useful to have some legitimate ways of diffusing information about what is happening. But this should not be done. as a part of publicity. Publicity may, in fact, become a threat to the proximate systems and as a result, the experiment may be adversely affected.

If the power of the proximate system is threatened at the action stage, there may be opposition to the experiment being planned. Power can be threatened at the action stage, if there is a feeling in the members of the proximate systems that the experiment which is being tried out, is likely to reduce their power in their own systems. Again, several factors may contribute to this. At the stage of acceptance, one factor which is likely to contribute to this feeling is lack of proper knowledge about the experiment. If the members of the proximate system do not really know what is being tried out, and as a result different rumours are floated, through those members of the focal system who feel less secure with the experiment and therefore spread both rumours and distorted information—the proximate systems' members are likely to exaggerate the rumours if they also feel threatened by the experiment. Continuous, but carefully planned information sharing, therefore, may be useful throughout the experiment with the proximate systems. This can be done in various forms. There may be open seminars on the experiment, in which several members of the focal system may be able to participate and speak about the results they are achieving; share some of the problems they are coming across and also how these problems are being solved. This may help in clearing misgivings amongst members of the proximate systems. Secondly, the members of the proximate systems can be helped to feel some increase in the power, if their own expertise is utilized for solving some problems which the focal system is facing, in relation to the change being implemented. For example, the members of the proximate systems can be invited to give their ideas and contribute to the solution, either as members of a task force, which may be set up to solve some difficulties, or as advisers on some aspects of the change experiment. This may help the members of the proximate systems to feel important. In the third place, the experiment should not do anything, which is likely to affect the proximate systems directly. Threat to the proximate systems can also be produced, if the experiment invokes a great deal of enthusiasm in the members of the focal system; and they may perceive the experiment as a crusade against some general defects of bureaucracy. Once that happens, the proximate systems are likely to feel threatened. Care may, therefore, be taken to see that the experiment does not pose any threats to the proximate systems in terms of exposing their weaknesses.

The power of the proximate systems may be threatened even at the stage of the stabilization of change. After the change has been well tried out, and it becomes obvious that the change will be helpful, and when it is becoming a part of the system, the proximate systems can withdraw their support and may ensure that the change is not legitimized in the system.

This can happen when they feel that if the system gets stabilized, they will also have to undergo similar change. One way to help in reducing this threat, is to involve at this stage, a group of people from the proximate systems who are able to study the change and discuss in what different forms their systems can accept some of the ideas. This process of diffusion, may not be regarded as the process of acceptance in toto, of what has been tried out and has been found useful in one system. This is a wrong concept of the diffusion of change. A more functional concept of diffusion is that change is seen as an important way to respond to the needs and fulfils the needs of a particular system. Learning from the experience in the form of diffusion of ideas in another system, may be in the form of adaptation, accepting various aspects which have been tried out with some modifications to suit a particular system. At the stage of stabilization, therefore, it may by useful to have an arrangement for members from the proximate systems to come and discuss, the various aspects of the change and also see what modifications need to be made to use this experience in their own system. It is unfortunate, that in bureaucracy, the tendency towards a uniform procedure is very high. Uniformity should be reinterpreted to mean the minimum common approach, but at the same time with enough variations to suit the needs of the sub-system, of course, without sacrificing the main advantages of a particular practice. This approach may help in reducing threat to some extent.

Monitoring (Fear of Impuissance)

The need to have some monitoring mechanism, to get the necessary information from time to time, for various purposes is a legitimate need of all the three systems. In the absence of good monitoring mechanisms, members of a system may feel weak. The fear of impuissance has to be reckoned with. Let us take the political system first, In the political system, the feeling that the necessary information which the political system wants, may not be available as a result of the introduction of the change, can produce, some difficulties and the acceptance may be greatly reduced. It may be useful to find out what information the political system people want and whether the flow of such information to the political system will be affected. There can be two approaches to this problem. In the first place, it can be seen as what is essential for the political system people to know, and such essential information can be provided. Sometimes, the members of the political system may want information which is not essential and gives them satisfaction only because they have a greater volume of information. If such information is not crucial for monitoring and control purposes, the information may only be a burden, In such a case, they may be helped to understand, how a different but simple system of information may be more effective for them to have control over various aspects. This may be an educative approach, helping them to identify information which may increase the control functions. They may be helped to see how the new system may provide them such information in a more efficient and faster way, than what they were getting before the new system was introduced. Necessary modifications may also be made in the proposed experiment in such a way that whatever information the political system wants, can be provided by making slight readjustment in the change.

This may also be necessary at the action stage. If the political system feels during the experiment, that as a result of it, they are not having the same monitoring control over the information they want for various purposes, some threat may be produced and the support may not be forthcoming. The continued involvement of the political system, and discussing with them as to how the new change or the experiment can help them in better monitoring the crucial information, can be of help. Even when the action is being taken, change in the experiment itself can be brought about, or more information can be provided to the members of the political system. For example, when a new system of performance appraisal is being introduced in a particular department, the concerned minister may feel that the information which he wanted about the people who are working in the department is not reaching him, because according to the new system, most of the information remains only with the immediate boss of the employee, after the assessment has been made. In the first place, it may be discussed with the minister, why such information may be required at his level. It may also be sorted out with him, what kind of information he would like to have. For example, if he is interested in knowing how the various persons at a particular level in his own department are doing, a form can be devised for collecting such information in a summary, to be sent to the minister. It may be useful to ensure that this information goes much faster than what the minister was getting before, and that the information is also in a more usable form. For example, instead of all the files of all the people going to the minister, a summary statement can be prepared which gives the necessary data of several people on the same sheet so that one can have a comparative view of the performance of the various people. If the performance appraisal procedure can be linked with the computer system, a summary print out sheet can be designed and this can quickly go up to the minister. Thus, if the minister is helped to see that the experiment which is being implemented, not only gives him the crucial information; but gives it much faster, and in a manageable form, which can be quickly looked at and used, rather than the huge data which he was getting previously; he may in fact become convinced that this may be a more efficient form of monitoring at his level. He is likely to provide support and get involved in ensuring that the experiment succeeds.

The problem of monitoring at the stage of stabilization is also important. When a change is getting stabilized, it may be seen what problems of monitoring or control remain unresolved for the political system and can be resolved at this stage. The follow-up at the level of the political system may also be necessary. One important action which can be taken at this stage is to follow-up and see what kind of information is needed, how much time the information takes to reach the Minister, how that information is being made use of and so on. At the stage of stabilization, the follow-up programme is useful, not only within the system, but also at the level of the political system.

Let us consider the monitoring dimension in relation to the proximate systems. Proximate systems may also have the need of having some monitoring control over various kinds of information they may want. This may be useful in several ways. At the stage of acceptance, if the proximate systems feel that necessary information is not being provided as a result of change, they may not have enough motivation to pay attention to the system, and in fact may come in the way of the implementation of change. As with the political system, an attempt may be made to find out what information is needed by different proximate systems, which have interface-relationship with the focal system and how that information can be facilitated, both in terms of the systems getting the information much faster, as well as the information being given in a better form. This applies to all the three stages of the change process at the stages of acceptance, action and stabilization. Three aspects which are important in relation to the monitoring system should be attended to at all the three stages, viz., getting information in time, whether the information they are getting is sufficient, and whether the form in which they are getting information is usable.

The problems of monitoring are equally important within the focal system, in which the change is being introduced. The focal system also has various problems. People who are important at various levels in the focal system, also want information from time to time; and if they feel that a system would deprive them of such information, they would resist it. As far as the focal system people are concerned, a continuous discussion of what information is needed by whom and why, may be very useful. More often, people want information which they cannot use. Sometimes, information is a source of power. It may be found out what information is functional and for what roles, then it may be ensured that such information reaches those roles in proper time. If people do not have enough information, they may not be able to act effectively. But, at the same time, it may be necessary for people to understand that information-overload is equally dysfunctional and may not be helpful. At the same time, the necessary information needed for monitoring purposes, by several people in the internal system, may also lead to modification of the change, so that the experiment can also help in providing necessary information to people to take decisions. This may provide the necessary support from inside the system and people are likely to become more creative in their approach, as well as accept the change to a great extent.

Knowledge (Fear of Obsolescence)

The last dimension of power dynamics is the feeling of having relevant knowledge and skills. People have fear of obsolescence in relation to a change. When people in any of the three systems feel that the new system which is being devised is beyond their comprehension, or that they do not have the necessary skills to use it, they are likely to feel threatened.

Let us take the political system first. If the change which is being tried out is too sophisticated and beyond the comprehension of the people in the political system, it is likely to pose some threat. They may lack understanding of the proposed change and may complain that the system is too sophisticated, and it may not be practicable for the Indian conditions or the conditions in a particular state.

At the stage of acceptance, obsolescence will play an important role in preventing innovations to be effective. Let us take the political system. If the members of the political system feel that an innovation which is being introduced is something about which they do not know, and that it poses several problems which their present knowledge is incapable to cope with, there will be resistance to the introduction of such an innovation. This is true of proximate systems also. For the political system members, it may be useful to organize some demonstrations and explanation of the innovation and its effectiveness to solve some problems. Where it is possible, persons of similar background may be brought of explain the implications of the change as experienced by another system. For example, when a particular change is being introduced in one state, and if there has been experience of a similar nature in another State Government, the minister from the other state who knows about such a system, may be invited to talk to the ministers of the state, where the system is being introduced explaining how the change was brought about and with what results. When a member of the political system may be able to gain more knowledge, he may not resist the change.

This holds true for the proximate systems also. If members of the proximate systems feel that their present knowledge and skills are incapable of coping with the proposed system of change, they are likely to create noises which will adversely affect the initial stages of the programme of change. For example, if it is proposed to introduce a computer system for handling some problems, the members of the proximate systems may be against the idea because they do not know how the computer operates. But if the proximate system members are given a short exposure to such a programme, they may be motivated to accept it.

This applies equally to the focal system. In one case, a programme of using computers for transfer of teachers was proposed. This was laughed at because the important persons in the focal system did not think this would be possible. Their knowledge about computers was very limited. In order to deal with this problem, a special programme was organized at the Indian Institute of Management, Ahmedabad, where a case was given and they worked with the data of the case on the computer. They handled the data, used several alternatives and worked out the results of their alternative proposals on the computer. This experience thrilled them. They were very enthused and asked for the Institute's help in the experiment with the new system. They requested the Institute to send some persons to visit their state and look at the data available to see if such a computer programme could be worked out. Their knowledge to some extent and in a limited way their skills to use the computer as an aid in decision making for complex problems, was helpful in the acceptance of change.

Similarly, if at the stage of action there is a fear of obsolescence in any of the three systems, the programme may not go ahead and problems may arise. While the programme is being implemented, obsolescence may be in terms of specific elements, when the details are to be worked out and are being implemented. Obsolescence may greatly affect the programme. If the members of the focal system feel that their present knowledge or skills are not adequate to cope with the change being introduced, they are likely to resist the change a great deal. For example, if a system of performance feedback and counselling to the employees is to be introduced, the members of the focal system are likely to resist this change at the stage of implementation, if they do not have adequate skill of providing guidance and counselling to their employees. They are likely to raise doubts and indicate that such counselling may be dysfunctional. The most effective way to deal with the problem of obsolescence is, of course, by providing adequate training and using other ways of developing the knowledge and skills of the people involved; to help them realize that they have adequate knowledge or skills to deal with the problems which may be thrown up by change. People who do not have the necessary knowledge or skills, feel threatened when they think of coping with problems which are likely to arise, as a result of the introduction of the change.

At the stage of consolidation or stabilization, the problem of dealing with obsolescence may still continue. This is particularly important as more and more people would be involved at the stage of stabilization. If most people at the stage of stabilization, fear that the change introduced in the focal system may eventually make them obsolete, they are likely to resist the change. As long as the proposed change is at the experimental stage, the threat to the three systems is not as high as at the stage of stabilization of the change. The fear may be that once the change becomes a part of the system, it would be difficult to go back. This would be particularly so, if the change requires increasing sophistication, and is likely to become a problem with the members of the focal system, who may be apprehensive of being irrelevant in due course. For example, if a new potential appraisal and promotion system like the assessment centre has been tried out in an organization and is now becoming part of it, persons administering appraisals and promotions may feel uneasy, because the new system would require increasing sophistication. and their present level of knowledge, skills and experience may be inadequate to cope with the requirements. The proximate systems may also disturb the stabilization process if they feel that once the change is accepted as a part of one system, they may also be under pressure to adopt it. In both cases, it may be useful to organize programmes to update the knowledge and skills of the members of the focal system, and also of the proximate systems. It may be better if such training precedes the stabilization stage so that the members feel confident and positive about the change being internalized in the system.

15

Indian Bureaucracy: A Short Critique

P.K. CHAUBEY

Bureaucracy is defined as a body of non-elective government officials. In India they may number around two crore with the following division: 40 lakh with the union government, 70 lakh with the state governments, 60 lakh with the quasi-government organizations and 20 lakh with local self-governments. In relation to the total labour force in the organized sector, their proportion is frightening 70 per cent. There is therefore very little non-administrative activity in the organized sector.[1] It is anybody's guess how much of administration is feeding onto itself. Adam Smith had considered it to be unproductive labour. While this was not accepted by and large, there are people who hold that much of it is in fact counterproductive, suggesting thereby that fewer people in administration could deliver better goods. Again, people worry how much of the resources of the society the bureaucracy gobbles up besides how much of the resources it controls.

II

Bureaucracy has a chequered history. It all started when the state, because of its increasing operation, found it necessary to convert some of the personal royal staff (staying in the palace) into the staff for public service (staying in their own household). To begin with, public service was a temporary measure and clerics who had celibate status and therefore were dependable, were appointed. This could be possible because of the development of university system, growth of money economy, legal system and representative government. But even as late as the beginning of the twentieth century, permission to marry was to be sought. This is all western history. We have simply borrowed the system.

Today, bureaucracy is a much maligned and condemned word. Officialism, red-tapism and proliferation are so accepted characteristics that they have entered the dictionaries. Other characteristics are said to be specialization of functions, adherence to fixed rules and a hierarchy of authority. Some people would add the traits of discretion, secrecy and conservatism. It is said to be inimical to people's development. It is caused to have been a fetter on German and French growth in the nineteenth century. Marx is reported to have held the view that this separate class of administrative officers and clerks in whose hands chief power is concentrated, stands in opposition to all other classes.[2] If this be taken to be the leftist view, we have the most tightest of all Milton Friedman in 1994, to hold that the Americans have a government of the people, by the bureaucrats, for the bureaucrats.[3] Of course, he includes among the bureaucrats the legislators who, he thinks, of late become bureaucrats.

Though there is need to distinguish between the term 'bureaucracy' in technical sense and pejorative usage of word 'bureaucracy' which has now history of more than a century. Any critic of rigid rules, of blundering officials, of slow operation and buckpassing, of conflicting directives, of duplication of efforts, of empire building, and of concentration of control in the hands of a few, according to entry on bureaucracy in the International Encyclopaedia of Social Sciences, will hold pejorative views about bureaucracy. There are not many to say words of praise. Yet it is found to thrive and flourish. The question is: Why? There must then be positive factors for the social choice to use more of bureaucracy. The resolution to this paradox has been attempted in terms of market failure and information inadequacy in the case of social production function, resulting in overuse of government and thus of government bureaucracy.

Most bureaucrats in India retort to such charges and hold that they are made scapegoat. However, a senior retired IAS officer accepts that big industrialists consciously try to bribe and corrupt bureaucracy and that the election process is manipulated by the politicians with the help of bureaucrats.[4] Another IAS officer from Bihar cadre says that there are other powerful actors—the politicians, the local capitalist class and the landlords—responsible for the problems. According to him, the bureaucracy is still a kind of instrument of change and these powerful actors work upon it. And, the final charge is that they succeed in either corrupting it or paralyzing it.[5] These actors, it is alleged, first try to seek favours by offering some gifts to the bureaucrats and in case the latter refuse, they are not allowed to work. This may be true in many cases.

Now, let us note some common observations. Politicians, particularly those in power, are found to exhort the bureaucrats, and the politicians, not in power, are found to accuse them. They do so perhaps in the hope that these things would work to their advantage. Most often they do not. Bureaucrats, in turn, blame that they are being made scapegoat. Industrialists often blame the bureaucrats in public but grease the palm in private, sometimes even by offering jobs to the kith and kin of senior bureaucrats and promising jobs to them after their retirement from the government service. Senior bureaucrats are often found to have good relations with big politicians and junior ones often quarrel with small industrialists. High bred industrialists are often found to look down upon the bureaucrats. Common people have utter contempt for the bureaucrats as their experience is woeful without exception.

III

That bureaucrats alone are responsible for this kind of state of affairs, would be a gross misjudgment. Again, there is no reason to believe that we Indians are unique in this regard. Yet 1 feel tempted to three stylized facts about our system concerning the bureaucracy:[6]

1. Howsoever good a piece of work you choose to accomplish, you cannot do it without facing a hurdle or two if you are lucky. You may have too many otherwise. No matter even if you are yourself a bureaucrat, the hurdles are bound to be there.
2. Howsoever had a thing you plan to execute, you will succeed if you are dead determined; it is all the more easy if you are a bureaucrat.
3. There is a lot of misuse and abuse of resources all around. Checking it bureaucratically very often results into disuse, raising the capital ratio in the economy.

Who is responsible for all this malaise? Administration? The common feeling is: Yes, largely. But it is administration, the collective noun, not administration, the abstract noun. We know that a society organized on civil basis with a state cannot do without administration. And, as Parkinson's law states, official staff expands in inverse proportion to the work done.

Senior bureaucrats often point out to these problems posed by audit procedures which they say are most unimaginative. Rigid and rule-bound as their practitioners are, they follow the letters of instructions, not the spirit behind. And the rules they hold are based on the premise that the people are dishonest and out to take undue advantage.[7] That may be the case. But the most common observation suggests that the rules are so interpreted that they serve neither the society nor the state but the official who often succeeds in corrupting the party to benefit from the action. Many a time those who interpret most intricate philosophical treatises are made to look foolish.

IV

In the wake of present liberalization phase, many senior bureaucrats have started telling junior functionaries, "do not make laws which cannot be implemented". I do not know if they have much role in framing laws. But this admission is itself an ample testimony of muddled thinking or deliberate confusion. However, when a junior functionary is told both 'do' and 'don't' in the same breath, he gets either frustrated or insincere. He may find it better not to do anything. Officers blame clerks and clerks in their turn blame officers for inaction and/or misaction.

Now we are told that laws could be reduced with ease to one fourth of the present number.[8] The tendency so far developed suggests that it is easier to add to the codified rules than to delete. As a result they grow in number and complexity. They become, to borrow Kurien's phrase, those affairs of state in which bureaucracy develops a vested interest in protecting and interpreting.[9] Further, decisions are made without assignment of reasons for making them. Delay in making decisions and refusal to embark upon experimentation, are everybody's everyday experience. One often finds that discretion often assumes the shape of discrimination and antiquity is promoted in the name of experience. If mistakes are not deliberate, they are avoided by minimizing the sphere of novelty and innovation.

A common refrain is "simplify procedures and make them transparent". Senior bureaucrats are suggesting that non-official experts be associated in the exercise of framing the rules. The present position, it seems, is that they are first framed and then objections and suggestions are invited. Nobody asks as to who asked the bureaucracy to frame complicated laws and procedures in the first place. It must not have been Nehru. The possible answers could be colonial mindset, ruling instinct or vested interests. How to do away with these is a difficult issue.

It is a common observation that most often the rules are not followed to help the people. They are so interpreted by the official dealing with the matter as to make it easy to procure some favour. But it may come as a surprise that the rules could be made farcical simply because somebody misbehaved with some official whom he visited.[10]

V

On a deeper probing, perhaps one would find, there pervade all kinds of alienation in the society. Normally, people in bureaucracy get no satisfaction in doing their bit as they never find themselves finishing or accomplishing something which a mathematician, a poet or a painter does. Normally, they are not even recognized for good work that they sometime perform. The junior functionaries often make complaint is that big officers steal the show when actually they deserved the kudos.

Bureaucracy is said to have been a by-product of aristocracy which transferred the power into the hands of permanent officials. They were given security of tenure, higher age of superannuating, incremental salaries and annual vacations with a view to exhorting them to do good work. It is admitted that these incentives have petered out. We have just inherited the so-called steel frame. It did not evolve here. Our attempt to make good use of the instrument met only with partial success.

But we need perhaps to admit that the western thinking which gave rise to high level of operation of the modem state and the vastness of the services it seeks to render, is based on the premise that the state holds the society together. Otherwise there are fissiparous tendencies inherent in the society. This thinking does not admit any entity between an individual and the state. Community processes which were most important processes have been given a go-by.

Then, there is what may be called master-servant syndrome. We work through some organization. And organization is a wonderful thing in which every employee considers himself the master in relation to his subordinates and treats his subordinates as his personal servants. The subordinates tend to resent but find it expedient to submit. The servants, which most of us are, call themselves as officers and behave as masters of common people in their respective jurisdictions.

Someone could ask: Who is the master then? Politicians? Senior bureaucrats? Industrialists? Tax payers, the paymasters? Or people? I would prefer to articulate it as follows: we are all jointly and collectively our masters and individually and severally servants.

VI

If you are not serving your masters—the people, you may not be committing a crime as there may be a rule or two for your inaction or misaction. But you surely commit a sin. Ethics seem to be overruled by the rules. They need to be changed, they have to be changed. One may tend to agree with Laski (1931) who suggested among others, that (1) the political heads should stay in public life long enough so that they develop their own mind on matters of crucial importance, (2) there should be direct contact between the bureaucracy and the representative public associations in order that public criticism of its work is both well informed and coherent, (3) retiring age should be low that the older who are prisoners of routine give way to the younger who is expected to be innovative, and (4) there should be effective decentralization which is responsive to the need for innovation. Who is going to do it and how? Until there is an egress, what do you do?

Here are couple of advices to the friends who are there at the real helm of affairs in bureaucracy. First, see if there is a preamble to the book of the rules you are following or there is lying somewhere the original proposal or rationale for the set of rules you are given. Apply common sense. Put yourself in the client's/claimant's position. You will find the talisman. And it is: Go by objectives, not by objections.

Second, when you plan to do anything for a village, please consult the villagers. Their perception is based on 'feel' which you can never develop unless you become part of the village. The solutions that their wisdom may offer may be superior to your knowledge or your superior's knowledge. Therefore, cross-check. Your mistakes/misactions can cost them much. You may ask what if they commit a mistake ? They will suffer. Why should they suffer for your mistakes? In fact, the right to commit mistakes should lie with the people who have to bear the consequences.

Notes

1. It has to be noted that the size of administration in the non-governmental organized sector should also be large. It is pointed by many including Laski (1931) that the undesirable characteristics of the bureaucracy are not in the least confined to the service of state. They operate whenever there is large-scale organization. So much so that a great business corporation, as long as it earns a dividend, never has to bother about its shareholders. See H.J. Laski (1931), Bureaucracy, in *Encyclopedia* of *the Social Sciences*, Vol. III, Macmillan, New York.
2. Raj Krishna quoted it in a discussion on Seventh Plan Perspectives held in the India International Centre during 1984. See M.S. Adiseshiah (1985), *Seventh Plan Perspectives,* Lancer International, New Delhi.
3. See Milton Friedman (1994), Why *Government is the Problem,* Forum of Free Enterprise, Bombay.
4. See B.G. Deshmukh (1992), *Can Bureaucracy Meet the Challenge of Liberalization,* Forum of Free Enterprise, Bombay.
5. This was one Shri Pereira who retorted to Raj Krishna on the latter's observation. Raj Krishna however agreed to the former's observations about other actors.

6. A friend of mine Dr. U.D.N. Bajpai, who is no more, compared us with Japanese in following words: While people in Japan work hard, people in India hardly work. It can be true only of the people in the organized sector, some of whom specialize in deliberate dulling.
7. See B.G. Deshmukh (1992), *op.cit.*
8. An IAS officer of Madhya Pradesh cadre Shri Shankar Nath held this view when speaking in the deliberations on New Industrial Policy and Responsive Administration, held in the Academy of Administration, Madhya Pradesh, Bhopal on March 11,1995.
9. See C.T. Kurien (1992), *The Economy: In Interpretative Introduction,* Sage, New Delhi.
10. B.G. Deshmukh (1992), op.cit.

16

Bureaucratic Sensitivity and Human Rights

AMIT LODHA

In *Rigveda,* it is stated: "*Ajyestaso akanishtasa etc, Sam bhrataro va vridhuhu sowbhagya.*" It means, no one is superior or inferior. All are brothers who should strive collectively for common welfare.

The concept of human rights has been in vogue since time immemorial. Even ancient treatises like the *Rigveda* of India which speaks of values in an enlightened society eloquently championed the cause of human equality, dignity, fraternity and need for common effort to attain prosperity.

Presently, there is no universally accepted conception of human rights. But, a common understanding of the core concept is nevertheless feasible, viz., the human rights are the rights enjoyable by a person by virtue of his being a human being. Therefore, human rights are fundamental, since they existed before the society and the state. Human rights are mainly concerned with human dignity, freedom and participation in the society. Human rights are those which are moral and universal. According to John Rawls, "justice is the first virtue of social institutions". Human rights, of course, are an end of justice; consequently, the role of justice is crucial in understanding human rights.

These rights have widened in concept over the last few decades. Their concept is interactive, intensive and it has broadened so much that it encompasses the economic, social and cultural rights as well as civil and political rights. It also includes the right to a healthy environment, the right of sustainable development. It even provides for the right of future generations. The problem of human rights is intrinsically linked with social environments and the relationship that exists, at a given time, between a person and the institutions on which his social existence depends. Since conditions continue to change, so does, like any other social norm, the nature of human rights. Nonetheless, there remains one core concept—the right to life, the right to live as a human being. This demands the presence of the basic conditions essential for the protection of human dignity. From this primordial right spring all other rights—the right to liberty and security of person, freedom of movement, freedom of expression, etc.

Administration is one of the most ancient and pervasive of human behaviours. Directly and indirectly, through the mode of complex organizations or bureaucracies, it affects the quality of our lives. When done well, it enriches, liberates, civilizes; and when badly done it can destroy, dehumanize and degrade. Millions of people are trapped in a vicious circle, in both cause and consequence, poverty and malnutrition and disease. It is the job of the administration to provide succour to the under-privileged of any society. And, it is not any different in our country, more so when some 30 per cent of its population lives below the poverty line. There is a feeling that authoritarianism can bring about the desired results; so-called human rights are to be restricted for the broader goal of national development. Consequently, the bureaucracy lacks what is the foundation of the human rights system—the principle that the authority of the state shall be exercised by the will of the people themselves, and that their participation in the government shall be truly representative and genuine.

Today, a critical examination of Indian reality shows chronic signs of a multiplicity of crises, the collective gravity of which has implications of violent struggles for survival by the deprived sections of our democracy. The situation is also a serious threat to the continued survival of India's social, cultural and ecological diversity. The burning issues have been primarily: first, direct and indirect violations by the state or the bureaucracy; and secondly, denial in practice of legally stipulated rights as well as the inability of government institutions to perform their functions.

The accusation on the bureaucracy of being insensitive is not of recent times. During the British period, there were untold miseries suffered by the common people. The poverty of the masses, the big famines and thousands of deaths are all reminiscent of the insensitivity of the erstwhile bureaucracy. The Indian independence and our Constitution asked for a vital change in this attitude of callousness. The bureaucracy came to be postulated as a durable vehicle for bringing in a change—from insensitivity to sensitivity, from the massacre of human rights to their restoration.

To the great dismay of the poverty-stricken millions, independence was just a transfer of power from the White Sahibs to the Burra Sahibs with the same set of system of the Raj, the same repression, the same attitude and the same contempt for those whom they governed. It was rather a transfer of millions from frying pan into fire. Members of the bureaucracy are like soldiers on the battlefield who are trained not to ask questions, leave apart thinking in terms of values and ethics. Sometimes it appears that the law, the rule and an order are not meant for the benefit of the community but to be obeyed mechanically and its an end in itself. The bureaucrat's conscience is often not pricked and is indifferent to the damages it causes.

India continues to witness significant human rights abuses despite extensive. constitutional and statutory safeguards.

Many of them are generated by intense social tensions and violent secessionist movements. The authorities' attempts to repress them and the bureaucracy's insensitivity further aggravate the problems. The weaker sections of Indian society have been deprived of justice for long. They have no access to justice on account of their poverty, ignorance and illiteracy. They are not aware of their rights and benefits conferred upon them by the Indian Constitution and the law. On account of their socially and economically disadvantaged position, they lack the capacity to assert their rights.

There are innumerable instances of bureaucratic apathy towards the plight of the masses; in fact, the list could go on *ad infinitum.* A few examples of bureaucratic insensitivity are highlighted as follows:

Bhopal Revisited

Despite a settlement in 1989 and review in 1991, the gas survivors continue to suffer untold misery. Indeed, their lives are more insecure today than in 1984. The forces that wreaked havoc on the lives of the poorest and most vulnerable segments of the population have displayed callousness throughout the ten years after the disaster. The administration has been slow and inept in distribution interim relief, and created little employment for those injured in the disaster. There has been extensive corruption in the distribution of relief. Only 10 per cent of the affected persons have been able to get their paltry allowance. The poor have to suffer further ignominy when they have to wait endlessly outside the offices of the bureaucrats for making their petition.

The bureaucracy either puts very little mind in implementing policies or connives with MNCs, etc. Either way, it is the poor people who lose. It is a matter of great concern as to how a supposedly educated bureaucracy could allow the setting up of the Union Carbide Corporation its toxic producing plant in a thriving metro like Bhopal. The setting up of the plant led to the mushrooming of a number of slums around it, inhabited mostly by people belonging to the poor and backward classes.

Some years later, the bureaucracy in its great wisdom decided to embark upon a 'city beautification' and an anti-encroachment drive. This meant the eviction of the poor, even forcibly, from their sheds. They were shifted to the outskirts of the city where employment, food and medical facilities were almost non-existent. The Bhopal gas tragedy and its consequent handling amply testifies the callousness of the state administration.

Srikrishna Commission Report

The Srikrishna Commission was appointed to investigate the causes of the Mumbai riots happened after the Babri Masjid demolition. The Commission strongly criticized the role of the administration, particularly the police. It found out that the response of the administration to appeals from desperate victims was cynical and utterly indifferent. The alertness of police pickets left much to be desired. The police did not act on time; rather it shied away from its duty of protecting the innocent people. The commission also made an alarming disclosure that the administration, often at lower levels, had an inbuilt bias. The investigations conducted were also grossly unsatisfactory. The bureaucracy, by its own conduct, lost moral authority over the citizens. The most damning revelation was that despite the knowledge of the fact that communal virus had infected the administration, no effective curative steps were taken.

Bureaucratic Share in the Violation of Human Rights

The Dalits, particularly SCs and STs, have suffered a lot due to the neglect of the administration. The class committing atrocities generally enjoys the patronage of the bureaucracy. The victims are often told to shut their mouths and threatened with dire consequences. Even their reports are not lodged, forget any action taken against the culprits.

At a seminar in Delhi, over 400 class I SC and ST officers complained of racism in the government service by tempering with their confidential reports, etc. If this is the plight of the members of the civil services itself, then one shudders to imagine the conditions of the underprivileged.

In recent years, the Supreme Court has taken a serious note of the illegal conduct of the bureaucracy, particularly criticizing the police for its high-handedness and tyranny. The apex court had to strongly come down on the police stating that it would not be allowed to keep the citizens at its mercy. Members of the police are trained to behave as masters, in a manner that the very sight of a police uniform would strike terror in the hearts of the common people.

In the famous case of Hussain Ara Khatun vs. State of Bihar, the Supreme Court found that there were a number of women prisoners in jail. Ironically, they were not accused of any offence but were required for the purpose of giving evidence. In the language used by the Bihar Police, they were in 'protective custody'. The court held this so-called 'protective custody' nothing short of blatant violation of personal liberty.

It was indeed a day for great shame for all when the District Magistrate of Barelli stated that it was quite natural for a woman to be raped if she goes out alone in the fields. When the people who have been given powers by the state to protect the people utter such kind of things, it is indeed to much to ask from the people to have faith in the administration.

Bureaucratic interventions add insult to injury by indulging in rhetoric of rule of law and democracy. The steel frame of the bureaucracy reflects a case of a democratic state's undemocratic credentials. For instance, the immediate provocation for the state oppression of tribals living near the Sardar Sarovar dam could be assigned to the threat percepted by the officials over the attempts of the tribals to get mobilized. The villagers were unwilling to leave the land of their ancestors, moreover they were apprehensive of the rehabilitative measures taken by the administration. The officials forcibly evicted them causing gross violation of human dignity in the process.

To this list, one can add innumerable instances of human rights violations of individuals, groups of the population, which are repetitive, enduring and have almost become a permanent feature of the state system.

Natwar Singh's disclosures in his memoirs quoted Indira Gandhi's advice to him on his intention to enter politics, was that he should have a thick skin, like that of bureaucrats. The truism does have an element of wisdom. The attitude of insensitivity has a wide spectrum. Call it inaction, apathy, neglect, delay, victimization, discrimination or arbitrariness, it is all a manifestation of a behaviour pattern of those who are put to govern and administer, towards those who are to be administered, i.e., the public. Just as a peg is needed to hang a hat, the human rights are construed as the pegs for evaluating the bureaucratic conduct and functioning.

The shades of such attitudinal insensitivity ascribed to the bureaucracy are as many as can be conceived and the denial of human rights have no less quantum of variations. A bureaucrat is being assessed and subjected to sarcasm for his not upholding human fights. The wail on this issue is getting louder in recent times. The eloquent rebuke of the bureaucracy is motivated due to some very serious lapses in the attitude and functioning of the administration. The bureaucracy would have to ponder over the whole landscape of evolution of the many uncharitable epithets for its insensitivity.

The bureaucrats, as the executors and administrators, cannot absolve themselves of their duty to provide protection and a sense of well being to the public. It would be a wholly indefensible proposition that the administration could practice the retrograde attitudinal behaviour of insensitivity. Sensitivity is a vital trait for bureaucracy. Administrators, who are called upon to execute programmes of development, and also as a functionary of the Constitution, shall have to have the trait of positive sensitivity towards their fellow being, i.e., the public for whose welfare the administration is carved out. The bureaucracy is one of the most vital limbs in a functional democracy. The objectives have been engrafted in the Preamble of our Constitution and duties further described in Article 51-A and to add to it the whole panorama of fundamental rights. Any insensitivity to these constitutional ideals and directives would at once make a bureaucrat guilty of the oath taken by him under the Constitution and make him accountable to the people, for whose welfare he has been given an office.

Liberalization and globalization processes have accelerated the expectations of the people. Human rights have been realized as the most sacrosanct of all rights. Human rights have no specific limits; their definition is widening. The moot point is to fulfil them, protect them. The wide dimension and spectrum of this ethos of human rights as we find today is really awesome. The impetus for its demand has increased all the more because of the proclamation of the welfare of all, irrespective of the quantum jump in population and a host of other problems. Each one has to be provided protection, shelter, food, health care, job; the list goes ad nauseam. Any inaction or delay due to whatever reason is ridiculed as insensitivity.

The chasm between the violation and the protection of human rights is growing wide. Atrocities against the scheduled castes, minorities, the daring crimes, environmental hazards, suicides by farmers and numerous other tragic events that make the headlines of daily newspapers making the front page virtually an obituaries page, point to the failure of the bureaucracy. The problems look deep into the face of the modern mandarins. Their half-baked policies and not so impressive accomplishments cannot be put under the carpet. The bureaucrats cannot exculpate themselves of the maladies and the consequent violation of human rights. The modern-day mandarins or sahibs will have to let go the archaic systems of office noting at the lowest levels, the bell, the red light, the hard frown, and sundry other syndromes of power. The bureaucracy has to come close to the public, it should feel the people's pulse, empathize with them.

Undoubtedly, the bureaucracy has successfully matched many of the hopeless situations in a remarkable manner. It has displayed a strong sense of conviction and strength of character. The system is working. Some of those who cry out are themselves the violators of human rights. The growth of the demand of the public for its rights without any parallel realization of its two obligations is a serious point to think over for a valid evaluation of the insensitivity ascribed to the bureaucracy alone.

Truly, numerous obstacles-social, economic, political-hamper the bureaucracy. Add to these are various commissions and special courts working for the protection of the rights of the people. The attitudinal insensitivity spelled out to stigmatize the bureaucracy is rather to dub it as a stony institution without a feeling, a creature without a human soul. Rather many a bureaucrat is brimming with pulsating life. He is not in a state of sclerosis.

This insensitivity needs to be given a final look in the context of numerous development projects, be it JRY, IRDP, etc. The list may go on and on. A lot of successes for the welfare of the people and the upholding of democracy have all required the bureaucrat to feel the pulse of the people and ensure its accomplishment. If the much-maligned bureaucracy were as insensitive as it is made out to be, the advancement of the poor would not have been as manifest as is actually seen. The devotion, zeal and selflessness of the bureaucracy has certainly made India strong. The stability and secure environs in which we all live are a rich tribute to those who have carried out their duty with utmost devotion.

Today, we are passing through a difficult phase where the society is prone to violence. There is need for more positive and operational steps to preserve human rights and prevent their violation. The state faces situations of grave emergency when demands of order should override those of liberty. The rationale behind this is expressed by the maxim "Salus Populi, Suprema lex est"—safety of the people is the highest law. It must, however, be remembered that the violation of human rights does not necessarily occur only by state action. The wanton killing of innocents by terrorists or militants and the destruction of property of the innocent citizens are also illustrations of the violation of human rights. These call for deeper introspection though it must be admitted that state terrorism is no answer to it. In an era of expansion of human rights there is no place for state terrorism in human rights jurisprudence. In all events and at any cost the action of the state must be "right, just and fair" using any form of torture or debasing human rights would be impermissible. The fundamental human rights of the members of the security forces, and the bureaucracy also deserve proper attention. A delicate balance has to be struck between the pre-emptory needs of the stability of the state and the observance of human rights.

Administration is philosophy in action. It depends a lot on the nature of the man holding an administrative post. The essential raw material of administration is man. Human nature is the basic stuff of organizations, those goal-seeking collectivities which give rise to administration. Administrators should be excellent leaders. They should have power to inspire the common populace by creating faith—faith in a common understanding, faith in the ultimate satisfaction of personal motives, and faith in the integrity of objectives authority.

There are certain moot points on which the state apparatus can reflect upon to improve its functioning and increase the people's faith in it. They are as follows:

Gap between Government and People

It is always the state policy to respect the human rights by the bureaucracy even in terrorist-affected areas. In the absence of popular government in such areas, the accountability and credibility of the administration dilutes. There exists a gap between the people and the government which makes the problem even more acute. The human rights organizations and NGOs, instead of playing a positive role, create further problems. A lot of interaction is needed to bridge the gap between the government and the people's organizations.

Confidence and Support of People

The bureaucracy, particularly the police and security forces, face a massive challenge due to the propaganda and misinformation campaigns launched by the militants and their mentors. The local press further compounds the problems of the administration by being sympathetic to the anti-state groups. The Internet has provided further fuel to the fire. There are hundreds of sites on the Internet maintained by the terrorist groups which spew venom against the state. Even the Khalistani groups have their sites on the web. The various human rights groups further espouse the cause of the anti-state elements. It is, therefore, important that people themselves judge the things in the right perspective.

Credibility of State Agencies to be Restored

In terrorist-affected areas, there is a tendency to give summary punishment due to impossibility of judicial verdict. A lot of moderation and restraint is needed in this respect. Care should be taken not to cross the thin line between custodial deaths projected as encounters and killings after a chase. Such situations should be dealt in such a way that the credibility of the state is maintained. This will also increase the faith of the people in the state.

Need of Restraint and Moderation

Killing, disappearance, torture in custody, extorting confession, etc., are some of the human rights violations that generally happen in militancy-affected areas. It is imperative that the bureaucracy takes measures to strike balance between the realities of dealing with terrorist situations and restraint and moderation. For instance, in closely-knit society like Kashmir, the meetings between terrorists and their relations are allowed.

Check and Balance in the System: Role of Various Agencies

The Indian system has quite a few remedial forums like the National Human Rights Commission and the State Human Rights Commission. The quick police investigation, judicial determination, individual aberration, departmental action followed by punishment, available roles of human rights organizations, transparency in day-to-day work are already existing to act as check and balance in the system of our country.

Transparency and Credibility

The *suo moto* enquiries, action on media reports, revival of democratic rule and civil administration pose a major challenge in terrorist-affected areas. The rule of law has to be maintained to ensure people's faith in the government. They should be given information about all the government activities. The demand for openness is based on the fact that the orchestration of democracy has to be continuous and pervasive. This means that people exercise sound judgement in the conduct of the government and the merits of public policies. Members of a democratic society should be sufficiently informed that they may influence intelligently the decisions that may affect themselves.

The challenge of terrorism should be met with innovative ideas and approach. State terrorism is no answer to combat terrorism. The state must ensure that various agencies deployed by it are within the bounds of the law and not become law unto themselves.

For ensuring adherence to human rights norms by police, it is necessary to build up an organizational culture that frowns on abuse or misuse of force and authority. Human rights training to the police personnel, particularly of the subordinate ranks, is essential to make the police more responsive and people-friendly. The National Human Rights Commission has prepared a model training syllabus for police officers of all ranks. Appropriate training in human rights principles will have an elevating impact. Constant supervision and adherence to human rights norms by senior officers is necessary to build up such an organizational ethos and make policing ethical and humane.

Human rights are entitlements due to every man, woman or child because they are human. They include right pertaining to the security of the person, including the right not to be deprived of life or liberty without due process of law; and the right not to be tortured or subjected to cruel, inhuman or degrading treatment or punishment. These are non-derogable rights. Their violation can never by justified even by a state in national emergency. Human rights also include civil and political rights, viz., the right to freedom of thought, opinion and expression, freedom of peaceful assembly and association, and the right to take part in the governance of one's own country. There are also economic, social and cultural rights to which everyone is entitled. These include basic survival rights to food, shelter, health care and social services. These are not given to the people by the state and the state cannot deprive people of those rights. The reality, of course, is that throughout history, people have had to fight to win their rights because power holders are rarely magnanimous in granting them.

Human rights now have a prominent place on international agenda. The societies the world over are witnessing a paradigm shift; the concept of state sovereignty is getting eroded. In the context of human rights, this has meant that the state can no longer hide behind the shield of 'domestic jurisdiction' as they abuse the rights of their citizens. There is a discernible lack of commitment on the part of the government in upholding human rights.

There is an observed and expressed need by administrative practitioners in a variety of fields at all stages of their career for some kind of analysis of the problem of value in administration which might reach a little beyond the banalities or, worse, the sterilities which so often tend to pass as values or ethical training in the preparation of administrators. Every administrator knows, whether he be endowed with the benefits of professional training or not, the day-to-day activity of administration is often downright imprecise, unclean, non-quantitative, emotionally taxing and painful.

In the foreseeable future, the administrative system will be expected to reorient itself to the requirements of human rights protection. It may not be very difficult to change laws and rules for this purpose. What is crucial and more problematic is the instilling of judicious, positive and sympathetic attitudes and values into the government functionaries at all levels, but most importantly, at the cutting-edge level. Broad-based moral understanding between people and administration, safeguarded by legal and constitutional guarantee, can make the system work in a manner helpful to both the freedom of the individual and the imperatives of governance.

Truly, it is undeniable that the administration has other counter currents, be that politicians, etc., which also have a decisive role in their actions, One cannot be unmindful of the existing constraints of the economic and socials set-ups in which he is called upon to function and bring up the said well-being of all sections of the society. An officer often finds himself in the midst of such a complex conglomeration. He is often in a serious puzzle, having difficult or no choices left to him. The *Jan Adalats, Aapke Sawaal aur Jawaab,* displayed quite frequently on TV mirror the very unpalatable scrutiny. The administrator has to face the vortex of expectations and execution.

The bureaucrats have to perform under tremendous pressure but unfortunately no one seems to understand their problems. They have become the favourite whipping boys of everyone. It has become fashionable to blame them for all the ills of the society. The fact remains that it is easy to pass judgements sitting in the comfortable environs of one's drawing room but facing the reality is an altogether different ball game. The bureaucracy undoubtedly has to face a lot of problems in performing the onerous duties it is assigned. It requires a lot of conviction and strength of character. The bureaucracy has always been receiving brickbats; it is time that they get their share of bouquets also.

Ironically, even the minutest error on the part of officials is sufficient to raise a lot of hue and cry but their achievements and efforts are never lauded. The media have a very major role in portraying the government functionaries as insensitive. To add to the woes of the hapless administrators is the judiciary. The officers almost always work under the fear of the Damocles sword of the contempt of the court hanging over them. The number of public interest litigations has been piling up and the judiciary has been passing judgements. The scope and meaning of human rights has widened tremendously. The judiciary passes an order and the executive has to implement it. Many of the judgements are very difficult to follow and often put the officers in an ethical dilemma. The various kinds of national and international pressures further compound the problem for the executive. Agencies like Amnesty International condemn the state machinery every now and then. The state apparatus is put under microscopic scrutiny for the acts it did without taking into account the gravity of the situation prevailing during that action.

The bureaucrat has to do a very thankless job. Every section of the society, from the most downtrodden to the most powerful politician, blames it. It has been branded insensitive.

But apparently, there is no alternative to it. The bureaucracy *per se* is not the villain, it is rather the bureaucrat who at times is insensitive. Therefore, there is an urgent need for a paradigm shift in the thinking of the bureaucracy; it simple has to be more proactive, sensitive and progressive in nature.

17

Rural Bureaucracy in the Developing Countries of Asia: A Critical Review

RICHARD M. TOM

In the late forties and fifties, a number of nations in the South Asian region became free independent states from British rule. After experiencing the pang of birth, most of the nations underwent the excruciating period of nation and state building. With the wresting of political power from the colonial state, most of the countries were absolutely in miserable conditions on account of the colonial exploitation. An overwhelming majority of the population in colonially ruled countries were in abject poverty, suffered from mass hunger, malnutrition, illiteracy, unemployment and higher rate of fertility. All these evils in the realm of social and economic life made the rural people apathetic and plagued the countries for a considerable period of time. Colonialism left the countries divided and underdeveloped and dependent in almost every aspect. Due to these factors and depressing features of rural life in most of the countries demanded for greater public intervention. This became a great concern for the planners, policy makers and administrators.

In order to remove the inadequacies from the socio-economic system and to put the country on the path of development and growth, the national governments of the independent countries initiated a wide ranging measures for rural betterment on a large scale. A series of development programmes of varied nature were launched for the people living in rural areas. Thus, began the tumultuous era of national reconstruction.

As the approach of most of the countries for social and economic development was towards rural development, a need was felt for having an administrative system for effective planning, implementation and management of rural development programmes. Many countries in the Indian sub-continent introduced various administrative systems of heterogeneous patterns. Initially, the governments of most of the South Asian countries, except China and Nepal, did not realize for a separate administrative apparatus for the development of rural areas. The administrative pattern devised by the British to look after both law and order and revenue collection, which was the most efficient during that time, was adopted by most of the South Asian countries to bring radical changes in rural areas. The administration was geared up to the developmental needs and was extended to rural areas, resulting not only in the weakening of the traditional local machinery looking after the maintenance of law and order, but also weakened the development administration.

In the mid-fifties, some of the developing countries in the South Asian region made efforts in reforming and restructuring the administrative system. But most of the efforts made by these countries could not bring much changes in the administrative functioning.

This paper is a modest attempt to present an overview of endeavours made by South Asian countries like China, Nepal, Bhutan, Pakistan, Bangladesh, Sri Lanka and India in constituting a separate rural local self-government/rural development administration at the grassroots level. It also reviews the various administrative structures presently functioning and to assesses the administrative problems prevailing in these countries.

China

China, being a leviathan Communist state, adopted throughout its countryside a network of people's communes. These communes are the principal economic, administrative, social and political units in rural areas. These were created by consolidating agricultural cooperatives with the lowest administrative units called 'Hsiangs' (townships). The communes serve as the basic units for rural administration and for effective management of rural development programmes. For effective management and efficiency, the population of the communes are divided into large production brigades, which are further divided into production teams. At present, there are about 50,000 communes, each linked to central government through 2,000 counties and 22 provinces. Today, the communes are a three-tiered organization, with production teams at the lowest level, production brigades at the intermediate level, and commune at the apex level.

The production team is formally an organized unit consisting of some twenty to thirty households. It is the main unit that undertakes the work at the grassroots level. Each team corresponds roughly to a small village or a hamlet. The team is the basic agricultural production and accounting unit. It enjoys substantial responsibility and autonomy regarding investment, decisions, savings, labour utilization, machinery purchase and irrigation facilities. All production decisions are made at this level. Also, this unit is the main starting point for the 'bottom-up' planning process. It arouses the rural masses to involve themselves in developmental activities and chalk out development plans for attaining the goals of development. Furthermore, all the work of the production teams is coordinated by production brigade, and provides facilities and plan their activities. Thus, in short, the production teams are the heart of the commune.

The next organized unit, which is the second tier of the commune system, is the production brigade. This intermediate unit is composed of several production teams and serves as the basic planning and administrative unit. The brigade undertakes large-scale investment in development activities. It runs agricultural processing plants, farm machinery, repair shops and livestock enterprises. It also operates primary schools and health service centres. All annual production plans and reports prepared by the production teams are routed through production brigade to commune for scrutinization.

The commune, the next highest tier, is a composite unit of local government. It is an organization which integrates government administration and economic management. The commune as a mechanism provides the individual inhabitants to work jointly and share the fruits of their effort collectively This unit coordinates, supervises and guides all the activities of teams and brigades.

The functions of the commune are many. It engages in collective activities like increasing the productivity of land, labour and other resources. It also performs varied functions like registration of births, deaths, marriages, etc. The other major activities it carries out include providing bigger irrigation facilities creating of hydro-electric power plants, large-scale livestock enterprises, farm machine manufacturing units, tractor stations, nurseries and experimental farms. The other functions are to give military training, implement administrative policies and strengthen ideological-cum-political base of rural society. The commune runs middle schools and hospitals and has an elaborate financial system which determines not only the production costs and taxes that are needed but also sets aside revenues for welfare and further investment. As a large commune, it acts as the link between the production teams and production brigades on one hand and with higher administrative sub-divisions on the other.

The commune has an adequate mechanism for representing the people at all the three organized levels. The supreme body of the commune is the people's council. It consists of all members of the commune. This body elects about 100 to 120 members as representatives for people's commune. There is a representing organization known as the Communes Revolutionary Committee which manages the communes. It consists of about ten to twenty-five members. In these, there are four to five officials from production team and an accountant from production brigade. The other members are workers, people's liberation army, party members, youth of the villages and several other members. The committee is headed by a chairman of either sex. The production brigade has a revolutionary team and elects its own leader.

Thus, the entire structure of China's local government is simple and rudimentary that people at each level could control and participate in all decisions and activities that touches their lives. The rural administration, instead of getting things done through civil servants, involves people at all stages of development. The local leadership organizes and mobilizes themselves to meet their basic needs by utilizing their own resources. The local system in China has been materializing the triple goals of diversifying rural economy, absorbing excess labour force and generating additional income for populace. It also provides essential social services as well as rural infrastructure. Most importantly, it integrates communes' activities, priorities and policies with national targets through carefully devised linkages with higher politico-administrative levels. In this way, the communes represent as an autonomous-decentralized system and serve as an institutional vehicle in bringing about transition of rural China from traditionalism to modernization.

Nepal

Sandwiched between the Communist China and the democratic India, is the Himalayan kingdom of Nepal. While being under the ideological radiation effects of both giant neighbours, Nepal has been in the quest for a suitable political system and pattern for rural development administration. Experiencing violent swings between parliamentary democracy and monarchy, Nepal and forged the institutional frame of a partyless panchayat system.

The country is administratively divided into five development regions and each of these is further divided into three to five zones. These zones are again sub-divided into districts. In total, there are five development regions, 14 zones, 75 districts, and 4,022 directly-elected village panchayats in the country.

After the introduction of panchayat system in the country, several organizational changes have taken place. A multi-tier panchayat system comprising people's representatives and decision-makers exists in the country for both developmental and non-developmental activities. The local government system envisaged by Nepal composed of three tiers. They are: village panchayat at the local level, district assembly at the intermediate level, and zonal assembly at the apex level. The zonal assembly is the state government body. All executive powers and sovereignty of the panchayat system rests with the king.

At the grassroots, each village panchayat varies in size, accessibility and resources, and is composed of a *pradhan pancha,* a *upapradhan pancha* and nine *gram panchas* representing their panchayat areas. This unit is responsible for preparing village profiles, indicating village problems/development prospects, formulating local plans, exploring resource mobilization, and arranging sectoral support for development activity. They also carry out additional functions entrusted to it by district panchayats from time to time. Under the new district administration plan, a multi-purpose development worker was appointed, who took over the role from village panchayat secretary. This new worker provides the liaison between the government and the village panchayat and co-ordinates the village administration and development works.

The next unit is the district assembly. From each village panchayat and from town panchayats, one representative each is sent to the district assembly. The district assembly indirectly elects eleven members for an executive body called the district panchayat. In this panchayat, there is a president and a vice-president, and there is a local development officer (LDO) appointed by the Ministry of Panchayat and Local Government. As a member-secretary of the district panchayat, the LDO implements the programmes and projects formulated by the panchayat as well as carries out all decisions taken by the panchayat. He works under the guidance of the president of the panchayat. He is vested with executive and deliberative powers. The other development officers, besides LDO working at this level, are the district planning officer and district officers of various development departments. All these officers are directed and co-ordinated by the district panchayat for implementation of the programmes and projects. The district panchayat, as an important body, assesses the potentiality of the district and arranges for sectoral support for designing and implementing development programmes. This panchayat is the focal point of both regulatory and development administration. Also at this level, there are nine multi-service centres which provide technical assistance and supplies to village panchayats whenever development schemes and projects are implemented. Also, there are five subject committees which prepare base plans on the suggestions received from the village and town panchayats. Besides these subject committees, there are joint committee and district supervision committee. The former brings co-ordination in planning and all project proposals, while the latter supervises the district development plan, ensures economy measures and fiscal discipline during the course of implementation and initiates action in the event of faulty execution of programmes. Both these committees are chaired by a national member (member of parliament) hailing from the district.

The zonal assembly at the apex level has members from district panchayats and selects eligible members to national panchayat. The body has a chairman and a vice-chairman component. The main function of the zonal assembly is to review and coordinate the district level development activities.

With the expansion of bureaucracy to man the country's burgeoning administrative organization, the development personnel in Nepal are functioning and working more independently than before and are maintaining good rapport with all functionaries and representatives. They are effectively coordinating among themselves across the departments. At the same time, despite panchayat philosophy of decentralization, the institutional frame of rural development administration in Nepal has been more elitist and bureaucratic in character and to a great extent is influenced by Indian precedents.

Bhutan

Adjoining to Nepal is yet another kingdom called the Kingdom of Bhutan. In this country, the planned development started late in the early sixties. The development here began in a modest way to eradicate poverty and social backwardness. To achieve self-sufficiency in all spheres of development, India has been playing a major role in providing assistance (finances and experience) to Bhutan in a big way. It is only in recent years that the highly centralized monarchical system of government has been undergoing very limited demoralization. The country still is without any regular and written constitution.

The local administration in recent decades has been reorganized and empowered to play an increased role of maintaining law and order, local affairs and development processes. The country has 18 districts of varying size and population. The Ministry of Home Affairs exercises control over the working of district and block administration. The rural administration in Bhutan has a two-tier structure with district and block agencies.

Block is the lowest tier having a group of villages. At present, there are about 190 blocks in the country. In each block there is a block officer who is assisted by a number of village headmen, each representing a number of villages. The headman is elected for a term of three years by villagers on the basis of one vote per family. This agency implements all development programmes and supervises its working.

Above block agency, there is the district administration/agency. The head of the district administration *(dzongda)* has the responsibility to maintain law and order, revenue collection, general management and socio-economic development. He coordinates and channelizes the activity of various district offices of development departments and other public sector agencies. There is a district planning committee with *dzongda* as its chairman. This committee has members from legislature, representatives from group of villages and some village elders. The committee formulates local plans and programmes for rural development. It supervises the implementation of development programmes and projects and periodically assesses the progress of the schemes.

The development administration in Bhutan became an important integral part of the administrative system from national level to block and village levels. The Bhutan's local system gave more institutionalized access to middle farmers with bureaucracy after its initial success corruption and privileges to certain classes. Moreover, the local government is facing severe shortage of well-trained persons with appropriate specialization and expertise. Also there is less people's participation in the development administration.

Pakistan

In contrast to Nepal and Bhutan, Pakistan, due to reasons of national history and psyche, has tried to invent/devise a system of rural development administration which may appear dissimilar from that of India. But it could not easily shrunk off from British colonial heritage and pattern of regulatory administration which had been a handover from the predecessor to both India and Pakistan.

Pakistan's endeavour for rural reconstruction began with vigour and effort in the middle fifties. This system is associated with rural people in rural development. It was more like a political party than a system of local government. It gave more institutionalized access to middle farmers with bureaucracy after its initial success corruption and privileges to certain classes.

After thirty years, for the first time in 1979, a fully representative system was introduced in the country. To associate people's representatives with the local development processes, a new multi-tiered local council system was set up. The present hierarchical tier structure in Pakistan mainly consists of a union, district and divisional councils. At the lower level is the union of villages. The lowest tier is the union council which has ten directly elected councillors and an official from provincial local government department who functions as the secretary in the council. The council sends proposals of local schemes to be undertaken and sends the progress of development work for consideration to higher bodies.

The next tier is the tehsil council comprising about twenty-five union councils. Its member are mostly chairpersons of union councils and ten official members working at tehsil level. The chairman of the council is a subdivisional officer appointed from the district level. The bureaucrats and elected representatives play a cooperative role in the management of development activities under the overall guidance and direction of district level council and administration.

The next administrative unit in the local system is the district council. This unit is headed by a deputy commissioner who has a critical role to play in development administration. In addition to this, he has to play a traditional role as the head of law and order administration. There is also a deputy commissioner, who is traditionally being the embodiment of government, effectively coordinates and controls all activities of the subordinate organizations. To assist the district administration in the development process, there is a representative council consisting of elected members from tehsil councils. The deputy commissioner of district council acts as its chairman. The vice-chairman elected from the representatives of tehsil council assists the commissioner in his activities.

There are special bodies (corporations and commissions) at the district level to undertake specific development projects and programmes. In order to facilitate flexibility in their working, they have been given autonomy in financial and general management of their affairs. Their standards of management have been of a mixed quality by and large. The divisional council working above district level functions as a co-ordinating agency of all councils.

From the above, it can be concluded that from time to time, the Pakistan government has been trying to promote various administrative reforms to improve administrative capability and integrity of the local government. Despite periodic reforms, it remained weak and served as an informal coordinating and transmission agency. Most of the problems with the local government are mainly because of authoritarian attitude of bureaucrats, corrupt practices, inadequate co-ordination and lack of concern for the downtrodden and women. Besides, standards of efficiency and effectiveness of the administration is not of requisite quality and adequacy. Moreover, the civil bureaucracy in Pakistan is dominating the local government and is unwilling to associate people with administration and are unconcerned to state building. Many government departments have no permanent officials at village level and the bureaucracy is ill-equipped for development and institution building roles. Thus, institutional frame for rural development administration is devoid of a weak socio-economic base and is also organizationally weak.

Bangladesh

The local government system in Bangladesh has been in operation for a quite long time. Bangladesh, being formerly a part of undivided India and latter of Pakistan, attained nationhood by secession. But, the system of rural development administration adopted by it exhibited legacies of Pakistan and traces of Indian influences. After the country was liberated, the nascent Bangladesh government could not establish any new local government system. During Sheikh Mujib's regime, from 1971 to 1975, attempts were made to reorganize the field administration through district governors scheme and *swamivar gram sarkar*. Both these experiments, from political and administrative points of view, failed in their objectives and ended in fiasco.

It was in 1976 when the then President Zia-ul-Rahman promulgated a local government ordinance to provide a consistent framework for local government with three tiers at district, *thana* and union levels. Regardless of various limitations, President Rahman was the first to start the process of more representative and functionally autonomous local government units.

After Rahman's regime, General Ershad accentuated his process of manning more representative local government with administrative decentralization, development orientation and people's participation. On the recommendations of the Committee on Administrative Reorganization Reform (CARR), constituted by the Bangladesh government, a new system was introduced for local administration called the *'upazilla system'* in 1982. This new system was the extension of the Comilla Model (the first experiment for rural development in Bangladesh in the sixties). The new system was one of the most innovative systems and the most important administrative reforms in the history of rural development in Bangladesh.

At present, the country is divided into sixty-two districts, 460 *upazillas* and 4,354 unions. The three units working in the *upazilla* system are the *zilla parishad* (district council), *upazilla parishad* and the union council *(parishad).*

In the new system, the *upazilla is* the main pivot of administration and the responsibility of development is squarely placed on union council. Each *upazilla is* sub-divided into several unions, each having a union council. This is the lowest tier in the hierarchy of local self-government. The union council, as an elected local body, has nine elected members and one chairman directly elected by the people. The chairman of the union council is the ex-officio representative member of the *upazill parishad.* The union council continues to perform specified developmental functions under the overall supervision of the *upazilla parishad.*

The next subservient agency of the government is the *upazilla parishad.* It is the middle tier of a three-tier structure and is the focal point of all administrative activities. As a corporate body, it is responsible for project identification, initiation and implementation of programmes and mobilization of people's participation. Like the former *thana parishad,* it has both representative and official member components. The chairman of the *upazilla parishad* also acts as its chief executive officer. He is assisted by an executive officer, called *upazilla nirbali,* who is a civil servant. As secretary of the *upazilla parishad,* the executive officer provides professional management support to the chairman and also acts as the principal agent of the central government. At this level, there is a group of officers working on deputation basis to deal with the development subjects. Besides, a directly elected people's representative—the *upazilla* chairman, there are chairmen/members drawn from *pourashabhas* (municipalities), union councils and from *upazilla* central cooperative association. Three women are also nominated as members. A freedom fighter and officials of relevant ministries are also members. The *upazilla parishad* has the power to control and regulate union councils and *pourashabhas* within its jurisdiction. It also looks after developmental activities and has a supreme authority in the *upazilla* administration. It is solely responsible for making development schemes under the guidance of the national development plan. This unit approves and modifies the plan proposals of union council and submits it to the *zilla parishad* (district council) for their final approval.

Above *upazilla parishad,* there is the representative district council, which is the primary unit of development administration. This body plays a vital role in resource mobilization and generates popular enthusiasm for development. It is the approving authority for certain schemes and is also the planning and executive agency. This body is headed by a deputy commissioner. The assistant directors of rural development are its secretaries. These civil servants have practical role authority in project initiation and implementation. Also, there is a government representative (project implementation officer) from the Ministry of Relief Rehabilitation, who oversees all development projects. For coordinating and implementing the rural area projects, there is a separate co-ordination and development committee at both *upazilla* and *zilla* levels.

The popularly decentralized administrative *upazilla* system has been in existence for the last eight years. The system, though radical one, has maximum autonomy in the selection of development schemes and their execution. The new system confronts with many problems. The administrative dualism in the system created a dichotomous relationship between *upazilia* chairman and *upazilla nirbali*. Secondly, the very system of policy making is faulty because the *parishad* has to follow the government development plan ignoring the local realities and wants. Thirdly, the system has limited financial resources to run its development and service-oriented activities and depends on national government for financial grant. Lack of delegation of authority to officers of local government and ineffective participation of rural poor failed the system completely. Moreover, the system is hamstrung with unrealistic rules and regulations imposed from above. It is honeycombed with conflicts among the bureaucrats and politicians. Also, there is bureaucratic infighting and conflict between politicians themselves. On the top of all this, the government meddles in the day-to-day affairs of the local bodies. But one cannot lightly dismiss the fact that the extent and scope of decentralization of the *upazilla* system seems to be quite substantial. The restructuring of the administrative set-up has really laid the foundation for sustained decentralized effort.

With the recent political change in Bangladesh and with the disposition of Ershad's government, the newly elected democratic government, under the leadership of Khaleda Zia is planning to do away with the *upzilla* system and replace it with a new system.

Sri Lanka

Rural development administration in Sri Lanka is a production of nearly four decades of adjustment and adaptation. The successive governments left the process of development administration largely in the hands of the officials and this led to an agitation for a greater participation of people in development process. Various national governments tried out experimentation in decentralizing the administration, but to little success. The backdrop of the present system is marked by many changes in the administrative system that accrued during the intervening years.

For administering the island, the country is divided into twenty-four administrative districts. All these districts are further sub-divided into 244 divisions. The divisions are again sub-divided into small village level subdivisions, called the *gram sevaka niladhari* divisions, totally around 4,450.

The local government has two-tier system with divisional council at the sub-divisional level and development council *(kachehert)* at the apex level. The development administration is supported by a number of advisory committees and other agencies.

At the sub-regional or local level, the most operationally significant level in the whole development management framework is the divisional council. At this level, the divisional revenue officer, now designated as assistant government agent

(AGA), functions under the direct supervision of government agent (GA). The GA is a multi-functionary officer and chief coordinator of various government functions. Presently, there are about 250 AGAs, dealing directly with the people of the villages and towns. Another important multi-functioning personnel working at this level is the *gram sevaka niladhari* (GSN). There are about 14,000 GSNs in charge of a cluster of villages and attend mostly to specific regulatory functions. They report back or channel all matters to GA through the AGA. Some of the functional departments representing at the district *kacheheri* have their own officers at this level like extension officers at block level in order to assist the AGA in relevant fields. The other officers working with AGA include rural development officer, supervisor, land development officer, village level overseer, statistical investigator, divisional development officer, social science officer, and so on.

To assist the divisional and development councils in discharging their powers and functions, there are two new broad based village level advisory organizations, called the *pradesiya mandalayas* (PMs) and *gramodaya mandalayas* (GMs), set up at the divisional and village levels. The purpose of these two organizations was to carry out proper survey of local resources and to ensure effective participation of the people in project formulation and implementation.

The PM at the divisional level examines the proposals sent by the GMs and arranges them according to sectoral plans. It recommends the priorities of GMs to the division and to the development councils for inclusion in the annual development plan. This body comprises several members corresponding to the number of *gram sevaka* divisions failing within the division and government officials at the AGA division level. To supervise the functioning of this body, there is a chairman elected from amongst these members. The divisional assistant government agent functions as its ex-officio secretary. The government officials serving in this division assist the *mandalaya*, in deciding priorities of development proposals recommended by the GMs.

The GM, which is the other body functioning at the *gram sevaka* division, has a chairman/president. The chairman of GM is elected from amongst the members. The members are mostly from voluntary organizations. Officials serving at the *gram sevaka* division are also the official members of the GM. These official members assist the GM in identifying projects and recommend to the PM. There is also a special service officer, appointed to cover two *gram sevaka* divisions, and he is the ex-officio secretary of the GM.

Thus, both these local bodies submit the real needs and wishes of the people to the development council. With the assistance of both these bodies, there is proper survey of local resources and effective project formulation and implementation. They are efficiently using the resources, avoiding duplication and wastage and making the people as partners of governmental efforts in development.

When the Sri Lanka government felt that there was no effective people's participation in developmental activities, it enacted the Development Councils Act (1980) for ensuring more people's participation. Under this legislation, a separate corporate, legislative, local body called the development council was established at the district level. The council has five nominated official members known as the councillors in all the districts and some elected representatives on a proportionate basis. The development council depends on the executive committee constituted at the district level. This committee is the executive arm of the council and is headed by a district minister. The council also has a chairman and two nominated members. The district secretary as the secretary of the executive committee looks after the administration of the development council.

In order to assist the development council in the execution of the development programmes set out in the annual development plan, the executive committee meets once in a month. The main functions of the committee are financial control, supervision of development staff and monitoring the progress of development schemes. It is also responsible for the conduct of the administration of the development council.

District in Sri Lanka, being the intermediate level for development efforts and integration, is referred as the *kacheheri* (the traditional district head office) or the district secretariat. There are twenty-four *kacheheris in* the island.

In each of these administrative districts *(kacheheris),* there is a district minister (DM) who is a new political head, appointed by the president of the country and has the same status as that of a deputy minister at the centre. As a kingpin of the district administration, he reports directly to the president on all administrative and development matters. The appointment of DM as the head of the district administration gave a new dimension to management of the district administrative system. The reason for his appointment was to bring the much needed co-ordination in the local level policy formulation and planning. As a chief executive of the district, he looks after both development and regulatory functions and co-associates most of the development agencies and key district development departments. Several important departmental officers are functioning under his administrative control.

The actual functioning of the rural development administration in Sri Lanka reveals that the performance of the rural organization in the island remains below expectations. Though there has been intensified commitment by various national governments in Sri Lanka to develop and strengthen the rural institutions but the performance continue to remain uneven and ineffective in some areas. Though much drastic changes in the administrative structure and process underwent but there is still lack of integration between the bureaucratic structure and elected bodies. Multiplicity of agencies have resulted into confusion among the officials and non-officials. The other deficiency has been that of the financial instability, inadequate managerial capacity and also inadequate understanding and commitment to the goals of national development.

One great thing happened in the interest of the development administration is the introduction of district minister. This has strengthened the district administration. This change facilitated in controlling and securing expeditious functioning of the development administration. This system has cut through the bureaucratic red-tapism, elucidated the unnecessary delay and facilitated more in expeditious decisions and execution of development works. It is hoped that the innovative system of PMs and GMs would help in achieving efficient use of resources and greater participation of people in development process.

India

India, being a federal and democratic country, has a fairly stable political system. With the initiation of the planning process in 1951-52, rural development became the integral part of overall national development. From early sixties till the adoption of the Panchayati Raj, the system witnessed a series of experiments undertaken by religious agencies, voluntary organizations, nationalist leaders, native princes and enlightened British bureaucrats.

In India, two major administrative systems for rural development emerged on the national canvas were the introduction of community development administration in 1952 and the Panchayati Raj administration in 1961. Both these were the basis for rural development administration in India.

The government's first initiated multi-purpose integrated process for development was the Community Development Programme (CDP) in rural areas, which for the first time brought out a significant change in the public administration system in India. It changed the basic ethos of the administrative system which in the past was regulatory in character and became development in nature. The introduction of National Extension Service (NES) brought in an integrated development administration. Thus, the comprehensive unified administrative structure provided more congenial base for introducing the management approach in rural development administration.

Realizing the fact that the CDP failed to bring much needed participation in development management and the administration was more bureaucratic, a need was felt to have a democratic institution, with people's representatives in the process of development. Thus, a revolutionary system in the form of Panchayati Raj was introduced to accomplish the radical transformation of rural areas and to provide organizational support to the rural development administration.

With the introduction of Panchayati Raj, there was a shift from bureaucratic administration to democratic administration. The idea of adopting this system was to have a democratic (political) approach and to place the administration in the hands of both officials and elected representatives so as to make them as partners in the development process. This was a new experiment in the sphere of rural development administration. The system formulates and executes development programmes through people's participation and instills political consciousness among the rural people.

The distribution of Panchayati Raj Institutions (PRIs) in the country is fairly impressive. It is functioning in almost all the states of federal India, except in a few. There are about 2,17,300 *gram panchayats* (village level), 4,528 *panchayat samitis* (block level) and 344 *zilla parishads* (district level) in the country.

The institutional framework provided under the Panchayati Raj system is a three-tier interconnected elected local self-governing bodies with an organic linkage from village to district level. There is a great variation in the Panchayati Raj structures in some states. The existing three-tier Panchayati Raj system has inter-linked units which assist and guide the rural development administration in the implementation of development programmes at the district, block and village levels. In some of the states, these three units are functioning with varying degrees of power and functions.

In the hierarchical structure of Panchayati Raj, the lowest tier is the *gram panchayat.* It is an executive body which implements policies and decisions of the *gram sabha.* The *gram sabha,* as a statutory body, is assigned with specific functions to direct and supervise the activities of the *gram panchayats.*

The *gram panchayats* are purely indirectly/directly elected bodies having people's representatives in the form of *sarpanch/pradhan* and *sarpanchas/upapradhan.* In some notified *gram panchayats*, there are executive officers looking after the administration of the *gram panchayats.*

The next intermediary tier is the nerve centre of the Panchayati Raj, i.e., the *panchayat samiti* (representative wing of the block). This body has been created to take governmental and technical aid down to the people at the village level. This key unit provides an organic link between the *zilla parishads* and *gram panchayats* and is recognized as a focal point of planning and administration. This unit carries out large number of substantial type of functions.

The chief executive officer of the *panchayat samiti* is the block development officer (BDO), who is charged with carrying out the implementation of development activities. As head of the team specialists (extension officers), the BDO co-ordinates and looks after administrative work. The extension officers working at this level are consultants in their respective technical subjects. They are a direct link in the administrative-cum-technical chain of their departments. Thus, the extension officers are technically and administratively under the control of BDO. To attend the day-to-day work and to function as a live-link between the people and the extension agency, there is a village development officer.

The block organization functions under a popularly elected representative called the *pradhan*. He is the head of the body and is indirectly elected from amongst the members of the *panchayat samiti*. He is entrusted with special functions of management character like the administrative control over BDO, power to appoint lower category staff and impose penalties and inspect the *gram panchayats*. To assist him, there is an indirectly elected representative called the *upapradhan*. Furthermore, the ex-officio members of the *panchayat samiti* include the *sarpanchas* of the gram panchayats, one representative each from SCs/STs, and members from co-operative society, legislative assembly and legislative council.

The next popular tier is the *zilla parishad* whose powers and functions vary from state to state. In some states, the *zilla parishad* is a supervisory, coordinating and advisory body while in some other states it has only regulatory functions. As an elected body, the *zilla parishads* have to take stock of the needs, resources and potentialities of the blocks in the district on one hand, and evolve state policy and plan of development for the entire district on the other.

With the advent of Panchayati Raj, the district administration underwent some changes. The collector is still the supreme head of the district administration. His presence was felt necessary at the district level for getting complete cooperation from the district level officers and that the *zilla parishad* gets a new stature. The role of the collector as a coordinator of developmental activities had its ups and downs. While in a few states, he is still the main coordinator of all activities in the district, in some other states he coordinates only developmental activities. With the introduction of system, the responsibilities of the collector increased manifold. Besides being responsible for the implementation of development schemes, he is the chief liaison between the official and non-official agencies in the district and also incharge of regulatory administration. His position in the district administration was strengthened by making him the member of the *zilla parishad* and its standing committees. Thus, as chief official of the district, he is involved in the entire process of development.

Another immediate deputy of collector is a statutory functionary appointed by the state government called the deputy chief executive officer who is an ex-officio secretary. Being the personal assistant to collector, he assists him in the supervision of all developmental activities. He is also the administrative head of general administrative department of the *zilla parishad*.

Another set of functionaries working at the district includes the technical subject specialists. They assist the generalists and the representatives of the people in the development matters. Administratively, they are under the control of the collector and technically under the control of their state departmental heads. But, in some states, these officers were brought under the control of Panchayati Raj in order to bring effective co-ordination.

Besides sectoral-line departments, there is a separate autonomous body known as the District Rural Development Agency (DRDA), which functions as an important arm of rural development administration to implement Integrated Rural Development Programme (IRDP) and other related programmes. The DRDA supervises, monitors and implements development programmes. It is headed by district collector, who is the chairman. There is a full-time project director who is assisted by a team of assistant project officers specialized in various rural development subjects to carry out various development programmes. For the implementation of the programmes, the DRDA depends on the extension officers of various sectoral departments working at the block level.

The Panchayati Raj system, though considered as revolutionary in the history of rural development in India, gradually proved to be elusive. It has been greatly ecological on the event of its introduction, began to sag, stagnate and waned after it was put to operation. The system could not emerge as an effective vehicle of change. The momentous change of bringing a new wave of public enthusiasm was lost and the status and role of PRIs as units of self-government were eclipsed by combination of several factors of decay and disarray. It has thrown up a complex of problems which are still a begging solution. Most of the administrative problems were the inter and intra organizational relations, the interrelations between the state government and Panchayati Raj, equations between officials and non-officials, the local development bureaucracy and its management and control, co-ordination and integrated development, interaction with clientele and popular participation, planning process and development programmes as well as nexus of Panchayati Raj with district administration, especially with collector. Scant regard to procedures, political interference in day-to-day administration and parochial loyalties made the institutions inferior. Moreover, the creation of agencies to implement special programmes systematically bypassed the Panchayati Raj machinery and thus seriously limited the utility of Panchayati Raj. What was more worse was that the elections to the PRIs were not held regularly.

On the whole, one cannot say that the panchayati raj system in India has totally failed. It has contributed significantly in the formulation and implementation of local development plans and provided a new dimension to rural development. It introduced a structural change of the highest importance in the district administration. Both administration and the system not only helped the growth of social awakening in the rural society and in narrowing the distance between the bureaucracy and the people but also succeeded in drawing a development goal for the people.

Summing up

The survey of the rural development administration/rural local organizations of six nations leads to a conclusion that the traditional governmental institutions do not represent a majority of the rural people, particularly the rural poor. The institutional positions of rural development administration in these countries have been highly bureaucratized and are centralized patterns of authority and administration. Though the pattern varies with each function of the government, but in some countries both central and local authorities are weak and ineffective. Frequent and unpredictable changes in the administrative structures or procedures delayed or thwarted the institutionalization of local organization.

What is worth noting is that in contrast to the other South Asian countries, the local government systems in China and India are highly politicized. They have provided an institutional framework for greater participation. People were actively involved in all stages of development and implementation and they had greater control over resource mobilization and allocation. The commune system reduced the structural dualism of elites and masses, urban and rural rich and poor, which is the marked characteristics of most of the developing countries. In spite of restricted political and intellectual freedom in the country, the Chinese masses more particularly in rural areas enjoy a great measure of control over the local bodies.

Compared to China, the rural development administration in India contributed significantly to the formulation and implementation of local development plans and provided a new dimension to rural development. The administration helped the growth of social awakening in the rural society.

However, the institutional structure for rural development, though viable and useful, lacked effectiveness. The institution was reduced to an extremely peripheral status with considerable erosion of powers and functions, suffered from local factions.

Moreover, the existing rural institutions controlled by elitist power structure served only the elitist groups in the rural economy at the cost of the rural poor.

With the shaky parliamentary system of government and frequent changes, political scene in Pakistan and Bangladesh had a devastating effect on rural development, particularly on institutional development and popular participation. The political scene in both the countries has not been conducive for the development of people's institutions. The local government systems in these countries are disgruntled and disjoined leading to many administrative problems like inadequate coordination, less association of people in development works, and inadequate delegation of authority and resources. Also authoritarian attitude of bureaucrats, lack of concern for the poor and unrealistic rules and regulations imposed from above and so on made the rural development administration organizationally weak. Unless the governments of both the countries entrust responsibility of development of rural people and resources, no real development will take place.

Nepal, being an autocratic country, experienced violent swings of political changes which considerably affected the local system. Despite adopting the philosophy of decentralization, the institutional frame of rural development administration has been more elitist and bureaucratic in character.

Though the Bhutan's local government system gave easy access of bureaucracy to middle farmers, it failed to involve effective participation. Also, due to well-trained rural managers and due to privileges given to elite class, the administration failed to respond to the causes of the downtrodden.

Sri Lanka, after great deal of adjustment and adoption in the administration, finally tried out experiments in decentralizing the administration on a democratic basis, with greater participation of people in the development process. Though changes were brought in the administration, the actual performance of the rural administration remains still below expectations. There is lack of integration between the bureaucratic structure and elected bodies. Multiplicity of local bodies resulted to confusion. Financial stability and inadequate managerial capacity and understanding among the officials and non-officials resulted in ineffective performance of the rural institutions.

To modernize the rural local government systems and to make the administration more responsive and representative, what is actually needed is a decentralized institution building which should be vigorously advocated by all South Asian countries. There should be persistent efforts from governments of Asian countries to enhance the administrative capabilities of rural governments. Suitable institutional structures and operational principles need to be worked out so that the local democratic institutions become vibrant for planning and development. The central elites interested in rural development should allow the rural local organizations to function effectively and freely with full autonomy for an extended period of time and must avoid the temptation to indulge in frequent and sharp structural changes which is not healthy from development point of view. Experimentation and innovation with the local organization are needed only when there is a necessity of strengthening the hierarchical structure of rural administration. Frequent tampering with the structure and revamping of institutional framework will only lead to confusion and disintegration of the developmental activities.

Secondly, instead of multi-tiers, the governments in these countries should give a serious thought of having a two-tiered approach to local organization. This approach can combine the benefits of solidarity and scale, both for mobilizing resources and for organizing and implementing development projects. In this two-tier pattern, the lower tier will perform functions at the neighbourhood or small group level, while the other would undertake more complex business activities. This pattern would provide the best base for the system of rural development organization. In addition to this, the local organization should be vested with multiple functions in order to achieve benefits of development on a large scale and to facilitate local integration of services. Also, there should be full devolution of authority accomplished with substantial central and state resources to the local bodies which are fundamentally necessary for effective and efficient functioning of the local bodies. Furthermore, the jurisdiction on resource mobilization and allocation should be extended to the local bodies. Greater opportunities for local planning and programme implementation should be granted to rural governments. More people's participation in the development process should be brought in by giving adequate representation to the disadvantaged sections of the society. There should be a clear-cut demarcation of rules and regulations to each unit in the hierarchical structure of the local government or by providing an organizational mechanism by constituting project steering or project co-ordination committees at each level to achieve better co-ordination in developmental efforts.

Finally, in addition to this, there should be the political will and commitment on the part of the political leadership to bring in a radical overhaul in the colonial archaic administrative system, if at all the system exists.

References

A Report on Agriculture and the People's Commune of China, An FAO Study of the United Nations, Bangkok, 1977, p. 15.

A Report on Ministries Meeting on RD in Asia and Pacific, Centre on Integrated Rural Development for Asia and Pacific, 1987, p.57.

A Report on Toward Improved Multilevel Planning for Agriculture and Rural Development in Asia and Pacific, FAO of UNS Italy, p. 22.

Akbar Ali Khan, 'Decentralization for RD in Bangladesh,' *Bangladesh Journal of Public Administration,* Vol. III, No. 1, January 1989, p. 16.

Balaikia, M.P., 'The Struggle for Basic Needs in Nepal,' Development Centre of the Organisation for Economic Cooperation and Development, p. 24.

Bhooshan, B.S., *The Development of Nepal,* Concept Publishing Company, New Delhi, p. 37.

D. Potter, *Rural India: An Introduction, Contemporary Development Administration,* G. Bell and Sons, London, 1964, p. 139.

Dubhashi, P.R., *Rural Development Administration in India,* Chugh Publications, Allahabad, p. 93.

Government of Bangladesh, Report of the Committee for Administrative Reorganization/Room (CARR), Dhaka, June, 1982.

Government of India, Ministry of Agriculture, *Panchayati Raj at a Glance. 1989*-90, New Delhi, 1990.

Inayatullah et. al, Approaches to Rural Development in Asia. The *Comparative Perspective,* Vol. 1, Asian Centre for Development Administration, Kualalumpur, Malaysia, p. 128.

Khanna, B.S., *Rural Development in South Asia,* Deep & Deep Publication, New Delhi, 1991, p. 8.

Lokendra Prasad Dandyal, 'Experience of Training for Decentralized Planning in Nepal, *'Public Administration and Development Journal,* Vol. 1, No. 2 (March and April, 1991), p. 173.

Metra Pal Jain, *Rural Reconstruction in India and China,* MacMillan Press Ltd., London, p. 48.

Munner Ahmed, 'Rural Self-Government in Pakistan: An Experiment in Political Development through Bureaucracy,' in Robert D. Stevens (Ed.), *Rural Development in Bangladesh and Pakistan,* East-West Centre, Honolulu, 1976, p. 222.

Navarante, V.T., 'The District Minister System: Strategy for Decentralization and Co-ordination at District Level', *Sri Lanka Journal of Development Administration,* p. 25.

Norman K. Nicholson and Dilwar Ali Khan, *Basic Democracies and RD in Pak,* Center for International Studies, Cornell University, Ithaca, New York, p. 310.

Porage, I., *Rural Development in Selected Countries,* Asian Centre for Development Administration, Kualalumpur, Malaysia, p. 144.

Sartaj Aziz, *Rural Development Learning from China,* MacMillan Press Ltd., London, p. 48.

Tarek Ahmad Muslehuddin and Firoz Ahmad, 'Local Government Upazilla System in Bangladesh: An Overview,' *Quarterly Journal of the All India Institute of Local Self-Government,* Bombay, Vol. XII, No. 2 (April-June, 1991), p. 102.

Uphoff T. Norman, *Rural Development and Local Organisation in Asia,* Part-II, East Asia, p. 50.

Uphoff T. Norman, *Rural Development and Local Organisation,* MacMillan Co., Ltd., London, p. 50.

Wickramiscyla I. Kamala, 'The Role of the Government Agent in Sri Lanka Changing Perspectives, 1796-1896', *Sri Lanka Journal of Development Administration,* 1988, p. 17.

18

Delays in Disposal

RAJENDRA BHANAWAT

Nani A. Palkhiwala, an eminent constitutional expert, observed once in his address, that in Bihar, nothing moves except the Ganges. This led the author to think, whether the situation is really different in other parts of the country. The same statement can probably be applied to the whole of the country with one amendment that even when a file moves, we cannot be sure whether the matter really moves. It is often said that delay breeds corruption. This cannot be more relevant to the public delivery system whether of the government or any other agency. While the delay has become an accepted way of life in almost all spheres of public utility services, still it would be worthwhile to look into some of the dimensions of the problem.

Before we suggest any prescription, which in any case is not possible, it would be useful if a searching look at the present scenario is taken.

Consequences of Delay

The delay in itself leads to a number of evils. Some of the important ones are:

1. Image of the organization goes down
2. Harassment to the public
3. Encourages corruption
4. Increased leg-pulling
5. Desired benefit denied
6. Justice delayed is justice denied

These are discussed in some detail in the following paragraphs.

It is very difficult for any organization to build up goodwill, but it is very easy to lose it by a simple method, i.e., by delaying the matters. Persons who get aggrieved because of non-disposal of the case, will talk in several circles about the image of the organization. What most of the departments face today is a crisis of credibility. You talk to anybody having some dealing with a public service organization and he will take no time in telling you of the manner, in which the things are delayed, whether it is issuing of a licence, no objection certificate, getting a loan, etc.

The condition of a villager, who comes to the office from a distant village and is told in the evening after waiting for six to seven hours, that he must come the next day, can only be imagined. His plight becomes more pitiable when this is repeated time and again. In a country, where a large chunk of the population is not even able to arrange square meals a day, calling people again and again to the office (which is a very normal affair) is to say the least, torturous. When sitting on one side of the table, we often forget that we can be on the other side also, at some other point of time. A Railway Officer could be a client for the Telephone Department whereas an officer of the Telephone Department could become a client for the Railways.

If the matters are not decided in time, the client will go back with the feeling that the delay is because of a 'demand,

Thus, even if the intention of the dealing person may not be malafide; yet, the very fact that the delay occurs, leads clients to think this way. The more the delay, the more would be the possibility of corruption. A common man always weighs the pros and cons of staying overnight for work, or to pay some amount and get the work done. This leads us to an obvious conclusion, that in order to minimise corruption, delays will have to be curtailed.

Whenever there are delays, there are efforts to find out the defaulters. The postmortem of a delay will encourage the officer to shift blame from one to the other. Consequently, harmonious atmosphere in an organization will tend to get converted to one, where everybody is busy in pulling the other's leg.

When the delay takes place, the expected outcome may not be forthcoming. It is a common knowledge that a number of projects have to be abandoned, due to price escalation, as a result of not getting sanctioned in time. A minor delay on one front tends to get reflected in greater delays in other related areas.

When the application of any applicant does not generate timely response and action, the next time the clients or the public will think twice before believing the department or the organization. When this faith gets reduced, the other activities of the organization and the credibility suffer a set-back. This is precisely the reason, why it is very rare to see any one showing an element of faith in our public delivery systems, specially those run by the government.

The saying "a stitch in time saves nine" is quite relevant for the service organization. Any help which does not come in time is almost useless. For example, if a loan to a farmer for improved seeds is made available after the sowing season is over, it is going to have a doubly negative effect on him: (i) he will not be able to utilize the loan amount for the desired purpose; and (ii) the possibility of repayment will be remote, as the money would be squandered on other undesired purposes.

As has been discussed above, even if the delay might be unintentional, the impression carried by the public because of delays in disposal would be that the employees of the organization want to exploit their positions. Thus, without there being a malafide attitude, the image of the organization will be seen as such.

What can be done to curtail delays?

One of the major causes of inordinate delays in an organization is a very high degree of paper work—necessary as well as unnecessary. While accepting that in a bureaucratic set-up, some paper work is bound to be there; still, there is a lot of scope of minimizing the paper work at all levels. Because of unnecessary creation of papers, on the one hand the physical climate of the office gets spoilt, on the other hand, the relevant important papers cannot be retrieved in time, whenever required. For early retrieval of papers, for deciding a case/file/application, it is very important that the record is maintained systematically. This would imply that the staff dealing with the record must be well trained for this purpose. Once a proper climate is created, many modern techniques of record management can be adopted.

While reduced paper work and systematic management of records are important, weeding of outdated records is also to be continuously carried out, in order to keep the office clean and more manageable. This job of weeding is, unfortunately, considered by most people as unimportant. The retention schedules for different papers and files do exist on papers in almost all the offices, yet the physical weeding hardly takes place.

The tendency of centralization in an organization makes the middle and lower level functionaries feel that they are unimportant and unwanted. Therefore, a proper decentralization and delegation of authority is a must for an organization wanting to expedite the finalization of cases. While delegating authority, one must not forget the basic principle of delegation.

These days, at many places, it is the responsibility which is getting delegated and not the authority. The desirable situation is one where both authority and responsibility are delegated together.

Sometimes, it is also seen that the non-availability of a person also contributes in delaying the matters. This can be remedied in two ways. One, by ensuring that alternative arrangements are made, whenever an official is on leave; and second, by encouraging the tendency to share the information with fellow colleagues. Truly speaking, there is very little information which really needs to be kept confidential. But in the name of confidentiality, quite often, the officials do not disclose/share whatever little information/papers they possess. This artificial indispensability might make a few persons feel 'important', but it does a lot of harm to the system.

One of the allegations against the government and similar organizations is the total absence of human touch in dealing with the public. Exceptions may be there, but the fact is that, we often deal with files considering them only as pieces of paper, losing sight of the human being behind every paper. While dealing with the files or papers, if one could keep in mind the human element behind the papers and consider them as live issues rather than dead things, it is expected that the approach would be much more realistic and humanistic, which in turn, would minimize delays.

The government officials can be heard complaining about the possible problems they might have to face if they did anything beyond the rules, even for a good cause. This is far from the truth, as there are cases, where the officers have circumvented the procedures and rules with bonafide intentions to help a deserving man, without attracting any charge sheet or the like. The need is to learn that the rules and procedures were created for human beings and not vice versa.

There is also a great need of demystifying the atmosphere that prevails in most of the government and public organizations. A villager or a farmer or for that matter any common man who happens to visit a government office, feels so much confused about the mystery which surrounds different sections that he gets lost in it. After running from pillar to post in an effort to unveil the mystery of the departmental functioning he ultimately lands up with a 'tout', who in turn will suggest ways and means to solve the problem. These 'ways and means' are anybody's guess. If the procedures of the organizations can be simplified and made known to all concerned, in simple language, it would go a long way in reducing the subsequent delays. An example from the university would be relevant here. The university lays down instructions for a first year student, on application forms in English, which are difficult to comprehend even by seniors. Expecting a first year student, mostly coming out from a vernacular school, to fill in such a form correctly, might be asking for too much. As a result, lie makes many mistakes which leads to a number of problems at the time of examinations and declaration of results. Why can't we have instructions in simple Hindi and English?

It is also observed that the officers do not use judicious discretion while inviting persons of the public to their offices. It is seen that large number of persons are required to reach office at 10 a.m. sharp. The same applies to the courts. It is an admitted situation that most of the persons wait till the end of the day, only to be informed, that they have to come some other day. Some thinking and concern on the part of the inviting officers would have saved a lot of manpower, time and money from going waste. They could be given different timings and only those persons might have been called, as could possibly be listened to on that day. The situation is especially pathetic, with reference to the courts—revenue or civil.

Whenever the beneficiaries or the clients come to the office for any problem, they are generally directed by the officers to meet the dealing clerks. This approach will not only keep the persons dissatisfied, but also, will not allow the concerned clerk to carry on with his normal work. Instead, the officers can call concerned officials, find out the facts and decide the matter at their own level. Another reason for delay is the lack of clarity about the job. The files keep on shuffling between the different tables without reaching the right persons at the right time. This can be avoided, if all officers are clear about their job descriptions and their powers. Similarly, all employees of the organization must be clear about the procedures of business, so that the file or the matter keeps on moving smoothly.

The measures suggested in this article for reducing the delays in disposal are certainly not exhaustive, only illustrative. Every organization will have to evolve its own strategy to combat this ever-increasing menace.

Contributors

T.N. CHATURVEDI, Governor, Government of Karnataka, Bangalore.

B. MEHTA, former Chief Secretary, Government of Rajasthan, Jaipur.

C. RICHARD PARKINS, former Ford Foundation Consultant, HCM Rajasthan State Institute of Public Administration, Jaipur.

MOHAN MUKERJI, former Chief Secretary, Government of Rajasthan, Jaipur.

R.G. SOOD, an officer in the District Gazetteers, Government of Himachal Pradesh, Shimla.

K.K. PARNAMI, Publication Officer, HCM Rajasthan State Institute of Public Administration, Jaipur.

B.K. KHUNTETA, former Professor of Economics, HCM Rajasthan State Institute of Public Administration, Jaipur.

A.N. KRISHNAMURTHY, Human Settlement Management Institute, New Delhi.

HARRY A. MENGERS, Project Leader, Decentralized Training Programme, Karnataka.

DHARMA VIRA, a former ICS officer.

G.B.K. HOOJA, former Vice Chancellor, Gurukul Kangri University, Haridwar.

R.K. MISHRA, Professor, Institute of Public Enterprises, Hyderabad.

V. JAGANNADHAM, former Professor, Indian Institute of Public Administration, New Delhi.

RAKESH HOOJA, Director, HCM Rajasthan State Institute of Public Administration, Jaipur.

UDAI PAREEK, former Professor, Indian Institute of Management, Ahmedabad.

P.K. CHAUBEY, Govind Ballabh Pant Social Science Institute, Allahabad.

AMIT LODHA, an IPS officer.

RICHARD M. TOM, National Institute of Rural Development, Hyderabad.

RAJENDRA BHANAWAT, Secretary, Animal Husbandry, Government of Rajasthan, Jaipur.